MORRIS AUTOMATED INFORMATION NETWORK

W9-ADY-568

OCT 23 2009

Chester
Library

DISCARD

250 West Main Street
Chester, NJ 07930

DOWNSIZED LUXURY
HOME PLANS

CREATIVE HOMEOWNER®, Upper Saddle River, New Jersey

COPYRIGHT © 2008

A Division of Federal Marketing Corp.
Upper Saddle River, NJ

All floor plans and elevations copyright by the individual designers and may not be reproduced by any means without permission. All text and other illustrative material ©2008 Creative Homeowner and may not be reproduced, either in part or in its entirety, in any form, by any means, without written permission from the publisher, with the exception of brief excerpts for purposes of radio, television, or published review. All rights, including the right of translation, are reserved. Although all possible measures have been taken to ensure the accuracy of the material presented, the publisher is not liable in case of misinterpretation or typographical error.

Creative Homeowner® is a registered trademark of Federal Marketing Corporation.

Home Plans Editor: Kenneth D. Stuts
Home Plans Consultant: James McNair
Home Plans Designer Liaison: Sara Markowitz

Design and Layout: Arrowhead Direct (David Kroha, Cindy DiPierdomenico, Judith Kroha); Maureen Mulligan

Cover Design: David Geer

Vice President and Publisher: Timothy O. Bakke
Production Director: Kimberly H. Vivas

Current Printing (last digit)
10 9 8 7 6 5 4 3 2

Downsized Luxury Home Plans
Library of Congress Control Number: 2007932958
ISBN-10: 1-58011-387-7
ISBN-13: 978-1-58011-387-8

CREATIVE HOMEOWNER®
A Division of Federal Marketing Corp.
24 Park Way
Upper Saddle River, NJ 07458
www.creativehomeowner.com

Note: The homes as shown in the photographs and renderings in this book may differ from the actual blueprints. When studying the house of your choice, please check the floor plans carefully.

PHOTO CREDITS

Front cover: *top* plan 161035, page 135; *bottom far left* plan 221155, page 186; *bottom left* plan 661007, page 185; *bottom right* plan 121019, page 208; *bottom far right* plan 181640, page 155 **page 1:** plan 121024, page 16 **page 3:** *top* plan 151034, page 24; *center* plan 131050, page 27; *bottom* plan 151019, page 38 **page 4:** plan 131026, page 42 **page 5:** plan 161002, page 36 **page 6:** *top* plan 121062, page 39; *bottom* plan 131032, page 22 **page 7:** plan 321049, page 46 **page 8:** plan 161025, page 45 **page 74:** Brian Vanden Brink **page 75:** *both* Walter Chandoha **page 76:** *top right* Tony Giammarino/Giammarino & Dworkin, design: Maureen Klein; *bottom right* Tony Giammarino/Giammarino & Dworkin; *bottom left* Brian Vanden Brink, design: Ron Forest Fences **page 77:** *illustrations* Nancy Hull **page 78:** *top* Jessie Walker; *illustrations* Nancy Hull **page 79:** *top* Roy Inman, stylist: Susan Andrews; *bottom both* Walter Chandoha **page 122:** Gabrielle Kessler, courtesy of Quintessentials, design: Elsa Kessler, cabinetry: Brookhaven "Vista" **page 123:** *top* courtesy of Granite Transformations; *bottom both* Gabrielle Kessler, courtesy of Quintessentials, design: Elsa Kessler, cabinetry: Brookhaven "Vista" **page 124:** EVERETT & SOULE, design: Joan DesCombes, CKD, Architectural Artworks Incorporated **page 125:** *top left & bottom* EVERETT & SOULE, design: Joan Descombes, CKD, Architectural Artworks Incorporated; *top right* courtesy of Granite Transformations **pages 126–127:** *all* EVERETT & SOULE, design: Jean DesCombes, CKD, Architectural Artworks Incorporated **page 128:** Todd Caverly **page 129:** *top left & bottom right* Dave Adams, design: Shasta Smith, Allied ASID, Delicate Design; *top right* design: John Buscarello, ASID; *bottom left* Todd Caverly **page 164:** Eric Roth **page 165:** *both* courtesy of GarageTek **page 166:** *top* Tony Giammarino/Giammarino & Dworkin, stylist: Christine McCabe; *bottom* courtesy of Rubbermaid **page 167:** *top* courtesy of Gladiator; *inset* courtesy of GarageTek **page 168:** *top* Bradley Olman; *bottom* courtesy of The Container Store **page 169:** *top left & bottom* courtesy of GarageTek; *top right* Mark Lohman **page 170:** *top* Eric Roth, architect: Ben Nutter; *bottom right* courtesy of Osram-Sylvania; *bottom left* melabee m miller, design/builder: Doyle Builders **page 171:** Eric Roth, architect: Ben Nutter **page 229:** plan 181081, page 117 **page 233:** *top* plan 131014, page 72; *center* plan 191001, page 96; *bottom* plan 551179, page 99 **page 240:** *top* plan 161184, page 51; *center* plan 271081, page 57; *bottom* plan 321048, page 61 **back cover:** *top right* plan 151015, page 41; *center right* plan 131081, page 132; *bottom right* plan 481028, page 50; *bottom center* plan 161018, page 40; *bottom left* plan 111004, page 19

Contents

Getting Started

Maybe you can't wait to bang the first nail. Or you may be just as happy leaving town until the windows are cleaned. The extent of your involvement with the construction phase is up to you. Your time, interests, and abilities can help you decide how to get the project from lines on paper to reality. But building a house requires more than putting pieces together. Whoever is in charge of the process must competently manage people as well as supplies, materials, and construction. He or she will have to

- Make a project schedule to plan the orderly progress of the work. This can be a bar chart that shows the time period of activity by each trade.
- Establish a budget for each category of work, such as foundation, framing, and finish carpentry.
- Arrange for a source of construction financing.
- Get a building permit and post it conspicuously at the construction site.
- Line up supply sources and order materials.
- Find subcontractors and negotiate their contracts.
- Coordinate the work so that it progresses smoothly with the fewest conflicts.
- Notify inspectors at the appropriate milestones.
- Make payments to suppliers and subcontractors.

Acting as the builder, above, requires the ability to hire and manage subcontractors.

Building a home, opposite, includes the need to schedule building inspections at the appropriate milestones.

You as the Builder

You'll have to take care of every logistical detail yourself if you decide to act as your own builder or general contractor. But along with the responsibilities of managing the project, you gain the flexibility to do as much of your own work as you want and subcontract out the rest. Before taking this path, however, be sure you have the time and capabilities. Do you also have the time and ability to schedule the work, hire and coordinate subs, order materials, and keep ahead of the accounting required to manage the project successfully? If you do, you stand to save the amount that a general contractor would charge to take on these responsibilities, normally 15 to 30 percent of the construction cost. If you take this responsibility on but mismanage the project, the potential savings will erode and may even cost you more than if you had hired a builder in the first place. A subcontractor might charge extra for having to return to the site to complete work that was originally scheduled for an earlier date. Or perhaps because you didn't order the windows at the beginning, you now have to pay for a recent cost increase. (If you had hired a builder in the first place he or she would absorb the increase.)

Hiring a Builder to Handle Construction

A builder or general contractor will manage every aspect of the construction process. Your role after signing the construction contract will be to make regular progress payments and ensure that the work for which you are paying has been completed. You will also consult with the builder and agree to any changes that may have to be made along the way.

Leads for finding builders might come from friends or neighbors who have had contractors build, remodel, or add to their homes. Real-estate agents and bankers may have some names handy but are more likely familiar with the builder's ability to complete projects on time and budget than the quality of the work itself.

The next step is to narrow your list of candidates to three or four who you think can do a quality job and work harmoniously with you. Phone each builder to see whether he or she is interested in being considered for your project. If so, invite the builder to an interview at your home. The meeting will serve two purposes. You'll be able to ask the candidate about his or her experience, and you'll be able to see whether or not your personalities are compatible. Go over the plans with the builder to make certain that he or she understands the scope of the project. Ask if they have constructed similar houses. Get references, and check the builder's standing with the Better Business Bureau. Develop a short list of builders, say three, and ask them to submit bids for the project.

Contracts

Lump-Sum Contracts

A lump-sum, or fixed-fee, contract lets you know from the beginning just what the project will cost, barring any changes made because of your requests or unforeseen conditions. This form works well for projects that promise few surprises and are well defined from the outset by a complete set of contract documents. You can enter into a fixed-price contract by negotiating with a single builder on your short list or by obtaining bids from three or four builders. If you go the latter route, give each bidder a set of documents and allow at least two weeks for them to submit their bids. When you get the bids, decide who you want and call the others to thank them for their efforts. You don't have to accept the lowest bid, but it probably makes sense to do so since you have already honed the list to builders you trust. Inform this builder of your intentions to finalize a contract.

Cost-Plus-Fee Contracts

Under a cost-plus-fee contract, you agree to pay the builder for the costs of labor and materials, as verified by receipts, plus a fee that represents the builder's overhead and profit. This arrangement is sometimes referred to as "time and materials." The fee can range between 15 and 30 percent of the incurred costs. Because you ultimately pick up the tab—whatever the costs—the contractor is never at risk, as he is with a lump-sum contract. You won't know the final total cost of a cost-plus-fee contract until the project is built and paid for. If you can live with that uncertainty, there are offsetting advantages. First, this form allows you to accommodate unknown conditions much more easily than does a lump-sum contract. And rather than being tied down by the project documents, you will be free to make changes at any point along the way. This can be a trap, though. Watching the project take shape will spark the desire to add something or do something differently. Each change costs more, and the accumulation can easily exceed your budget. Because of the uncertainty of the final tab and the built-in advantage to the contractor, you should think twice before entering into this form of contract.

Contract Content

The conditions of your agreement should be spelled out thoroughly in writing and signed by both parties, whatever contractual arrangement you make with your builder. Your contract should include provisions for the following:

- The names and addresses of the owner and builder.
- A description of the work to be included ("As described in the plans and specifications dated . . .").
- The date that the work will be completed if time is of the essence.
- The contract price for lump-sum contracts and the builder's allowed profit and overhead costs for changes.
- The builder's fee for cost-plus-fee contracts and the method of accounting and requesting payment.
- The criteria for progress payments (monthly, by project milestones) and the conditions of final payment.
- A list of each drawing and specification section that is to be included as part of the contract.
- Requirements for guarantees. (One year is the standard period for which contractors guarantee the entire project, but you may require specific guarantees on

When submitting bids, all of the builders should base their estimates on the same specifications. Once the work begins, communicate with your builder to keep the work proceeding smoothly.

certain parts of the project, such as a 20-year guarantee on the roofing.)

■ Provisions for insurance.

■ A description of how changes in the work orders will be handled.

The builder may have a standard contract that you can tailor to the specifics of your project. These contain complete specific conditions with blanks that you can fill in to fit your project and a set of "general conditions" that cover a host of issues from insurance to termination provisions. It's always a good idea to have an attorney review the draft of your completed contract before signing it.

Working with Your Builder

The construction phase officially begins when you have a signed copy of the contract and copies of any insurance required from the builder. It's not unheard of for a builder to request an initial payment of 10 to 20 percent of the total cost to cover mobilization costs, those costs associated with obtaining permits and getting set up to begin the actual construction. If you agree to this, keep a careful eye on the progress of the work to ensure that the total paid out at any one time doesn't get too far out of sync with the actual work completed.

What about changes? From here on, it's up to you and your builder to proceed in good faith and to keep the channels of communication open. Even so, changes of one sort or another beset every project, and they usually add to its cost.

Light at the End of the Tunnel.

The builder's request for a final inspection marks the end of the construction phase—almost. At the final inspection meeting, you and the builder will inspect the work, noting any defects or incomplete items on a "punch list." When the builder tidies up the punch list items, you should reinspect. Sometimes, builders go on to another job and take forever to clean up the last few details, so only after all items on the list have been completed satisfactorily should you release the final payment, which often accounts for the builder's profit.

Some Final Words

Having a positive attitude is important when undertaking a project as large as building a home. A positive attitude can help you ride out the rigors and stress of the construction process.

Stay Flexible. Expect problems, because they certainly will occur. Weather can upset the schedule you have established for subcontractors. A supplier may get behind on deliveries, which also affects the schedule. An unexpected pipe may surprise you during excavation. Just as certain, every problem that comes along has a solution if you are open to it.

Be Patient. The extra days it may take to resolve a construction problem will be forgotten once the project is completed.

Express Yourself. If what you see isn't exactly what you thought you were getting, don't be afraid to look into changing it. Or you may spot an unforeseen opportunity for an improvement. Changes usually cost more money, though, so don't make frivolous decisions.

Finally, watching your home go up is exciting, so stay upbeat. Get away from your project from time to time. Dine out. Take time to relax. A positive attitude will make for smoother relations with your builder. An optimistic outlook will yield better-quality work if you are doing your own construction. And though the project might seem endless while it is under way, keep in mind that all the planning and construction will fade to a faint memory at some time in the future, and you will be getting a lifetime of pleasure from a home that is just right for you.

Ten Steps You Should Do Before Submitting Your Plans For a Permit

1.Check Your Plans to Make Sure That You Received What You Ordered

You should immediately check your plans to make sure that you received exactly what you ordered. All plans are checked for content prior to shipping, but mistakes can happen. If you find an error in your plans call 1-800-523-6789. All plans are drawn on a particular type of foundation and all details of the plan will illustrate that particular foundation. If you ordered an alternate foundation type. It should be included immediately after the original foundation. Tell your builder which foundation you wish to use and disregard the other foundation.

2.Check to Make Sure You Have Purchased the Proper Plan License

If you purchased prints, your plan will have a round red stamp stating, "If this stamp is not red it is an illegal set of plans." This license grants the purchaser the right to build one home using these construction drawings. It is illegal to make copies, doing so is punishable up to $150,000 per offense plus attorney fees. If you need more prints, call 1-800-523-6789. The House Plans Market Association monitors the home building industry for illegal prints.

It is also illegal to modify or redraw the plan if you purchased a print. If you purchased prints and need to modify the plan, you can upgrade to the reproducible master or CAD file — call 1-800-523-6789. If you purchased a reproducible master or CAD file you have the right to modify the plan and make up to 10 copies. A reproducible master or CAD files comes with a license that you must surrender to the printer or architect making your changes.

3.Complete the "Owner Selection" Portion of the Building Process

The working drawings are very complete, but there are items that you must decide upon. For example, the plans show a toilet in the bathroom, but there are hundreds of models from which to choose. Your individual selection should be made based upon the color, style, and price you wish to pay. This same thing is true for all of the plumbing fixtures, light fixtures, appliances, and interior finishes (for the floors. walls and ceilings) and the exterior finishes. The selection of these items are required in order to obtain accurate competitive bids for the construction of your home

4.Complete Your Permit Package by Adding Other Documents That May Be Required

Your permit department, lender, and builder will need other drawings or documents that must be obtained locally. These items are explained in the next three items.

5.Obtain a Heating & Cooling Calculation and Layout

The heating and cooling system must be calculated and designed for your exact home and your location. Even the orientation of your home can affect the system size. This service is normally provided free of charge by the mechanical company that is supplying the equipment and installation. However, to get an unbiased calculation and equipment recommendation, we suggest employing the services of a mechanical engineer.

6.Obtain a Site Plan

A site plan is a document that shows the relationship of your home to your property. It may be as simple as the document your surveyor provides, or it can be a complex collection of drawings such as those prepared by a landscape architect. Typically, the document prepared by a surveyor will only show the property boundaries and the footprint of the home. Landscape architects can provide planning and drawings for all site amenities, such as driveways and walkways, outdoor structures such as pools, planting plans, irrigation plans, and outdoor lighting.

7.Obtain Earthquake or Hurricane Engineering if You Are Planning to Build in an Earthquake or Hurricane Zone

If you are building in an earthquake or hurricane zone, your permit department will most likely require you to submit calculations and drawings to illustrate the ability of your home to withstand those forces. This information is never included with pre-drawn plans because it would penalize the vast majority of plan purchasers who do not build in those zones. A structural engineer licensed by the state where you are building usually provides this information.

8.Review Your Plan to See Whether Modifications Are Needed

These plans have been designed to assumed conditions and do not address the individual site where you are building. Conditions can vary greatly, including soil conditions, wind and snow loads, and temperature, and any one of these conditions may require some modifications of your plan. For example, if you live in an area that receives snow, structural changes may be necessary. We suggest:

(i)Have your soil tested by a soil-testing laboratory so that sub-surface conditions can be determined at your specific building site. The findings of the soil-testing laboratory should be reviewed by a structural engineer to determine if the existing plan foundation is suitable or if modifications are needed.

(ii)Have your entire plan reviewed by your builder or a structural engineer to determine if other design elements, such as load bearing beams, are sized appropriately for the conditions that exist at your site.

Now that you have the complete plan, you may discover items that you wish to modify to suit your own personal taste or decor. To change the drawings, you must have the reproducible masters or CAD files (see item 2). We can make the changes for you. For complete information regarding modifications, including our fees, go to www.ultimateplans.com and click the "resources" button on the home page; then click on "our custom services."

9.Record Your Blueprint License Number

Record your blueprint license number for easy reference. If you or your builder should need technical support, the license number is required.

10.Keep One Set of Plans as Long as You Own the Home

Be sure to file one copy of your home plan away for safe keeping. You may need a copy in the future if you remodel or sell the home. By filing a copy away for safe keeping, you can avoid the cost of having to purchase plans later.

Plan #151050

Dimensions: 69'2" W x 74'10" D

Levels: 1

Square Footage: 2,096

Bedrooms: 3

Bathrooms: 2½

Foundation: Crawl space, slab, basement, or walkout

CompleteCost List Available: Yes

Price Category: F

Images provided by designer/architect.

You'll love this spacious home for both its elegance and its convenient design.

Features:

- Ceiling Height: 8 ft.

- Great Room: A 9-ft. boxed ceiling complements this large room, which sits just beyond the front gallery. A fireplace and door to the rear porch make it a natural gathering spot.

- Kitchen: This well-designed kitchen includes a central work island and shares an angled eating bar with the adjacent breakfast room.

- Breakfast Room: This room's bay window is gorgeous, and the door to the garage is practical.

- Master Suite: You'll love the 9-ft. boxed ceiling in the bedroom and the vaulted ceiling in the bath, which also includes two walk-in closets, a corner whirlpool tub, split vanities, a shower, and a separate toilet room.

- Workshop: A huge workshop with half-bath is ideal for anyone who loves to build or repair.

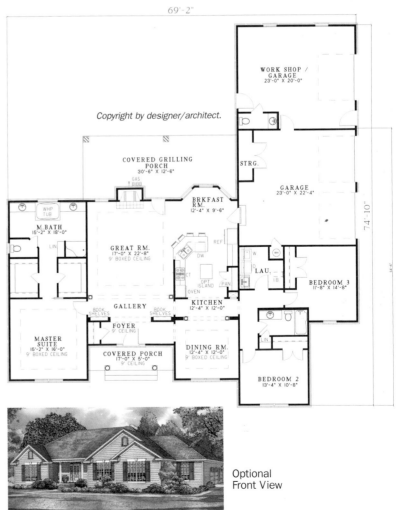

Optional Front View

Plan #101011

Dimensions: 71'2" W x 58'1" D

Levels: 1

Square Footage: 2,184

Bedrooms: 3

Bathrooms: 3

Foundation: Crawl space, slab, basement, or walkout

Materials List Available: Yes

Price Category: E

A classic design and spacious interior add up to a flexible design suitable to any modern lifestyle.

Features:

- Ceiling Height: 9 ft. unless otherwise noted.

- Dining Room: A decorative square column and a tray ceiling adorn this elegant dining room.

- Screened Porch: Enjoy summer breezes in style by stepping out of the French doors into this vaulted screened porch.

- Kitchen: Does everyone want to hang out in the kitchen while you are cooking? No problem. True to the home's country style, this huge 14-ft.-3-in. x 22-ft.-6-in. has plenty of room for helpers. This area is open to the vaulted family room.

- Patio or Deck: This pleasant outdoor area is accessible from both the screened porch and the master bedroom.

- Master Suite: This luxurious suite includes a double tray ceiling, a sitting area, two walk-in closets, and an exquisite bath.

Images provided by designer/architect.

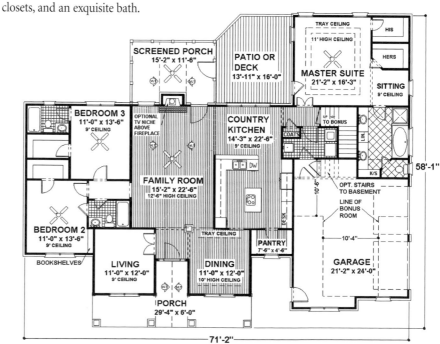

Copyright by designer/architect.

Kitchen

Dining Room

Family Room

Living Room

Master Bath

Master Bedroom

Plan #351001

Dimensions: 72'8" W x 51' D
Levels: 1
Square Footage: 1,855
Bedrooms: 3
Bathrooms: 2½
Foundation: Crawl space, slab, or basement
Materials List Available: Yes
Price Category: D

Images provided by designer/architect.

From the lovely arched windows on the front to the front and back covered porches, this home is as comfortable as it is beautiful.

Features:

• Great Room: Come into this room with 12-ft. ceilings, and you're sure to admire the corner gas fireplace and three windows overlooking the porch.

• Dining Room: Set off from the open design, this room is designed to be used formally or not.

• Kitchen: You'll love the practical walk-in pantry, broom closet, and angled snack bar here.

• Breakfast Room: Brightly lit and leading to the covered porch, this room will be a favorite spot.

• Bonus Room: Develop a playroom or study in this area.

• Master Suite: The large bedroom is complemented by the private bath with garden tub, separate shower, double vanity, and spacious walk-in closet.

Copyright by designer/architect.

Kitchen

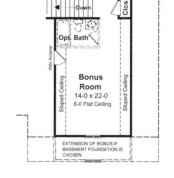

Bonus Area Floor Plan

Plan #351008

Dimensions: 64'6" W x 61'4" D

Levels: 1

Square Footage: 2,002

Bedrooms: 3

Bathrooms: 2

Foundation: Crawl space or basement

Materials List Available: Yes

Price Category: E

Images provided by designer/architect.

This home has the charming appeal of a quaint cottage that you might find in an old village in the English countryside. It's a unique design that maximizes every inch of its usable space.

Features:

• Great Room: This room has a vaulted ceiling and built-in units on each side of the fireplace.

• Kitchen: This kitchen boasts a raised bar open to the breakfast area; the room is also open to the dining room.

• Master Suite: This bedroom retreat features a raised ceiling and a walk-in closet. The bathroom has a double vanity, large walk-in closet, and soaking tub.

• Bedrooms: Two bedrooms share a common bathroom and have large closets.

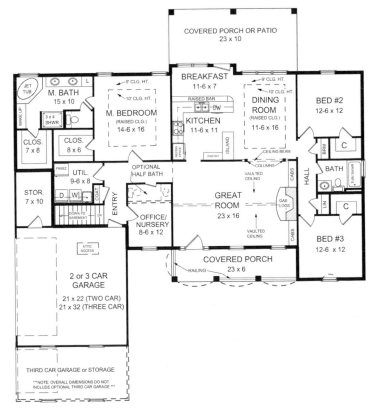

Copyright by designer/architect.

Plan #161051

Dimensions: 57'8" W x 58' D

Levels: 2

Square Footage: 2,484

Main Level Sq. Ft.: 1,710

Upper Level Sq. Ft.: 774

Bedrooms: 4

Bathrooms: 3½

Foundation: Basement; crawl space for fee

Materials List Available: Yes

Price Category: E

Images provided by designer/architect.

Upper Level Floor Plan

Bedroom 14'2" x 11'
Great Room Below
Bath
Bedroom 13' x 11'2"
Balcony
Bath
Foyer Below
Bedroom 11'6" x 12'1"

Main Level Floor Plan

Copyright by designer/architect.

Porch
Master Bedroom 15' x 13'1"
Breakfast 11'5" x 11'3"
Office 8'3" x 5'2"
Great Room 18'4" x 18'10"
Bath
Dressing
Kitchen 13'7" x 12'1"
Laun. 8'3" x 9'6"
Dining Room 11'6" x 14'6"
Foyer
Porch
Two-Car Garage 21' x 24'

57'-8"

58'-0"

Plan #371042

Dimensions: 71'6" W x 49' D

Levels: 1

Square Footage: 1,999

Bedrooms: 3

Bathrooms: 2

Foundation: Slab

Materials List Available: No

Price Category: D

Images provided by designer/architect.

CAD FILE AVAILABLE

71'-5½"

51'-0"

PORCH
NOOK 9'-2" x 10'-7"
KITCH. 10'-0" x 12'-6"
LIVING RM. 15'-0" x 23'-4"
DOUBLE STEP UP CEILING
MASTER SUITE 12'-0" x 16'-2"
W. I. CLOSET
STEP CEILING UP 11'0"
B. 1
UTIL.
WASH DRY
STOR.
PANTRY
STOR.
STAIRCASE
BUTLER'S PANTRY
STORAGE
MEDIA CENTER
STEP DOWN
W. I. CLOSET
GARAGE 20'-8" x 22'-7"
DINING RM. 15'-4" x 12'-7"
ENTRY
BED RM.3 10'-2" x 11'-4"
B.2
LINEN STOR.
DESK & BOOKS
BED RM.2 11'-0" x 14'-4"
BARREL CEILING RAISE FLOOR 7 1/2"
BARREL CEILING
PORCH
WINDOW SEAT

Copyright by designer/architect.

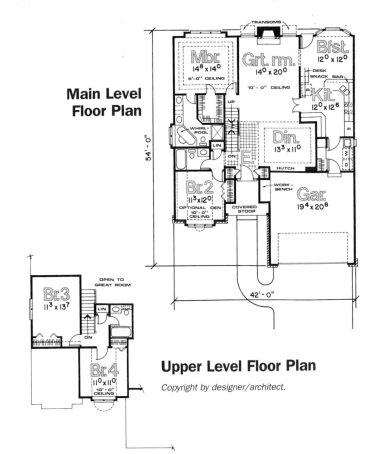

Main Level Floor Plan

Upper Level Floor Plan

Copyright by designer/architect.

Plan #121085

Dimensions: 42' W x 54' D

Levels: 2

Square Footage: 1,948

Main Level Sq. Ft.: 1,517

Upper Level Sq. Ft.: 431

Bedrooms: 4

Bathrooms: 3

Foundation: Basement

Materials List Available: Yes

Price Category: D

Images provided by designer/architect.

CAD FILE AVAILABLE CAD

Upper Level Floor Plan

Main Level Floor Plan

Copyright by designer/architect.

Plan #221025

Dimensions: 69'8" W x 72' D

Levels: 2

Square Footage: 3,009

Main Level Sq. Ft.: 2,039

Upper Level Sq. Ft.: 970

Bedrooms: 4

Bathrooms: 2½

Foundation: Basement

Materials List Available: No

Price Category: G

Images provided by designer/architect.

CAD FILE AVAILABLE CAD

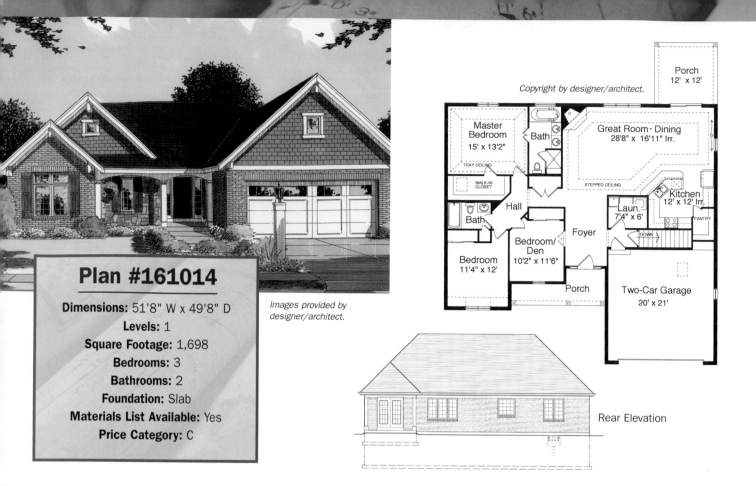

Plan #161014

Dimensions: 51'8" W x 49'8" D

Levels: 1

Square Footage: 1,698

Bedrooms: 3

Bathrooms: 2

Foundation: Slab

Materials List Available: Yes

Price Category: C

Images provided by designer/architect.

Copyright by designer/architect.

Rear Elevation

Plan #121024

Dimensions: 60' W x 58' D

Levels: 2

Square Footage: 3,057

Main Level Sq. Ft.: 1,631

Second Level Sq. Ft.: 1,426

Bedrooms: 4

Bathrooms: 2½

Foundation: Basement; crawl space for fee

Materials List Available: Yes

Price Category: G

Images provided by designer/architect.

Upper Level Floor Plan

Copyright by designer/architect.

Plan #221017

Dimensions: 65' W x 56' D

Levels: 1

Square Footage: 2,229

Bedrooms: 3

Bathrooms: 2

Foundation: Basement

Materials List Available: No

Price Category: E

Images provided by designer/architect.

CAD FILE AVAILABLE

Copyright by designer/architect.

Rear Elevation

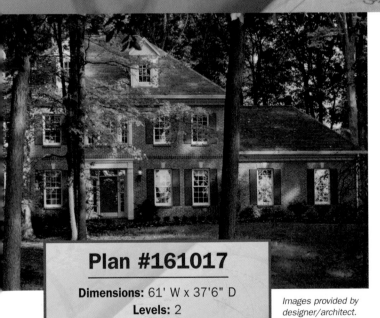

Plan #161017

Dimensions: 61' W x 37'6" D

Levels: 2

Square Footage: 2,653

Main Level Sq. Ft.: 1,365

Upper Level Sq. Ft.: 1,288

Bedrooms: 4

Bathrooms: 2½

Foundation: Basement

Materials List Available: Yes

Price Category: F

Images provided by designer/architect.

CAD FILE AVAILABLE

Main Level Floor Plan

Upper Level Floor Plan

Copyright by designer/architect.

Plan #151179

Dimensions: 66'4" W x 67'2" D

Levels: 1.5

Square Footage: 2,405

Opt. Bonus Level Sq. Ft.: 358

Bedrooms: 4

Bathrooms: 3

Foundation: Crawl space, slab; basement or walkout for fee

CompleteCost List Available: Yes

Price Category: E

Images provided by designer/architect.

As beautiful inside as it is outside, this home will delight the most discerning family.

Features:

- Great Room: This room has a 10-ft. ceiling, door to the porch, fireplace, and built-ins.

- Dining Room: You'll love the way the columns set off this room from the great room and foyer.

- Kitchen: An L-shaped work area, central dining, and working island add to your efficiency.

- Hearth Room: A fireplace and computer center make this room a natural gathering spot.

- Breakfast Room: This lovely room is lit by large windows and a door that opens to the rear porch.

- Master Suite: You'll love the sitting room in the bayed area, walk-in closet, and luxury bath.

- Rear Porch: Use this porch for grilling, dining, and just relaxing—it's large enough to do it all.

Copyright by designer/architect.

Bonus Area Floor Plan

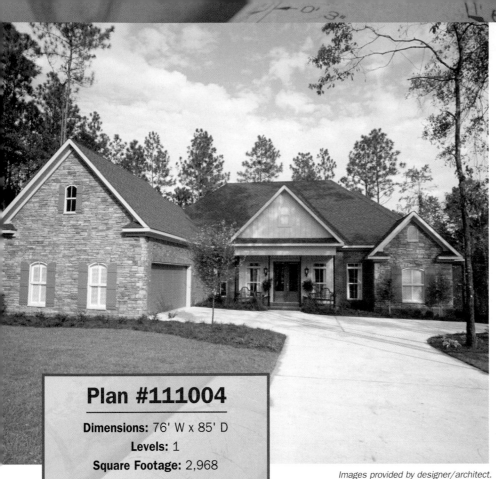

Images provided by designer/architect. Living Room

Plan #111004

Dimensions: 76' W x 85' D
Levels: 1
Square Footage: 2,968
Bedrooms: 4
Full Bathrooms: 3½
Foundation: Basement or slab
Materials List Available: No
Price Category: G

If you've been looking for a home that includes a special master suite, this one could be the answer to your dreams.

Features:

- **Living Room:** Make a sitting area around the fireplace here so that the whole family can enjoy the warmth on chilly days and winter evenings. A door from this room leads to the rear covered porch, making this room the heart of your home.

- **Kitchen:** An island with a cooktop makes cooking a pleasure in this well-designed kitchen, and the breakfast bar invites visitors at all times of day.

- **Utility Room:** A sink and a built-in ironing board make this room totally practical.

- **Master Suite:** A private fireplace in the corner sets a romantic tone for this bedroom, and the door to the covered porch allows you to sit outside on warm summer nights. The bath has two vanities, a divided walk-in closet, a standing shower, and a deluxe corner bathtub.

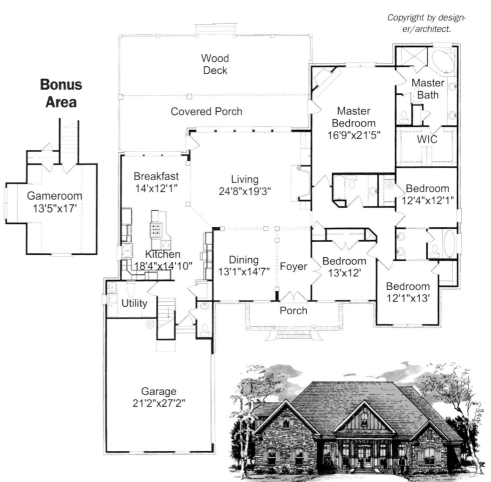

Copyright by designer/architect.

Bonus Area

Gameroom 13'5"x17'

Wood Deck

Covered Porch

Master Bedroom 16'9"x21'5"

Master Bath

WIC

Breakfast 14'x12'1"

Living 24'8"x19'3"

Bedroom 12'4"x12'1"

Kitchen 18'4"x14'10"

Dining 13'1"x14'7"

Foyer

Bedroom 13'x12'

Bedroom 12'1"x13'

Utility

Porch

Garage 21'2"x27'2"

Plan #151170

Dimensions: 57' W x 64'4" D

Levels: 1

Square Footage: 1,965

Bedrooms: 4

Bathrooms: 2

Foundation: Crawl space, slab; basement or daylight basement for fee

CompleteCost List Available: Yes

Price Category: E

Images provided by designer/architect.

The clean lines of the open floor plan and high ceilings match the classic good looks of this home's exterior.

Features:

• Foyer: The 10-ft. ceiling here sets the stage for the open, airy feeling of this lovely home.

• Dining Room: Set off by columns from the foyer and great room, this area is ideal for entertaining.

• Great Room: Open to the breakfast room beyond, this great room features a masonry fireplace and a door to the rear grilling porch.

• Breakfast Room: A deep bay overlooking the porch is the focal point here.

• Kitchen: Planned for efficiency, the kitchen has an angled island with storage and snack bar.

• Master Suite: A boxed ceiling adds elegance to the bedroom, and the bath features a whirlpool tub, double vanity, and separate shower.

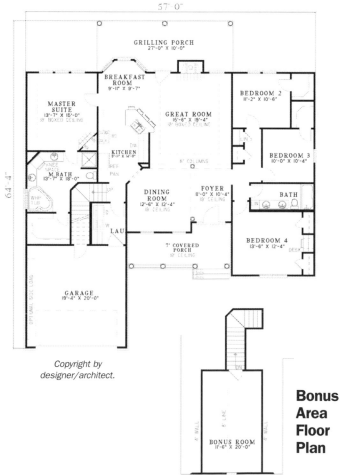

Copyright by designer/architect.

Bonus Area Floor Plan

Images provided by designer/architect.

Plan #241008

Dimensions: 65' W x 56'8" D
Levels: 1
Square Footage: 2,526
Bedrooms: 4
Bathrooms: 3
Foundation: Crawl space, slab, or basement
Materials List Available: No
Price Category: E

A covered back porch—with access from the master suite and the breakfast area—makes this traditional home ideal for sitting near a golf course or with a backyard pool.

Features:

- **Great Room:** From the foyer, guests enter this spacious and comfortable great room, which features a handsome fireplace.

- **Kitchen:** This kitchen—the hub of this family-oriented home—is a joy in which to work, thanks to abundant counter space, a pantry, a convenient eating bar, and an adjoining breakfast area and sunroom.

- **Master Suite:** Enjoy the quiet comfort of this coffered-ceiling master suite, which features dual vanities and separate walk-in closets.

- **Additional Bedrooms:** Two secondary bedrooms, which share a full bath, are located at the opposite end of the house from the master suite. Bedroom 4—in front of the house—can be converted into a study.

Copyright by designer/architect.

SMARTtip

Traditional-Style Kitchen Cabinetry

You can modify stock kitchen cabinetry to enjoy fine furniture-quality details. Prefabricated trims may be purchased at local lumber mills and home centers. For example, crown molding, applied to the top of stock cabinetry and stained or painted to match the door style, may be all you need. Likewise, you can replace hardware with reproduction polished-brass door and drawer knobs or pulls for a finishing touch.

Plan #131032

Dimensions: 69'2" W x 46' D

Levels: 2

Square Footage: 2,455

Main Level Sq. Ft.: 1,499

Upper Level Sq. Ft.: 956

Bedrooms: 4

Bathrooms: 3

Foundation: Crawl space, slab, or basement

Materials List Available: Yes

Price Category: F

If you love Victorian styling, you'll be charmed by the ornate, rounded front porch and the two-story bay that distinguish this home.

Images provided by designer/architect.

Features:

- **Living Room:** You'll love the 13-ft. ceiling in this room, as well as the panoramic view it gives of the front porch and yard.

- **Kitchen:** Sunlight streams into this room, where an angled island with a cooktop eases both prepping and cooking.

- **Breakfast Room:** This room shares an eating bar with the kitchen, making it easy for the family to congregate while the family chef is cooking.

- **Guest Room:** Use this lovely room on the first level as a home office or study if you wish.

- **Master Suite:** The dramatic bayed sitting area with a high ceiling has an octagonal shape that you'll adore, and the amenities in the private bath will soothe you at the end of a busy day.

Rear View

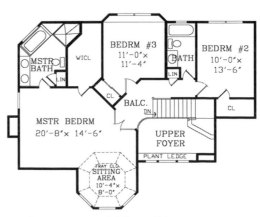

Main Level Floor Plan

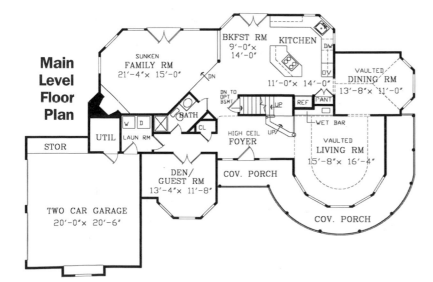

Upper Level Floor Plan

Copyright by designer/architect.

Plan #101017

Dimensions: 57' W x 51' D
Levels: 2
Square Footage: 2,253
Main Level Sq. Ft.: 1,719
Upper Level Sq. Ft.: 534
Opt. Upper Level Bonus Sq. Ft.: 247
Bedrooms: 4
Bathrooms: 3
Foundation: Basement
Materials List Available: No
Price Category: E

Images provided by designer/architect.

This alluring two-story "master-down" design blends a spectacular floor plan with a lovely facade to create a home that's simply irresistible.

Features:

- **Entry:** You're welcomed by an inviting front porch and greeted by a beautiful leaded glass door leading to this two-story entry.

- **Family Room:** A corner fireplace and a window wall with arched transoms accent this dramatic room.

- **Master Suite:** This sumptuous suite includes a double tray ceiling, sitting area, and his and her walk-in closets. The master bathroom features dual vanities, a corner tub, and a shower.

- **Bedrooms:** Located upstairs, these two additional bedrooms share a Jack-and-Jill bathroom.

Main Level Floor Plan

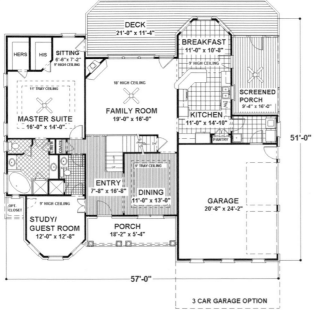

Upper Level Floor Plan

Copyright by designer/architect.

Plan #151034

Dimensions: 58'6" W x 64'6" D

Levels: 1

Square Footage: 2,133

Bedrooms: 3

Bathrooms: 2

Foundation: Crawl space, slab, basement, or walkout

Materials List Available: Yes

Price Category: D

 This home, as shown in the photograph, may differ from the actual blueprints. For more detailed information, please check the floor plans carefully.

Images provided by designer/architect.

You'll love the high ceilings, open floor plan, and contemporary design features in this home.

Features:

- **Great Room:** A pass-through tiled fireplace between this lovely large room and the adjacent hearth room allows you to notice the mirror effect created by the 10-ft. boxed ceilings in both rooms.

- **Dining Room:** An 11-ft. ceiling and 8-in. boxed column give formality to this lovely room, where you're certain to entertain.

- **Kitchen:** If you're a cook, this room may become your favorite spot in the house, thanks to its great design, which includes plenty of work and storage space, and a very practical layout.

- **Master Suite:** A 10-ft. boxed ceiling gives elegance to this room. A pocket door opens to the private bath, with its huge walk-in closet, glass-blocked whirlpool tub, separate glass shower, and private toilet room.

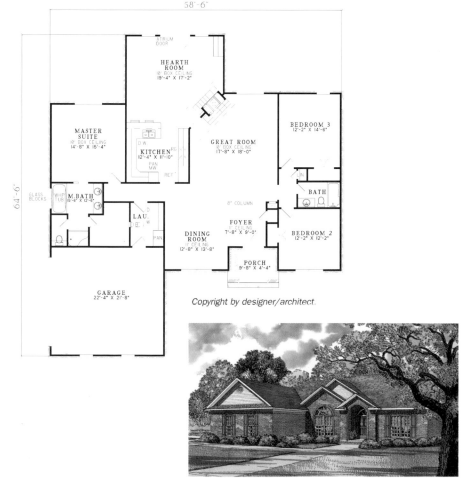

Copyright by designer/architect.

Rendering reflects floor plan

Plan #261001

Dimensions: 77'8" W x 49' D

Levels: 2

Square Footage: 3,746

Main Level Sq. Ft.: 1,965

Upper Level Sq. Ft.: 1,781

Bedrooms: 4

Bathrooms: 3½

Foundation: Basement

Materials List Available: No

Price Category: H

If contemporary designs appeal to you, you're sure to love this stunning home.

Features:

- Foyer: A volume ceiling here announces the spaciousness of this gracious home.

- Family Room: Also with a volume ceiling, this family room features a fireplace where you can create a cozy sitting area.

- Kitchen: Designed for the pleasure of the family cooks, this room features a large pantry, ample counter and cabinet space, and a dining bar.

- Dinette: Serve the family in style, or host casual, informal dinners for friends in this dinette with its gracious volume ceiling.

- Master Suite: You'll love this room's spaciousness and walk-in closet. The bath features dual vanities, a whirlpool tub, and a separate shower.

Images provided by designer/architect.

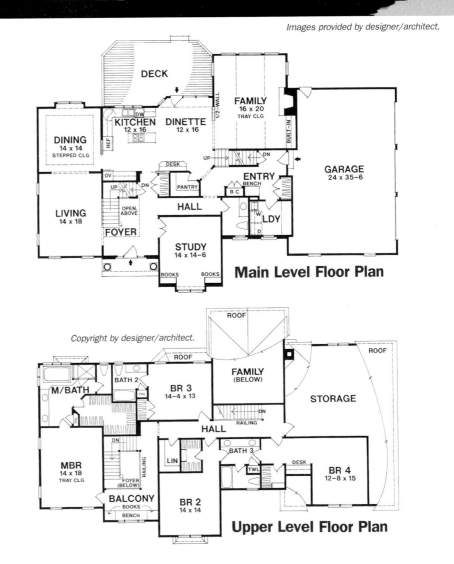

Main Level Floor Plan

Copyright by designer/architect.

Upper Level Floor Plan

Plan #161045

Dimensions: 57' W x 49'8" D

Levels: 2

Square Footage: 2,077

Main Level Sq. Ft.: 1,532

Upper Level Sq. Ft.: 545

Bedrooms: 3

Bathrooms: 2½

Foundation: Basement; crawl space for fee

Materials List Available: No

Price Category: D

Images provided by designer/architect.

Multiple gables, arched windows, and the stone accents that adorn the exterior of this lovely two-story home create a dramatic first impression.

Features:

• Great Room: With multiple windows to light your way, grand openings, varied ceiling treatments, and angled walls let you flow from room to room. Enjoy the warmth of the gas fireplace in both this great room and the dining area.

• Master Suite: Experience the luxurious atmosphere of this master suite, with its coffered ceiling and deluxe bath.

• Additional Bedrooms: Angled stairs lead to a balcony with writing desk and to two additional bedrooms.

• Porch: Exit two sets of French doors to the rear yard and a covered porch, perfect for relaxing in comfortable weather.

Main Level Floor Plan

Copyright by designer/architect.

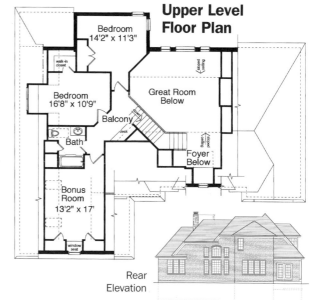

Upper Level Floor Plan

Rear Elevation

Plan #131050

Dimensions: 72'8" W x 47' D
Levels: 2
Square Footage: 2,874
Main Level Sq. Ft.: 2,146
Upper Level Sq. Ft.: 728
Bedrooms: 4
Bathrooms: 3
Foundation: Crawl space, slab, or basement
Materials List Available: Yes
Price Category: G

A gazebo and long covered porch at the entry let you know that this is a spectacular design.

Images provided by designer/architect.

Features:

- Foyer: This vaulted foyer divides the formal living room and dining room, setting the stage for guests to feel welcome in your home.

- Great Room: This large room is defined by several columns; a corner fireplace and vaulted ceiling add to its drama.

- Kitchen: An island work space separates this area from the bayed breakfast nook.

- Master Suite: You'll have privacy in this main-floor suite, which features two walk-in closets and a separate toilet room with a dual-sink vanity.

- Upper Level: The two large bedrooms share a bath and a dramatic balcony.

- Bonus Room: Walk down a few steps into this large bonus room over the 3-car garage.

Rear Elevation

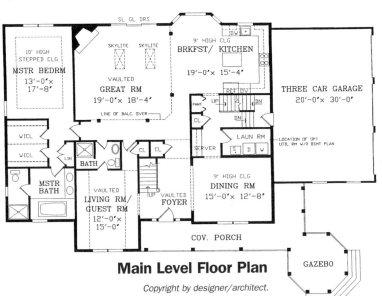

Main Level Floor Plan

Copyright by designer/architect.

Upper Level Floor Plan

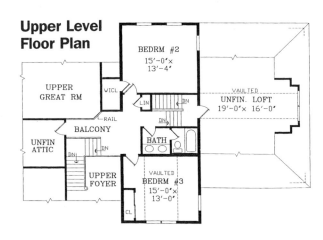

Plan #121001

Dimensions: 56' W x 58' D

Levels: 1

Square Footage: 1,911

Bedrooms: 3

Bathrooms: 2

Foundation: Basement

Materials List Available: Yes

Price Category: D

Detailed, soaring ceilings and top-notch amenities set this distinctive home apart.

Features:

- Ceiling Height: 8 ft. except as noted.

- Great Room: A soaring ceiling and six tall transom-topped windows make this a light and airy spot for entertaining.

- Formal Dining Room: The entry enjoys a pleasing view of this dining room's detailed 12-ft. ceiling and picture window.

- Great Room: At the back of the home, a see-through fireplace in this great room is joined by a built-in entertainment center.

- Hearth Room: This bayed room shares the see-through fireplace with the great room.

- Master Suite: Enjoy the stars and the sun in the private bath's whirlpool and separate shower. The bath features the same decorative ceiling as the dining room.

Images provided by designer/architect.

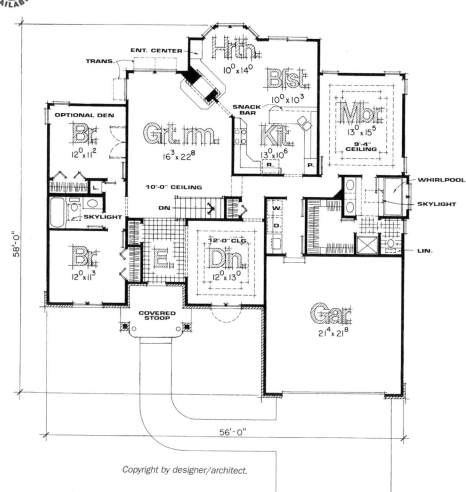

Copyright by designer/architect.

Plan #151117

Dimensions: 66' W x 55' D

Levels: 1

Square Footage: 1,957

Bedrooms: 3

Bathrooms: 3

Foundation: Crawl space, slab, or basement

CompleteCost List Available: Yes

Price Category: D

You'll love this home if you have a family-centered lifestyle and enjoy an active social life.

Features:

- Foyer: A 10-ft. ceiling sets the tone for this home.

- Great Room: A 10-ft. boxed ceiling and fireplace are the highlights of this room, which also has a door leading to the rear covered porch.

- Dining Room: Columns mark the entry from the foyer to this lovely formal dining room.

- Study: Add the French doors from the foyer to transform bedroom 3, with its vaulted ceiling, into a quiet study.

- Kitchen: This large kitchen includes a pantry and shares an eating bar with the adjoining, bayed breakfast room.

- Master Suite: You'll love the access to the rear porch, as well as the bath with every amenity, in this suite.

CAD FILE AVAILABLE

Images provided by designer/architect.

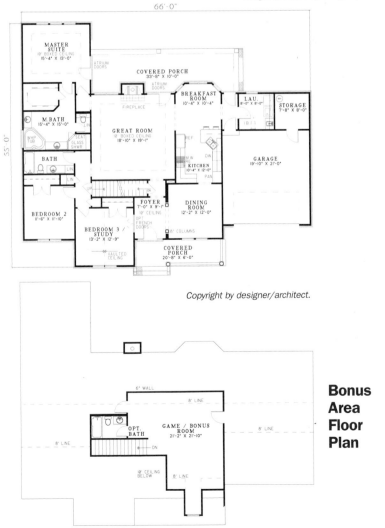

Copyright by designer/architect.

Bonus Area Floor Plan

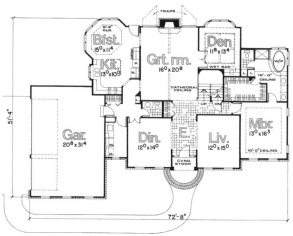

Main Level Floor Plan

Plan #121071

Dimensions: 72'8" W x 51'4" D

Levels: 2

Square Footage: 2,957

Main Level Sq. Ft.: 2,063

Upper Level Sq. Ft.: 894

Bedrooms: 4

Bathrooms: 4½

Foundation: Basement

Materials List Available: Yes

Price Category: F

Images provided by designer/architect.

Upper Level Floor Plan

Copyright by designer/architect.

Plan #211086

Dimensions: 71' W x 50' D

Levels: 1

Square Footage: 1,704

Bedrooms: 3

Bathrooms: 2½

Foundation: Crawl space

Materials List Available: Yes

Price Category: C

Images provided by designer/architect.

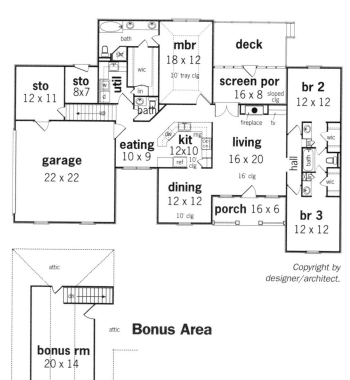

Bonus Area

Copyright by designer/architect.

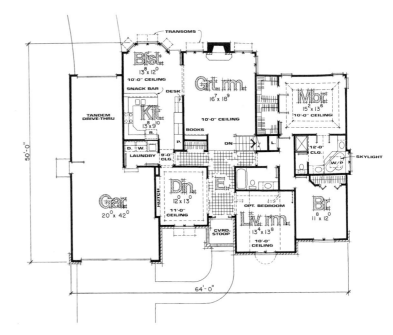

Plan #121050

Dimensions: 64' W x 50' D

Levels: 1

Square Footage: 1,996

Bedrooms: 2

Bathrooms: 2

Foundation: Basement; crawl space for fee

Materials List Available: Yes

Price Category: D

Images provided by designer/architect.

Copyright by designer/architect.

Upper Level Floor Plan

Plan #161020

Dimensions: 60' W" x 50'4" D

Levels: 2

Square Footage: 2,082; 2,349 with bonus space

Main Level Sq. Ft.: 1,524

Upper Level Sq. Ft.: 558

Bedrooms: 3

Bathrooms: 2½

Foundation: Basement

Materials List Available: Yes

Price Category: D

Images provided by designer/architect.

CAD FILE AVAILABLE

Main Level Floor Plan

Copyright by designer/architect.

Images provided by designer/architect.

Copyright by designer/architect.

Plan #271073

Dimensions: 69' W x 56' D

Levels: 1

Square Footage: 1,920

Bedrooms: 3

Bathrooms: 2½

Foundation: Walkout basement

Materials List Available: No

Price Category: D

Basement Level Floor Plan

Plan #211090

Dimensions: 66' W x 72' D

Levels: 1

Square Footage: 1,932

Bedrooms: 3

Bathrooms: 2

Foundation: Crawl space

Materials List Available: No

Price Category: D

Images provided by designer/architect.

CAD FILE AVAILABLE

Bonus Area

Copyright by designer/architect.

Plan #121095

Dimensions: 65'4" W x 48'8" D

Levels: 2

Square Footage: 2,282

Main Level Sq. Ft.: 1,597

Upper Level Sq. Ft.: 685

Bedrooms: 4

Bathrooms: 2½

Foundation: Basement

Materials List Available: Yes

Price Category: E

Images provided by designer/architect.

CAD FILE AVAILABLE

Main Level Floor Plan

Copyright by designer/architect.

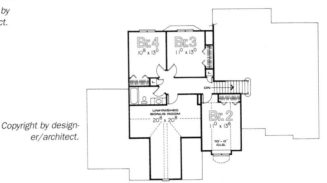

Upper Level Floor Plan

Plan #211037

Dimensions: 66' W x 60' D

Levels: 1

Square Footage: 1,800

Bedrooms: 3

Bathrooms: 2

Foundation: Crawl space or basement; slab available for fee

Materials List Available: Yes

Price Category: D

Images provided by designer/architect.

CAD FILE AVAILABLE

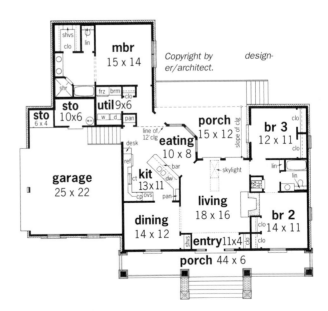

Copyright by designer/architect.

SMARTtip

Reflected Light in the Bathroom

The addition of a large mirror can bring reflected light into a small bathroom, adding the illusion of space without the expense of renovation.

Plan #121093

Dimensions: 62' W x 60'8" D

Levels: 1.5

Square Footage: 2,603

Main Level Sq. Ft.: 1,800

Upper Level Sq. Ft.: 803

Bedrooms: 4

Bathrooms: 3½

Foundation: Basement

Materials List Available: Yes

Price Category: F

Images provided by designer/architect.

If you love family life but also treasure your privacy, you'll appreciate the layout of this home.

Features:

• Entry: This two-story, open area features plant shelves to display your favorite plants and flowers.

• Dining Room: Open to the entry, this room features 12-ft. ceilings and corner hutches.

• Den: French doors lead to this quiet room, with its bowed window and spider-beamed ceiling.

• Gathering Room: A three-sided fireplace, shared with both the kitchen and the breakfast area, is the highlight of this room.

• Master Suite: Secluded for privacy, this suite also has a private covered deck where you can sit and recharge at any time of day. A walk-in closet is practical, and a whirlpool tub is pure comfort.

Main Level Floor Plan

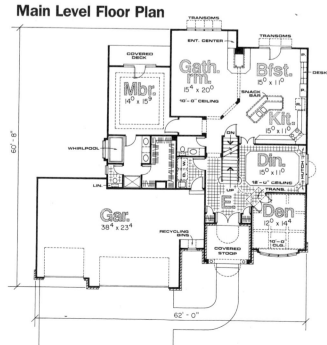

Upper Level Floor Plan

Copyright by designer/architect.

Plan #101012

Dimensions: 69'4" W x 62'9" D

Levels: 1

Square Footage: 2,288

Bedrooms: 3

Bathrooms: 2½

Foundation: Crawl space, slab, basement, or walkout

Materials List Available: No

Price Category: E

Images provided by designer/architect.

This classic brick ranch boasts traditional styling and an exciting up-to-date floor plan.

CAD FILE AVAILABLE

Features:

- Ceiling Height: 9 ft. unless otherwise noted.

- Front Porch: Guests will be welcome by this inviting front porch, which features a 12-ft. ceiling.

- Family Room: This warm and inviting room measures 16 ft. x 19 ft. It features a 14-ft. ceiling and a rear wall of windows. French doors lead to an enormous deck.

- Kitchen: This unique angled kitchen is open to the hearth room and eating areas, all of which enjoy vaulted ceilings and are surrounded by windows. The hearth room has a TV niche.

- Master Suite: This 16-ft. x 15-ft. master suite is truly sumptuous, with its 12-ft. ceiling, sitting area, two walk-in closets, and full-featured bath.

- Bonus Room: Here is plenty of storage or room for future expansion. Just beyond the entry are stairs leading to a bonus room measuring approximately 12 ft. x 21 ft.

Copyright by designer/architect.

Living Room

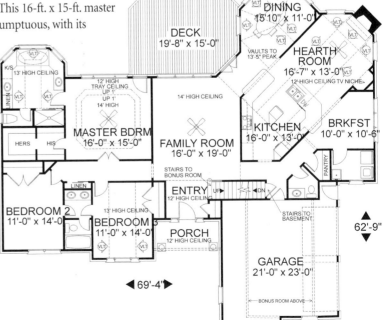

Plan #161002

Dimensions: 64'2" W x 44'2" D

Levels: 1

Square Footage: 1,860

Bedrooms: 3

Bathrooms: 2

Foundation: Basement

Materials List Available: Yes

Price Category: D

Images provided by designer/architect.

The brick, stone, and cedar shake facade provides color and texture to the exterior, while the unique nooks and angles inside this delightful one-level home give it character.

Features:

- Great Room/Dining Room: This spacious great room is furnished with a wood-burning fireplace, a high ceiling, and French doors. Wide entrances to the breakfast room and dining room expand its space to comfortably hold large gatherings.

- Kitchen: The breakfast bar offers additional seating. The covered porch lets you enjoy a view of the landscape and is conveniently located for outdoor meals off this kitchen and breakfast area.

- Master Suite: The master suite is a private retreat. An alcove creates a comfortable sitting area, and an angled entry leads to the bath with whirlpool and a double-bowl vanity.

Great Room/Foyer

Rear Elevation

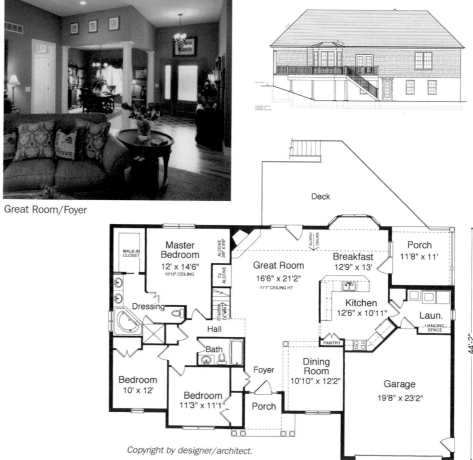

Copyright by designer/architect.

Plan #121078

Dimensions: 50' W x 48' D
Levels: 2
Square Footage: 2,248
Main Level Sq. Ft.: 1,568
Upper Level Sq. Ft.: 680
Bedrooms: 4
Bathrooms: 2½
Foundation: Slab;
crawl space or basement for fee
Materials List Available: Yes
Price Category: E

Images provided by designer/architect.

This home, as shown in the photograph, may differ from the actual blueprints. For more detailed information, please check the floor plans carefully.

This design is wonderful for any family but has features that make it ideal for one with teens.

Features:

- Family Room: A vaulted ceiling gives a touch of elegance here and a corner fireplace makes it comfortable, especially when the weather's cool.

- Living Room: Both this room and the dining room have a formal feeling, but don't let that stop you from making them a family gathering spot.

- Kitchen: A built-in desk, butler's pantry, and a walk-in pantry make this kitchen easy to organize. The breakfast nook shares an angled eating bar with the family room.

- Master Suite: A walk-in closet and corner tub and shower make this suite feel luxurious.

Main Level Floor Plan

Copyright by designer/architect.

Upper Level Floor Plan

Plan #151019

Dimensions: 63'4" W x 53'10" D

Levels: 2

Square Footage: 2,653

Main Level Sq. Ft.: 1,407

Upper Level Sq. Ft.: 1,246

Bedrooms: 3

Bathrooms: 2½

Foundation: Crawl space or slab; full basement for fee

CompleteCost List Available: Yes

Price Category: F

Images provided by designer/architect.

Majestic French doors at the entry and a balcony overlooking the open foyer set the gracious tone that marks every aspect of this fabulous design.

Features:

- Great Room: Step down into this large room with its gas fireplace and atrium door to the patio.
- Study: Sliding doors and a 9-ft. ceiling give presence to this room.
- Dining Room: Entertaining is easy in this conveniently-placed room with sliding glass doors leading to a rear screened porch as well as the patio.
- Upper Level: Bedrooms 2 and 3 share access to a bath and the balcony that overlooks the foyer.
- Master Suite: A 10-ft. pan ceiling and French doors give elegance to the spacious suite, and you'll enjoy practicality and luxury in the bath, with its two walk-in closets, a corner whirlpool tub, and split vanities.

Main Level Floor Plan

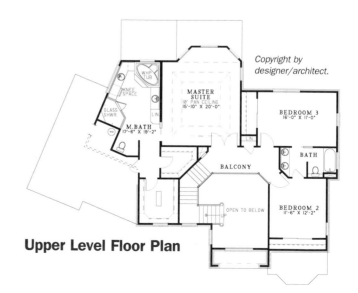

Copyright by designer/architect.

Upper Level Floor Plan

Plan #121062

Dimensions: 70' W x 62' D
Levels: 1.5
Square Footage: 3,448
Main Level Sq. Ft.: 2,375
Upper Level Sq. Ft.: 1,073
Bedrooms: 4
Bathrooms: 3½
Foundation: Basement
Materials List Available: Yes
Price Category: G

Images provided by designer/architect.

You'll love this design if you're looking for a comfortable home with dimensions and details that create a sense of grandeur.

Features:

- Entry: A soaring ceiling, curved staircase, and balcony that overlooks a tall plant shelf combine to create your first impression of grandeur in this home.

- Great Room: A transom-topped bowed window highlights this room, with its 11-ft., beamed ceiling, built-in wet bar, and see-through fireplace.

- Kitchen: Designed for the gourmet cook, this kitchen has every amenity you could desire.

- Breakfast Room: Adjacent to the great room and the kitchen, this gazebo-shaped breakfast area lights both the kitchen and hearth room.

Main Level Floor Plan

Upper Level Floor Plan

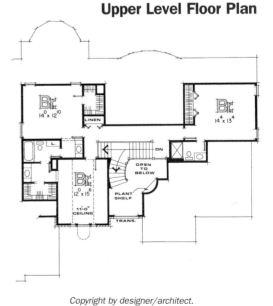

Copyright by designer/architect.

www.ultimateplans.com

Plan #161018

Dimensions: 74'4" W x 69'11" D

Levels: 1.5

Square Footage: 2,816
+ 325 Sq. Ft. bonus room

Main Level Sq. Ft.: 2,231

Upper Level Sq. Ft.: 624

Bedrooms: 3

Bathrooms: 2 full, 2 half

Foundation: Basement, or walkout

Materials List Available: No

Price Category: F

If you love classic European designs, look closely at this home with its multiple gables and countless conveniences and luxuries.

Images provided by designer/architect.

Features:

- Foyer: Open to the great room, the 2-story foyer offers a view all the way to the rear windows.

- Great Room: A fireplace makes this room cozy in any kind of weather.

- Kitchen: This large room features an island with a sink, and an angled wall with French doors to the back yard.

- Dining Room: The furniture alcove and raised ceiling make this room both formal and practical.

- Master Suite: You'll love the quiet in the bedroom and the luxuries—a tub, separate shower, and double vanities—in the bath.

- Basement: The door from the basement to the side yard adds convenience to outdoor work.

Rear View

Main Level Floor Plan

Upper Level Floor Plan

Copyright by designer/architect.

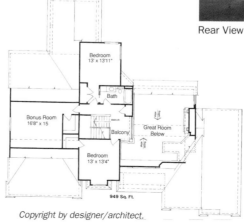

Foyer/Dining Room

Plan #151015

Dimensions: 72'4" W x 48'4" D
Levels: 1.5
Square Footage: 2,789
Main Level Sq. Ft.: 1,977
Upper Level Sq. Ft.: 812
Bedrooms: 4
Bathrooms: 3
Foundation: Crawl space, slab, or basement
CompleteCost List Available: Yes
Price Category: F

Images provided by designer/architect.

The spacious kitchen that opens to the breakfast room and the hearth room make this family home ideal for entertaining.

Features:

- Great Room: The fireplace will make a cozy winter focal point in this versatile space.

- Hearth Room: Enjoy the built-in entertainment center, built-in shelving, and fireplace here.

- Dining Room: A swing door leading to the kitchen is as attractive as it is practical.

- Study: A private bath and walk-in closet make this room an ideal spot for guests when needed.

- Kitchen: An island work area, a computer desk, and an eat-in bar add convenience and utility.

- Master Suite: Two vanities, two walk-in closets, a shower with a seat, and a whirlpool tub highlight this private space.

Upper Level Floor Plan

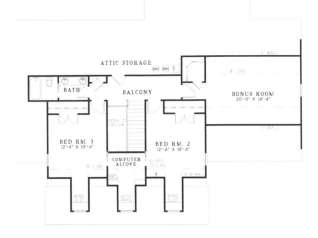

Main Level Floor Plan

Plan #131026

Dimensions: 55'10" W x 41' D
Levels: 2
Square Footage: 2,796
Main Level Sq. Ft.: 1,481
Upper level Sq. Ft.: 1,315
Bedrooms: 4
Bathrooms: 2½
Foundation: Crawl space, slab, or basement
Materials List Available: Yes
Price Category: G

Images provided by designer/architect.

Handsome half rounds add to curb appeal.

Features:

• Ceiling Height: 8 ft.

• Library: This room features a 10-ft. ceiling with a bright bay window.

• Family Room: A 10-ft. ceiling adds to the spacious feeling of this room, while the fireplace gives it an intimate feeling. Sliding glass doors at the rear of the room open to the backyard.

• Dining Room: This formal room adjoins the family room, allowing guests and family to flow between the rooms, and it opens to the backyard through sliding glass doors.

• Breakfast Room: Turrets add a Victorian feeling to this room, which is just off the kitchen and overlooks the front porch.

• Master Suite: Privacy is assured in this suite, which is separated from the main part of the house. A separate toilet room and large walk-in closet add convenience to its beauty.

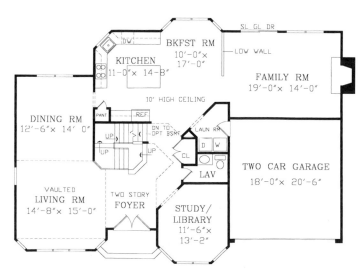

Main Level Floor Plan

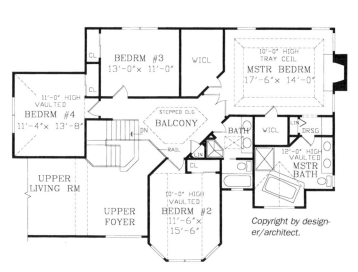

Upper Level Floor Plan

Plan #121079

Dimensions: 50' W x 60' D
Levels: 2
Square Footage: 2,688
Main Level Sq. Ft.: 1,650
Upper Level Sq. Ft.: 1,038
Bedrooms: 4
Bathrooms: 3½
Foundation: Slab
Materials List Available: Yes
Price Category: F

You'll love this open design if you're looking for a home that gives a spacious feeling while also providing private areas.

Features:

• Entry: The cased openings and corner columns here give an attractive view into the dining room.

• Living Room: Another cased opening defines the entry to this living room but lets traffic flow into it.

• Kitchen: This well-designed kitchen is built around a center island that gives you extra work space. A snack bar makes an easy, open transition between the sunny dining nook and the kitchen.

• Master Suite: An 11-ft. ceiling sets the tone for this private space. With a walk-in closet and adjoining full bath, it will delight you.

Images provided by designer/architect.

This home, as shown in the photograph, may differ from the actual blueprints. For more detailed information, please check the floor plans carefully.

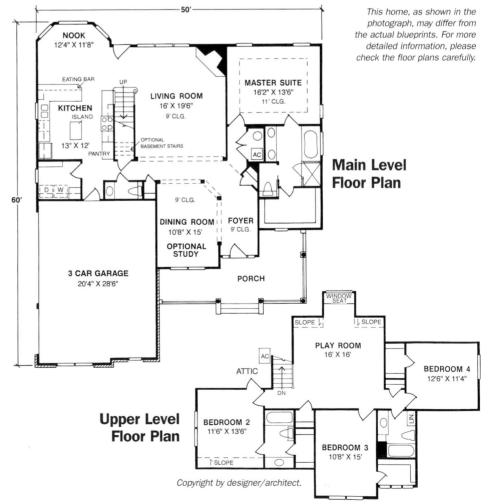

Copyright by designer/architect.

Plan #131019

Dimensions: 83'6" W x 53'4" D
Levels: 1
Square Footage: 2,243
Bedrooms: 3
Bathrooms: 2½
Foundation: Crawl space, slab, or basement
Materials List Available: Yes
Price Category: F

Drama marks this contemporary, angled ranch-style home which can be placed to suit any site, even the most difficult.

Images provided by designer/architect.

Features:

- **Great Room:** Imagine having an octagonal great room! The shape alone makes it spectacular, but the view to the backyard from its four exterior sides adds to the impression it creates, and you'll love its 16-ft. tray ceiling, fireplace, and wall designed to fit a large entertainment center.

- **Kitchen:** This room is adjacent to and visually connected to the great room but has excellent features of its own that make it an easy place to cook or clean.

- **Master Suite:** Separated from the other bedrooms, this suite is planned for privacy. You'll love the bath here and look forward to the quiet you can find at the end of the day.

- **Additional Bedrooms:** In a wing of their own, the other two bedrooms share a bath.

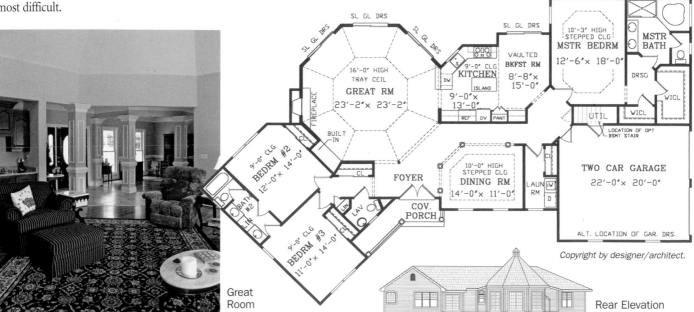

Great Room

Copyright by designer/architect.

Rear Elevation

Plan #161025

Dimensions: 63'4" W x 48' D
Levels: 1.5
Square Footage: 2,738
Main Level Sq. Ft.: 1,915
Upper Level Sq. Ft.: 823
Bedrooms: 4
Bathrooms: 3½
Foundation: Basement
Materials List Available: No
Price Category: F

This home, as shown in the photograph, may differ from the actual blueprints. For more detailed information, please check the floor plans carefully.

Images provided by designer/architect.

One look at the octagonal tower, boxed window, and wood-and-stone trim, and you'll know how much your family will love this home.

Features:

- Foyer: View the high windows across the rear wall, a fireplace, and open stairs as you come in.

- Great Room: Gather in this two-story-high area.

- Hearth Room: Open to the breakfast room, it's close to both the kitchen and dining room.

- Kitchen: A snack bar and an island make the kitchen ideal for family living.

- Master Suite: You'll love the 9-ft. ceiling in the bedroom and 11-ft. ceiling in the sitting area. The bath has a tub, double-bowl vanity, and walk-in closet.

- Upper Level: A balcony leads to a bedroom with a private bath and 2 other rooms with private access to a shared bath.

Main Level Floor Plan

Upper Level Floor Plan

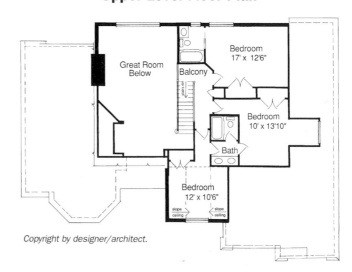

Copyright by designer/architect.

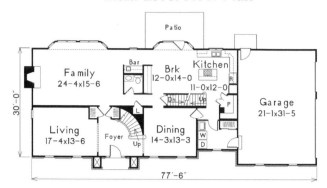

Main Level Floor Plan

Plan #321049

Dimensions: 77'6" W x 30' D

Levels: 2

Square Footage: 3,144

Main Level Sq. Ft.: 1,724

Upper Level Sq. Ft.: 1,420

Bedrooms: 4

Bathrooms: 3½

Foundation: Basement

Materials List Available: Yes

Price Category: G

Images provided by designer/architect.

CAD FILE AVAILABLE

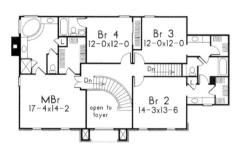

Upper Level Floor Plan

Copyright by designer/architect.

Plan #161015

Dimensions: 55'4" W x 40'4" D

Levels: 2

Square Footage: 1,768

Main Level Sq. Ft.: 960

Upper Level Sq. Ft.: 808

Bedrooms: 3

Bathrooms: 2½

Foundation: Basement

Materials List Available: Yes

Price Category: C

Images provided by designer/architect.

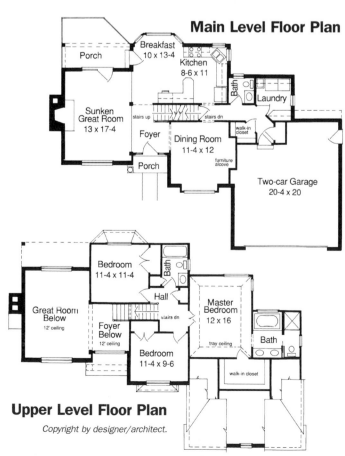

Main Level Floor Plan

Upper Level Floor Plan

Copyright by designer/architect.

Plan #291013

Dimensions: 72' W x 75' D

Levels: 2

Square Footage: 3,553

Main Level Sq. Ft.: 1,830

Upper Level Sq. Ft.: 1,723

Bedrooms: 4

Bathrooms: 2½

Foundation: Basement

Materials List Available: No

Price Category: H

Images provided by designer/architect.

Copyright by designer/architect.

Main Level Floor Plan

Upper Level Floor Plan

Plan #151087

Dimensions: 55'4" W x 53'10" D

Levels: 2

Square Footage: 2,942

Main Level Sq. Ft.: 1,547

Upper Level Sq. Ft.: 1,395

Bedrooms: 5

Bathrooms: 4

Foundation: Crawl space or slab; basement or walkout for fee

CompleteCost List Available: Yes

Price Category: F

Images provided by designer/architect.

CAD FILE AVAILABLE

Main Level Floor Plan

Upper Level Floor Plan

Copyright by designer/architect.

Plan #151656

Dimensions: 43'8" W x 71'6" D

Levels: 1

Square Footage: 1,806

Bedrooms: 3

Bathrooms: 2

Foundation: Crawl space or slab; basement or wwalkout for fee

CompleteCost List Available: Yes

Price Category: D

Images provided by designer/architect.

Copyright by designer/architect.

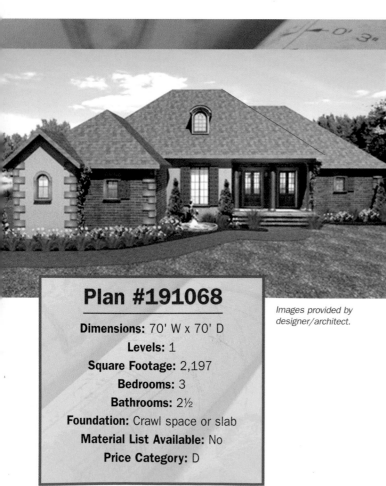

Plan #191068

Dimensions: 70' W x 70' D

Levels: 1

Square Footage: 2,197

Bedrooms: 3

Bathrooms: 2½

Foundation: Crawl space or slab

Material List Available: No

Price Category: D

Images provided by designer/architect.

Copyright by designer/architect.

Rear View

Main Level Floor Plan

Plan #221079

Dimensions: 69'8" W x 64'4" D

Levels: 2

Square Footage: 2,727

Main Level Sq. Ft.: 2,146

Upper Level Sq. Ft.: 581

Bedrooms: 3

Bathrooms: 2½

Foundation: Basement

Material List Available: No

Price Category: F

Images provided by designer/architect.

Rear Elevation

Upper Level Floor Plan

Copyright by designer/architect.

Plan #461174

Dimensions: 70'4" W x 67' D

Levels: 2

Square Footage: 3,753

Main Level Sq. Ft.: 2,519

Upper Level Sq. Ft.: 1,234

Bedrooms: 4

Bathrooms: 3½

Foundation: Crawl space, slab, or basement

Material List Available: No

Price Category: H

Images provided by designer/architect.

Main Level Floor Plan

Upper Level Floor Plan

Copyright by designer/architect.

Main Level Floor Plan

Upper Level Floor Plan

Copyright by designer/architect.

Plan #651064

Dimensions: 59' W x 62' D

Levels: 2

Square Footage: 2,504

Main Level Sq. Ft.: 1,858

Upper Level Sq. Ft.: 646

Bedrooms: 3

Bathrooms: 2½

Foundation: Slab

Material List Available: No

Price Category: E

Images provided by designer/architect.

CAD FILE AVAILABLE

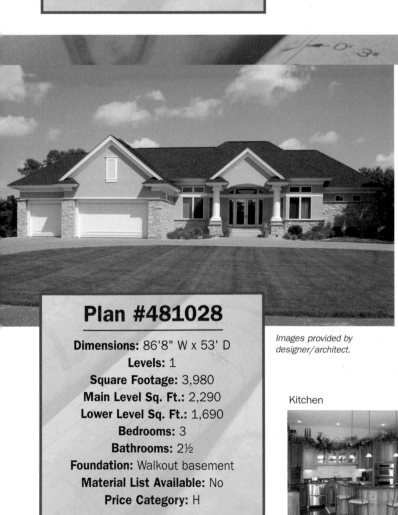

Plan #481028

Dimensions: 86'8" W x 53' D

Levels: 1

Square Footage: 3,980

Main Level Sq. Ft.: 2,290

Lower Level Sq. Ft.: 1,690

Bedrooms: 3

Bathrooms: 2½

Foundation: Walkout basement

Material List Available: No

Price Category: H

Images provided by designer/architect.

Kitchen

Rear View

Lower Level Floor Plan

Copyright by designer/architect.

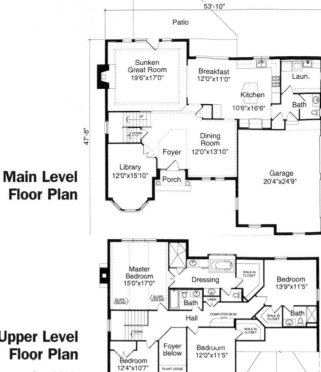

Main Level Floor Plan

Main Level floor plan rooms:
- Patio
- Sunken Great Room 19'6"x17'0"
- Breakfast 12'0"x11'0"
- Kitchen 10'6"x16'6"
- Laun.
- Bath
- Dining Room 12'0"x13'10"
- Foyer
- Library 12'0"x15'10"
- Porch
- Garage 20'4"x24'9"

53'-10"

47'-8"

Images provided by designer/architect.

Upper Level Floor Plan

Upper Level floor plan rooms:
- Master Bedroom 15'0"x17'0"
- Dressing
- Walk In Closet
- Bedroom 13'9"x11'5"
- Bath
- Linen
- Hall
- Computer Desk
- Walk In Closet
- Bath
- Slope Ceiling
- Bedroom 12'0"x11'5"
- Foyer Below
- Bedroom 12'4"x10'7"
- Plant Ledge

Copyright by designer/architect.

Plan #161184

Dimensions: 53'10" W x 47'8" D
Levels: 2
Square Footage: 2,843
Main Level Sq. Ft.: 1,437
Upper Level Sq. Ft.: 1,406
Bedrooms: 4
Bathrooms: 3½
Foundation: Basement; crawl space, slab, or walkout for fee
Material List Available: Yes
Price Category: F

Main Level Floor Plan

Main Level floor plan rooms:
- Covered Patio
- Family Room 25' x 25'
- Master Bedroom 15' x 14'
- Nook 11' x 8'
- w.i.c.
- Kitchen 12' x 11'
- Mstr. Bath
- Pwdr
- Foyer
- Laun.
- Dining Rm. 13' x 11'
- Entry
- 2 Car Garage 20' x 28'

Upper Level Floor Plan

Upper Level floor plan rooms:
- Bedroom 3 15' x 12'
- Bath 2
- Bedroom 2 11' x 11'
- open to below
- Loft 8' x 12'
- balcony
- Future Space 15' x 21'

Images provided by designer/architect.

CAD FILE AVAILABLE

Copyright by designer/architect.

Plan #661124

Dimensions: 45' W x 68'10" D
Levels: 1.5
Square Footage: 2,392
Main Level Sq. Ft.: 1,654
Upper Level Sq. Ft.: 738
Bedrooms: 3
Bathrooms: 2½
Foundation: Slab
Material List Available: No
Price Category: E

Plan #121091

Dimensions: 56' W x 50' D

Levels: 2

Square Footage: 2,689

Main Level Sq. Ft.: 1,415

Upper Level Sq. Ft.: 1,274

Bedrooms: 4

Bathrooms: 2½

Foundation: Basement

Materials List Available: Yes

Price Category: F

This home, as shown in the photograph, may differ from the actual blueprints. For more detailed information, please check the floor plans carefully.

Images provided by designer/architect.

You'll love the unusual details that make this home as elegant as it is comfortable.

Features:

- **Entry:** This two-story entry is filled with natural light that streams in through the sidelights and transom window.

- **Den:** To the right of the entry, French doors open to this room, with its 11-ft. high, spider-beamed ceiling. A triple-wide,

transom-topped window brightens this room during the daytime.

- **Family Room:** A fireplace and built-in entertainment center add comfort to this room, and the cased opening to the kitchen area makes it convenient.

- **Kitchen:** With an adjoining breakfast area, this kitchen is another natural gathering spot.

Main Level Floor Plan

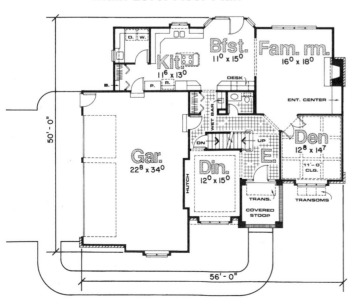

Upper Level Floor Plan

Copyright by designer/architect.

Images provided by designer/architect.

Plan #141020

Dimensions: 58' W x 40'4" D

Levels: 2

Square Footage: 3,140

Main Level Sq. Ft.: 1,553

Upper Level Sq. Ft.: 1,587

Bedrooms: 5

Bathrooms: 4

Foundation: Basement

Materials List Available: Yes

Price Category: G

This stately and spacious traditional home will add elegance to any neighborhood.

Features:

• Ceiling height: 9 ft. unless otherwise noted.

• Foyer: The angled staircase rises to this two-story entry and then overlooks the family room from a Juliet-style balcony. The stairs also break to allow direct access to the kitchen.

• Kitchen: This is a dream kitchen, with its oversize work island and walk-in pantry. The kitchen overlooks the breakfast room and family room.

• Master Suite: This luxurious retreat occupies its own side of the house for added privacy. It has its own sitting area and dual closets leading to the master bath.

• Guest Room: Your overnight guests will enjoy the privacy of this first floor bedroom.

• Secondary Bedrooms: All the upstairs bedrooms feature their own walk-in closets.

Main Level Floor Plan

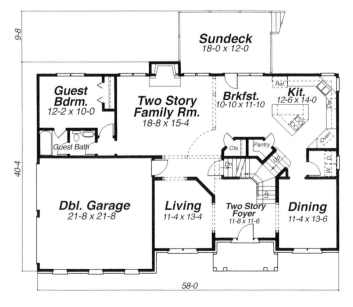

Upper Level Floor Plan

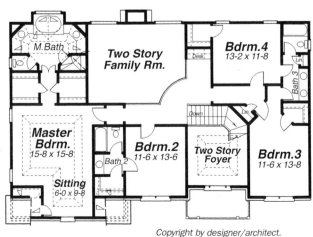

Copyright by designer/architect.

Plan #121090

Dimensions: 60' W x 58' D

Levels: 1.5

Square Footage: 2,645

Main Level Sq. Ft.: 1,972

Upper Level Sq. Ft.: 673

Bedrooms: 4

Bathrooms: 2½

Foundation: Basement

Materials List Available: Yes

Price Category: F

Images provided by designer/architect.

You'll be amazed at the amenities that have been designed into this lovely home.

Features:

- Den: French doors just off the entry lead to this lovely room, with its bowed window and spider-beamed ceiling.

- Great Room: A trio of graceful arched windows highlights the volume ceiling in this room. You might want to curl up to read next to the see-through fireplace into the hearth room.

- Kitchen: Enjoy the good design in this room.

- Hearth Room: The shared fireplace with the great room makes this a cozy spot in cool weather.

- Master Suite: French doors lead to this well-lit area, with its roomy walk-in closet, sunlit whirlpool tub, separate shower, and two vanities.

Main Level Floor Plan

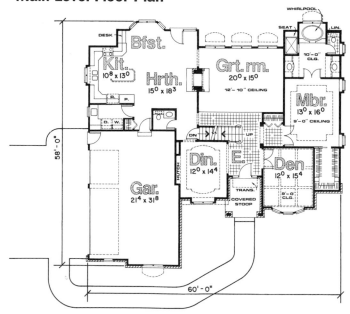

Upper Level Floor Plan

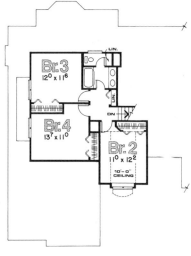

Copyright by designer/architect.

Plan #131044

Dimensions: 57'6" W x 42'4" D
Levels: 1
Square Footage: 1,994
Bedrooms: 4
Bathrooms: 2
Foundation: Crawl space, slab, or basement
Materials List Available: Yes
Price Category: E

Under a covered porch, Victorian-detailed bay windows grace each side of the brick-faced facade at the center of this ranch-style home, giving it a formal air.

Images provided by designer/architect.

Features:

- Ceiling Height: 10-ft. ceilings grace the central living area and the master bedroom of this home.

- Foyer: Round top windows make this area and the flanking rooms bright and cheery.

- Great Room: A fireplace and built-ins that are visible from anywhere in this large room make it a natural gathering place for friends and family.

- Optional Office: Use the room just off the central hall as a home office, fourth bedroom, or study.

- Master Suite: You'll love the bay window, tray ceiling, two walk-in closets, and private bath.

- Bonus Space: Finish this large area in the attic for extra living space, or use it for storage.

Rear Elevation

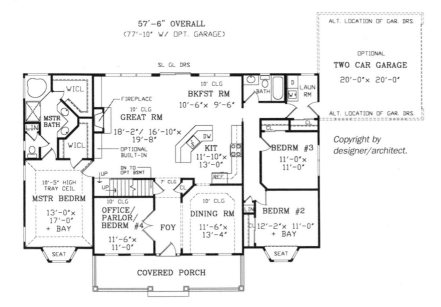

Copyright by designer/architect.

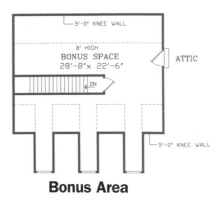

Bonus Area

Upper Level Floor Plan

DECK

SITTING

MSTR BEDRM.
24X14

OPEN TO FAMILY ROOM

BEDROOM 3
12X12

BEDROOM 2
12X12

BEDROOM 4
12X12

STORAGE

Images provided by designer/architect.

Copyright by designer/archite...

Plan #101116

Dimensions: 53' W x 51' D

Levels: 2

Square Footage: 3,012

Main Level Sq. Ft.: 1,600

Upper Level Sq. Ft.: 1,412

Bedrooms: 5

Bathrooms: 4

Foundation: Basement

Materials List Available: No

Price Category: G

Main Level Floor Plan

DECK

KITCHEN
13X14

BREAKFAST
11X14

FAMILY ROOM
16X20

MEDIA/
BEDROOM 5
12X13

PANTRY

LAUNDRY
7X11

GARAGE
20X22

DINING
12X15

FOYER

LIVING
12X12

51

53

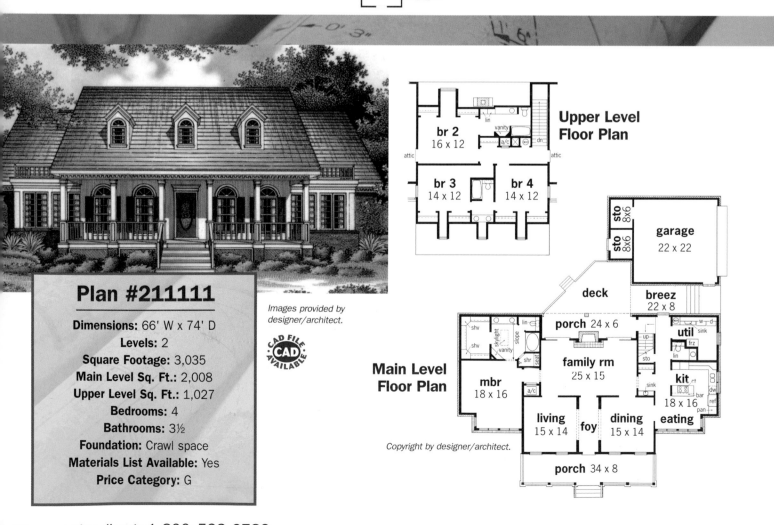

Upper Level Floor Plan

br 2
16 x 12

br 3
14 x 12

br 4
14 x 12

attic

attic

sto 8x6

sto 8x6

garage
22 x 22

deck

breez
22 x 8

porch 24 x 6

util

Plan #211111

Dimensions: 66' W x 74' D

Levels: 2

Square Footage: 3,035

Main Level Sq. Ft.: 2,008

Upper Level Sq. Ft.: 1,027

Bedrooms: 4

Bathrooms: 3½

Foundation: Crawl space

Materials List Available: Yes

Price Category: G

Images provided by designer/architect.

CAD FILE AVAILABLE

Main Level Floor Plan

family rm
25 x 15

mbr
18 x 16

kit
18 x 16

living
15 x 14

foy

dining
15 x 14

eating

porch 34 x 8

Copyright by designer/architect.

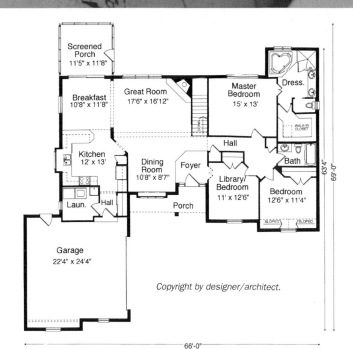

Images provided by designer/architect.

Copyright by designer/architect.

Plan #161011

Dimensions: 66' W x 69' D

Levels: 1

Square Footage: 1,788

Bedrooms: 3

Bathrooms: 2

Foundation: Basement

Materials List Available: Yes

Price Category: C

Rear Elevation

Images provided by designer/architect.

CAD FILE AVAILABLE — CAD

Copyright by designer/architect.

Plan #271081

Dimensions: 86' W x 54' D

Levels: 1

Square Footage: 2,539

Bedrooms: 3

Bathrooms: 2

Foundation: Slab

Materials List Available: No

Price Category: E

SMARTtip

Determining Curtain Length

Follow length guidelines for foolproof results, but remember that they're not rules. Go ahead and play with curtain and drapery lengths. Instead of shortening long panels at the hem, for instance, take up excess material by blousing them over tiebacks for a pleasing effect.

Plan #321006

Dimensions: 76' W x 45' D
Levels: 1, optional lower
Square Footage: 1,977
Optional Basement Level
Sq. Ft.: 1,416
Bedrooms: 4
Bathrooms: 2½
Foundation: Basement
Materials List Available: Yes
Price Category: E

Images provided by designer/architect.

76'-0"

45'-0"

MBr 14-6x15-5
open to below Dn
Brk 11-8x13-0
Deck

Br 2 10-7x 10-0
Great Rm 16-4x24-2 vaulted
Kit 11-3x 12-4
Garage 23-4x29-4

Dining

Br 3 11-4x11x8
Br 4 11-8x12-8 vaulted
Porch

CAD FILE AVAILABLE

Optional Basement Level Floor Plan

Copyright by designer/architect.

Br 5 15-3x15-6
Up Atrium
Study 10-9x 13-2

Family 18-4x23-6
storage

Br 6 11-5x12-7

storage

Plan #131025

Dimensions: 62'4" W x 65'10" D
Levels: 1.5
Square Footage: 3,204
Main Level Sq. Ft.: 2,196
Upper Level Sq. Ft.: 1,008
Bedrooms: 4
Bathrooms: 4
Foundation: Crawl space, slab, or basement
Materials List Available: Yes
Price Category: H

Images provided by designer/architect.

Rear Elevation

SITTING AREA
VAULTED BKFST RM 11'-8"x 12'-6"
BUILT-IN
VAULTED GREAT RM 29'-0"x 16'-10"
TRAY CEIL MSTR BEDRM 15'-4"x 17'-0"/ 21'-8"

BATH
KITCHEN 16'-8"x 13'-2" ISLAND
WICL
MSTR BATH

LAUN RM
W.I.PANT
UP
STEPPED CLG DINING RM 12'-0"x 14'-0"
OFFICE/ GUEST RM 12'-0"x 12'-0"
FOY

THREE CAR GARAGE 20'-0"x 32'-0"
COV. PORCH

Main Level Floor Plan
Copyright by designer/architect.

RAIL
UPPER GREAT RM CEILING
LOFT 20'-0"x 20'-0"
RAIL
BALCONY
BATH

DN
BEDRM #2 13'-2"x 12'-4" 17'-8"
BEDRM #3 13'-10"x 11'-0" 17'-8"

Upper Level Floor Plan

Images provided by designer/architect.

Main Level Floor Plan

Copyright by designer/architect.

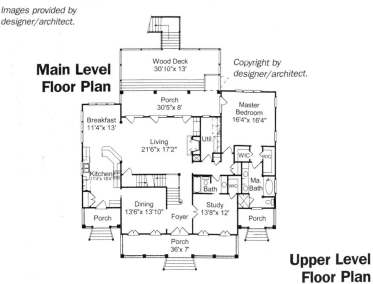

Upper Level Floor Plan

Plan #111039

Dimensions: 59' W x 64' D

Levels: 2

Square Footage: 3,335

Main Level Sq. Ft.: 2,129

Upper Level Sq. Ft.: 1,206

Bedrooms: 4

Bathrooms: 4

Foundation: Basement

Materials List Available: No

Price Category: H

Optional Lower Level Floor Plan

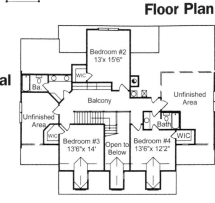

Plan #211008

Dimensions: 56' W x 93' D

Levels: 1

Square Footage: 2,259

Bedrooms: 3

Bathrooms: 2½

Foundation: Slab

Material List Available: Yes

Price Category: E

Images provided by designer/architect.

Copyright by designer/architect.

Front View

Plan #161013

Dimensions: 59'4" W x 46'4" D

Levels: 1

Square Footage: 1,509

Bedrooms: 3

Bathrooms: 2

Foundation: Basement; crawl space for fee

Materials List Available: Yes

Price Category: C

The unique roofline and stone accents make this home stand apart from the rest.

Features:

- Foyer: Just off the front porch, this entry opens to the great room.

- Great Room: This room warms up with a fireplace and is open to the dining area.

- Kitchen: This kitchen features a peninsula with a raised bar, creating more seating space for the adjacent dining room.

- Master Suite: This suite features a private bathroom with a walk-in closet and double vanities.

- Bedrooms: Two secondary bedrooms have large closets and share a hall bathroom.

Images provided by designer/architect.

Rear Elevation

Right Side Elevation

Left Side Elevation

Copyright by designer/architect.

Plan #321048

Dimensions: 77'6" W x 30' D

Levels: 2

Square Footage: 3,216

Main Level Sq. Ft.: 1,834

Upper Level Sq. Ft.: 1,382

Bedrooms: 4

Bathrooms: 4½

Foundation: Basement

Materials List Available: Yes

Price Category: G

Images provided by designer/architect.

You'll love the columns and well-proportioned dormers that grace the exterior of this home, which is as spacious as it is comfortable.

Features:

- **Family Room:** This large room, featuring a graceful bay window and a wet bar, is sure to be the heart of your home. On chilly evenings, the whole family will gather around the fireplace.

- **Dining Room:** Whether you're serving a family dinner or hosting a formal dinner party, everyone will feel at home in this lovely room.

- **Kitchen:** The family cooks will appreciate the thought that went into designing this kitchen, which includes ample work and storage space. A breakfast room adjoins the kitchen.

- **Hearth Room:** This room also adjoins the kitchen, creating a large area for informal entertaining.

- **Bedrooms:** Each bedroom is really a suite, because it includes a private, full bath.

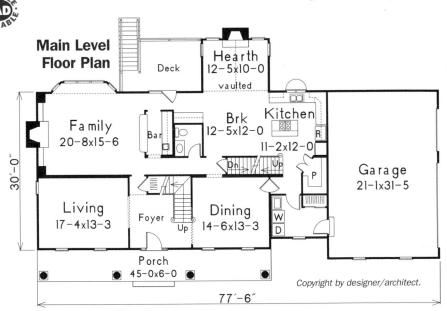

CAD FILE AVAILABLE

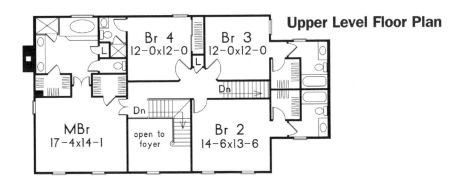

Copyright by designer/architect.

Plan #181080

Dimensions: 44'8" W x 36' D

Levels: 2

Square Footage: 2,042

Main Level Sq. Ft.: 934

Upper Level Sq. Ft.: 1,108

Bedrooms: 3

Bathrooms: 2½

Foundation: Full basement

Materials List Available: Yes

Price Category: E

Images provided by designer/architect.

The second-floor balcony and angled tower are only two of the many design elements you'll love in this beautiful home.

Features:

• Family Room: Corner windows and sliding glass doors to the backyard let natural light pour into this spacious, open area.

• Living Room: Decorate around the deep bay to separate it from the adjacent dining area.

• Dining Room: Large windows and French doors to the kitchen are highlights here.

• Kitchen: The U-shaped counter aids efficiency, as does the handy lunch counter.

• Master Suite: From the sitting area in the bay to the walk-in closet and bath with tub and shower, this suite will pamper you.

• Balcony: Set a row of potted plants and a table and chairs on this perch above the street.

Main Level Floor Plan

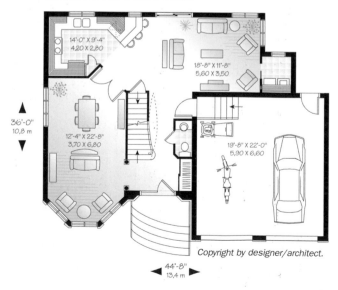

Copyright by designer/architect.

Upper Level Floor Plan

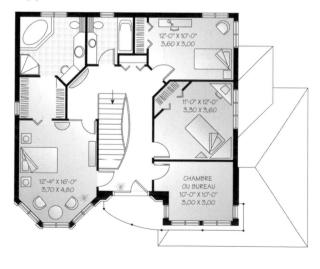

Plan #141032

Dimensions: 52' W x 44' D

Levels: 2

Square Footage: 2,476

Main Level Sq. Ft.: 1,160

Upper Level Sq. Ft.: 1,316

Bedrooms: 4

Bathrooms: 2½

Foundation: Basement

Materials List Available: Yes

Price Category: E

A refreshing design combines comfort, convenience, style, and modern innovations, inviting you to experience this family-oriented home.

Images provided by designer/architect.

Features:

- **Family Room:** Even as you enter the front door, you will be drawn to this impressive family room and its two-story fireplace wall.

- **Kitchen:** This well-designed kitchen with walk-in pantry makes meal preparation easy and enjoyable.

- **Computer Station:** An innovative assist to managing a complex lifestyle, this computer station, with its effective handling of additional work space and storage, will quickly become a family favorite.

- **Master Suite:** At the end of a busy day you can adjourn to the luxury and comfort of this master suite, which features a sitting room with a Palladian window.

Front View

Main Level Floor Plan

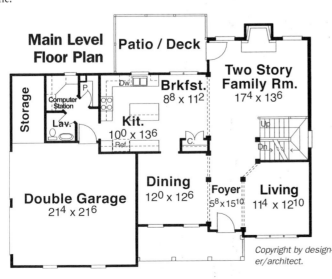

Patio / Deck

Storage

Computer Station

Lav.

Brkfst. 8⁸ x 11²

Kit. 10⁰ x 13⁶

Ref.

Two Story Family Rm. 17⁴ x 13⁶

Up

Dn

Double Garage 21⁴ x 21⁶

Dining 12⁰ x 12⁶

Foyer 5⁸ x 15¹⁰

Living 11⁴ x 12¹⁰

Copyright by designer/architect.

Upper Level Floor Plan

M. Bath Tray Ceil.

Bdrm.2 11⁰ x 11⁶ Opt. Vault W/ Plant Shelf

Bth.2

Two Story Family Rm.

Master Bdrm. 15⁴ x 14⁶ Tray Ceil.

Bdrm.3 11⁸ x 10⁶ Opt. Vault W/ Plant Shelf

W.I.C.

Laund.

Balcony Opt. Vault W/ Plant Shelf

Dn

Open To Foyer

Bdrm.4 11⁴ x 11⁰

Opt. Closet

Sitting 10⁰ x 7⁰

Plan #191002

Dimensions: 44' W x 65' D

Levels: 1

Square Footage: 1,716

Bedrooms: 3

Bathrooms: 2

Foundation: Crawl space, slab

Materials List Available: No

Price Category: C

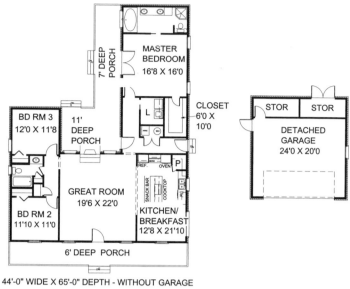

Images provided by designer/architect.

BD RM 3 12'0 X 11'8

11' DEEP PORCH

7' DEEP PORCH

MASTER BEDROOM 16'8 X 16'0

CLOSET 6'0 X 10'0

L

BD RM 2 11'10 X 11'0

GREAT ROOM 19'6 X 22'0

REF. OVEN P
SNACK BAR COOKTOP

KITCHEN/ BREAKFAST 12'8 X 21'10

6' DEEP PORCH

STOR STOR

DETACHED GARAGE 24'0 X 20'0

44'-0" WIDE X 65'-0" DEPTH - WITHOUT GARAGE

Copyright by designer/architect.

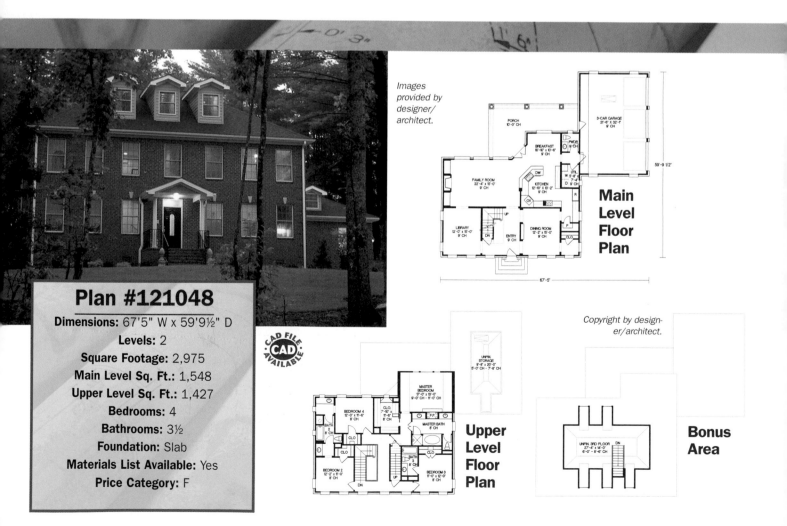

Plan #121048

Dimensions: 67'5" W x 59'9½" D

Levels: 2

Square Footage: 2,975

Main Level Sq. Ft.: 1,548

Upper Level Sq. Ft.: 1,427

Bedrooms: 4

Bathrooms: 3½

Foundation: Slab

Materials List Available: Yes

Price Category: F

Images provided by designer/architect.

Main Level Floor Plan

PORCH 10'-0" CH

3-CAR GARAGE 27'-8" X 32'-F 9' CH

BREAKFAST 10'-40" X 10'-6" 9' CH

PWDR 9' CH

FAMILY ROOM 22'-4" X 15'-0" 9' CH

KITCHEN 12'-6" X 13'-2" 9' CH

UTIL W S 7'-4"-F 9' CH

DW

LIBRARY 12'-0" X 15'-0" 9' CH

UP

DN

ENTRY 9' CH

DINING ROOM 12'-2" X 15'-0" 9' CH

F.P.

59'-9 1/2'

67'-5'

Copyright by designer/architect.

CAD FILE AVAILABLE

Upper Level Floor Plan

MASTER BEDROOM 17'-0" X 16'-0" 9'-0" CH - 11'-0" CH

BEDROOM 4 12'-0" X 11'-6" 8' CH

CLO 7'-6" 11'-6" 8'

F.P.

MASTER BATH 8' CH

BEDROOM 2 12'-2" X 11'-0" 8' CH

CLO

CLO

BATH 8'

CLO

BATH 8'

BEDROOM 3 11'-0" X 12'-0" 8' CH

DN

UP

DN

BATH 2 8' CH

UNFIN STORAGE 9'-8" X 20'-0" 5'-0" CH - 7'-6" CH

Bonus Area

UNFIN 3RD FLOOR 27'-4" X 14'-0" 6'-0" CH - 8'-6" CH

DN

Plan #321029

Dimensions: 50' W x 56' D

Levels: 1

Square Footage: 2,334

Bedrooms: 3

Bathrooms: 2

Foundation: Daylight basement

Materials List Available: Yes

Price Category: E

Rear View

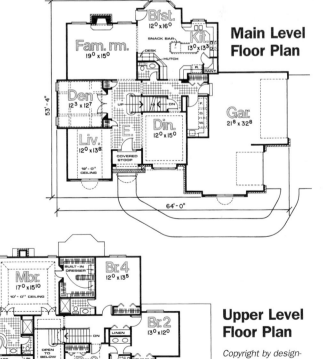

CAD FILE AVAILABLE

Images provided by designer/architect.

Optional Basement Level Floor Plan

Copyright by designer/architect.

Plan #121072

Dimensions: 64' W x 53'4" D

Levels: 2

Square Footage: 3,031

Main Level Sq. Ft.: 1,640

Upper Level Sq. Ft.: 1,391

Bedrooms: 4

Bathrooms: 3½

Foundation: Basement

Materials List Available: Yes

Price Category: G

Images provided by designer/architect.

Main Level Floor Plan

Upper Level Floor Plan

Copyright by designer/architect.

Plan #161052

Dimensions: 57'8" W x 58' D
Levels: 2
Square Footage: 2,484
Main Level Sq. Ft.: 1,710
Upper Level Sq. Ft.: 774
Bedrooms: 4
Bathrooms: 3½
Foundation: Basement
Materials List Available: Yes
Price Category: E

Images provided by designer/architect.

You'll love the airy feeling of the open floor plan in this spacious, comfortable home.

Features:

• Foyer: This elegant two-story space sets the gracious tone you'll find throughout this home.

• Great Room: A fireplace and decorative window highlight this room with a two-story ceiling.

• Dining Room: You'll find expansive windows in this formal dining room.

• Kitchen: This kitchen has an L-shaped work area for efficiency and access to the laundry room.

• Breakfast Room: A window area makes a perfect frame for table and chairs, and a door leads to the porch.

• Master Suite: A walk-in closet and bath with a double vanity impart luxury to this suite.

Main Level Floor Plan

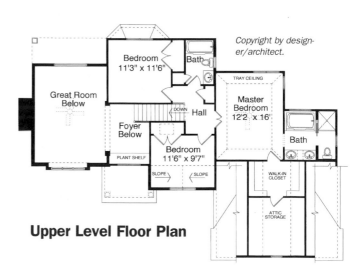

Copyright by designer/architect.

Upper Level Floor Plan

Plan #121034

Dimensions: 92'8" W x 59'4" D

Levels: 1

Square Footage: 2,223

Bedrooms: 1

Bathrooms: 2½

Foundation: Basement; crawl space for fee

Materials List Available: Yes

Price Category: E

CAD FILE AVAILABLE

Images provided by designer/architect.

This home features a flowing, open floor plan coupled with an abundance of amenities.

Features:

• Ceiling Height: 8 ft. unless otherwise noted.

• Foyer: This elegant entry features a curved staircase and a view of the formal dining room.

• Formal Dining Room: Magnificent arched openings lead from the foyer into this dining room. The boxed ceiling adds to the architectural interest.

• Great Room: A wall of windows, a see-through fireplace, and built-in entertainment center make this the perfect gathering place.

• Covered Deck: The view of this deck, through the wall of windows in the great room, will lure guests out to this large deck.

• Hearth Room: This room shares a panoramic view with the eating area.

• Kitchen: This kitchen features a corner pantry, a built-in desk, and a curved island.

Main Level Floor Plan

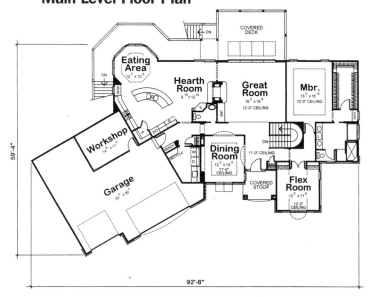

Optional Basement Level Floor Plan

Copyright by designer/architect.

Plan #351033

Dimensions: 64' W x 39' D

Levels: 1

Square Footage: 1,654

Bedrooms: 3

Bathrooms: 2

Foundation: Crawl space, slab, or basement

Materials List Available: Yes

Price Category: C

Images provided by designer/architect.

This gorgeous three-bedroom brick home would be the perfect place to raise your family.

Features:

- **Great Room:** This terrific room has a gas fireplace with built-in cabinets on either side.

- **Kitchen:** This island kitchen with breakfast area is open to the great room.

- **Master Suite:** This private room features a vaulted ceiling and a large walk-in closet. The bath area has a walk-in closet, jetted tub, and double vanities.

- **Bedrooms:** The two additional bedrooms share a bathroom located in the hall.

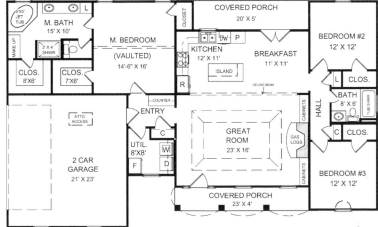

Copyright by designer/architect.

Plan #261004

Dimensions: 82' W x 48'8" D
Levels: 2
Square Footage: 2,707
Main Level Sq. Ft.: 1,484
Upper Level Sq. Ft.: 1,223
Bedrooms: 3
Bathrooms: 2½
Foundation: Basement
Materials List Available: No
Price Category: F

Inside the classic Victorian exterior is a spacious home filled with contemporary amenities that the whole family is sure to love.

Features:

- **Porch:** This wraparound porch provides space for entertaining or sitting out to enjoy the evening.

- **Foyer:** Two stories high, the foyer opens to the formal dining room and front parlor.

- **Family Room:** French doors open from the parlor into this room, with its cozy fireplace.

- **Sunroom:** A cathedral ceiling adds drama to this versatile room.

- **Kitchen:** A pantry and a work island make this well-planned kitchen even more convenient.

- **Master Suite:** A tray ceiling and French doors to the bath give the bedroom elegance, while the sumptuous bath features a deluxe tub, walk-in shower, and split vanities.

Images provided by designer/architect.

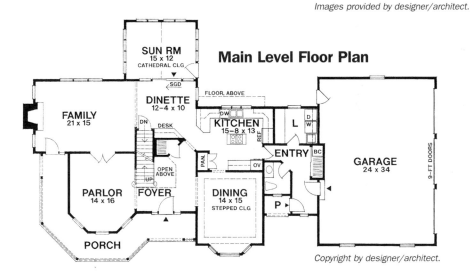

Main Level Floor Plan

Copyright by designer/architect.

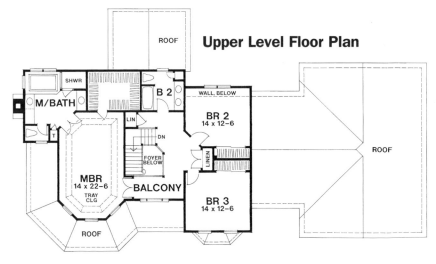

Upper Level Floor Plan

Plan #161012

Dimensions: 69' W x 50'10" D
Levels: 1
Square Footage: 1,648
Bedrooms: 3
Bathrooms: 2
Foundation: Basement
Materials List Available: Yes
Price Category: C

Images provided by designer/architect.

This delightful brick home, with multiple gables and an inviting front porch, offers an exciting interior with varied ceiling heights and an open floor plan.

Features:

- **Great Room:** This great room showcases an 11-ft. ceiling and a gas fireplace. Enjoy a beverage seated at the convenient bar, and move freely through a generous opening to the relaxed dining area.

- **Kitchen:** This galley kitchen is expanded by easy access to the garage and laundry room.

- **Master Suite:** You will appreciate the openness of this large master bedroom, which features an 11-ft. ceiling. You can also retreat to the privacy of an adjoining covered porch.

- **Library:** Thoughtful design allows you to exercise the option of converting the bedroom off the foyer into a library.

Right Side Elevation

Left Side Elevation

Rear Elevation

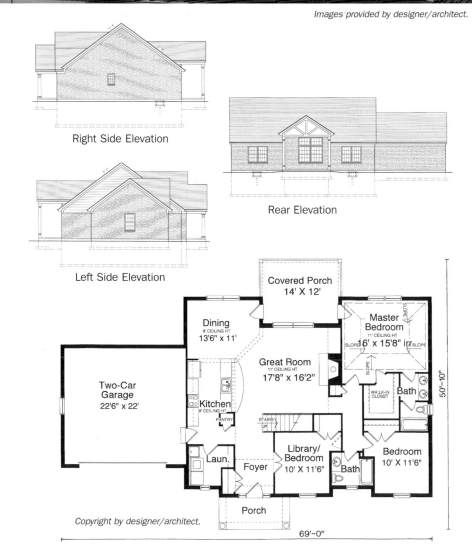

Copyright by designer/architect.

Plan #211029

Dimensions: 68' W x 60' D
Levels: 1
Square Footage: 1,672
Bedrooms: 3
Bathrooms: 2
Foundation: Crawl space
Materials List Available: Yes
Price Category: C

A large front porch adds charm to this three-bedroom home.

Features:

- Living Room: This large room features a corner fireplace.

- Kitchen: This efficient kitchen has lots of cabinet space and an adjoining eating area.

- Master Suite: This large bedroom boasts a spacious walk-in closet and a sloped ceiling. The bath features a double vanity and a sepa rate shower area.

- Bedrooms: Two additional bedrooms share a common bathroom.

Images provided by designer/architect.

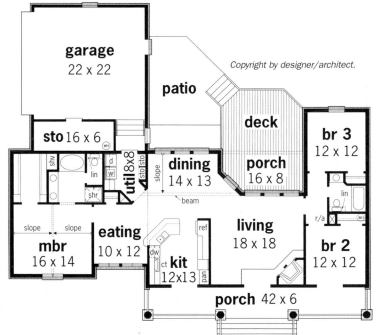

Copyright by designer/architect.

SMARTtip

Ponds

If a pond or small body of water already exists on your property, arrange your garden elements to take advantage of it. Build a bridge over it to connect it to other areas of the garden. If there's a dock already in place, make use of it for an instant midday picnic for one.

Plan #131014

Dimensions: 48' W x 43'4" D
Levels: 1
Square Footage: 1,380
Bedrooms: 3
Bathrooms: 2
Foundation: Crawl space, slab, or basement
Materials List Available: Yes
Price Category: C

Images provided by designer/architect.

Living Room

The exterior of this home looks formal, thanks to its twin dormers, gables, and the bay windows that flank the columned porch, but the inside is contemporary in both design and features.

Features:

- Great Room: Centrally located, this great room has a 10-ft. ceiling. A fireplace, built-in cabinets, and windows that overlook the rear covered porch make it as practical as it is attractive.

- Dining Room: A bay window adds to the charm of this versatile room.

- Kitchen: This U-shaped room is designed to make cooking and cleaning jobs efficient.

- Master Suite: With a bay window, a walk-in closet, and a private bath with an oval tub, the master suite may be your favorite area.

- Additional Bedrooms: Located on the opposite side of the house from the master suite, these rooms share a full bath in the hall.

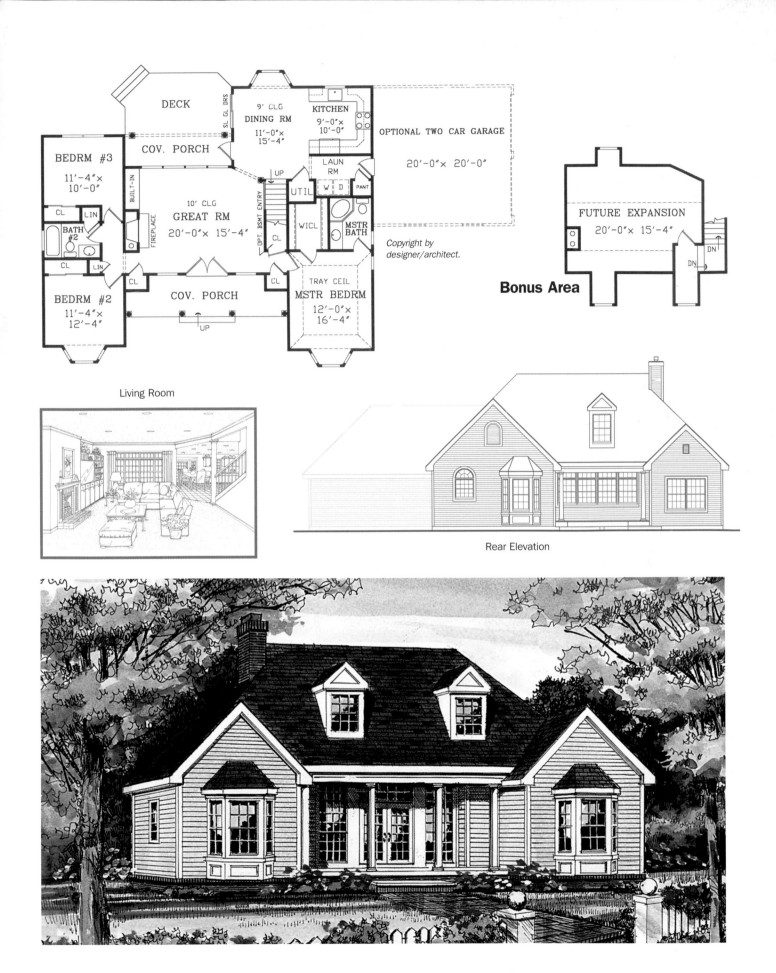

DECK

9' CLG
DINING RM
11'-0"×
15'-4"

KITCHEN
9'-0"×
10'-0"

OPTIONAL TWO CAR GARAGE
20'-0" × 20'-0"

COV. PORCH

BEDRM #3
11'-4"×
10'-0"

LAUN
RM

UTIL

W D

PANT

BUILT-IN

UP

CL LIN

BATH #2

FIREPLACE

10' CLG
GREAT RM
20'-0"× 15'-4"

OPT. BSMT ENTRY

WICL

CL

MSTR
BATH

CL LIN

BEDRM #2
11'-4"×
12'-4"

CL

COV. PORCH

UP

CL

TRAY CEIL
MSTR BEDRM
12'-0"×
16'-4"

Copyright by designer/architect.

FUTURE EXPANSION
20'-0"× 15'-4"

DN

DN

Bonus Area

Living Room

Rear Elevation

design ideas for   CRE▲TIVE HOMEOWNER®

Curb Appeal

architectural details ┃ color and paint ┃ landscaping and more

Megan Connolly

This article was reprinted from *Design Ideas for Curb Appeal* (Creative Homeowner 2006).

Hardscaping Your Yard

Landscape designs often benefit from vertical elements such as walls, fences, arches, arbors, pergolas, and decorative freestanding plant supports. Walls and fences help define boundaries while enclosing special spaces. Properly positioned, an arbor or arch is an eye-catching accent, adding visual drama to the scene and providing an attractive focal point or point of passage between two parts of the garden. A pergola transforms an ordinary path into a special, shaded, and sheltered passageway, while a freestanding plant support is like an exclamation point, drawing attention to itself and creating a pleasant focus.

As an added bonus, any one of these features provides an opportunity to grow and enjoy the wide range of climbing plants such as clematis, wisteria, climbing roses, honeysuckle, trumpet vine, and jasmine. These vertical plants add a sense of lushness to the garden as they scramble up walls and over trellised arches or droop heavy panicles of flowers through the open fretwork ceiling of a pergola. Here are some ideas for hardscaping your front yard with these elements.

Fences, opposite, not only serve as boundary markers, they are a design element in their own right. There are so many styles from which to choose that you should have no trouble finding one that is both functional and decorative. The posts on this classic style are topped with decorative finials.

The brick wall, above, that encloses this garden complements the brick pathway. Both have weathered to the point where they look as though they have always been part of the setting.

Consider installing a fence, below, as a backdrop to a group of lush plantings. This simple rail fence defines the garden path and separates the front yard from the side yard, but it also seems to support the flowering plants.

A traditional picket fence, right, serves as a backdrop for a group of border plants. In addition to their utilitarian functions, vertical elements such as fences and walls add texture and visual interest to a landscape.

The classic picket fence, below, can be used with a variety of house styles. A purely decorative section of fence spans an opening in a hedge that borders the front yard of this house.

Fence posts, bottom right, especially posts that mark an entry, can become focal points if you add special cap treatments or adorn one with fresh flowers.

order direct: 1-800-523-6789

Designing a Fence

Erecting a fence is the quickest and generally easiest way to define the boundary of your property. To be a successful part of a landscape design, a fence should be planned to complement the architecture of your house, possibly even echoing a distinctive design feature. Also bear in mind the character of your neighborhood and region. Your fence may be beautiful in and of itself but look out of place in the neighborhood where you live. In addition to style, other considerations for making a fence harmonious with its surroundings include height, color, and material.

With that in mind, the possibilities for fence designs are limitless. Traditional options include wrought iron, wooden pickets (or palings), stockade, split-rail, double- and triple-bar ranch fences, and even chain-link fences. Within those basic styles are many variations. For example, iron can be wrought in fanciful designs from modern clean-cut to the fancy curlicues of the Romanesque style. Picket points can take the form of arrows, fleurs-de-lis, or any other design. The pickets can be spaced in a variety of ways. Stockade fences can be closed- or open-board, or have angled paling boards. To add extra charm and interest, a solid wood-en fence can be topped with lattice. The main components of a board fence are pickets, horizontal rails, a top rail to protect the end grain of the pickets from moisture, the kickboard, and the support post.

Fence Anatomy

Capping Rail
Finial
Lattice Top
Top Rail
Picket, or Paling
4x4 Post
Bottom Rail
Kickboard
Horizontal Rail
Concrete
Gravel Footing

Building Fences on Slopes

A slope presents a special challenge for fence design as fence sections are generally straight and parallel with the ground. Three possible solutions include stepping the fence down the slope, allowing gaps to occur as the slope progresses downward; building the fence to follow the hillside so that the top of the fence is angled at the same degree as the slope; and custom-building the fence so each paling touches the ground, creating a wavy line across the fence top and bottom.

Stepped Fencing

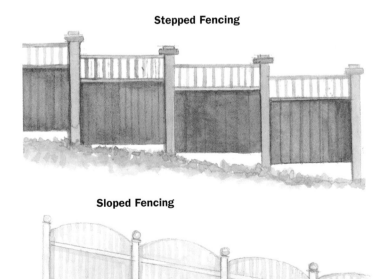

Sloped Fencing

Contour Fencing

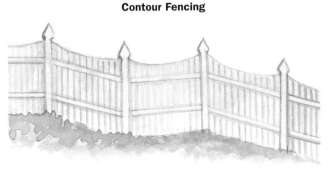

Designing a Gate

The garden gate meets many needs, from practical to aesthetic to psychological. It is a place of romance—where else would an ardent suitor steal a kiss or wait for a late-night romantic tryst but by the garden gate?

On the purely practical side, a gate allows passage to and between a front and back garden. This functional aspect is closely tied to a gate's symbolic meaning. A locked, solid gate set in a high wall or fence provides a sense of privacy, enclosure, and security. A gate with an open design, even when set into a solid wall, has a welcoming air about it.

An open gate beckons; a tall, solid gate adds mystery, suggesting the entrance to a secret garden. It can guide the eye to a focal point or add charm, intimacy, drama, or panache.

Gates, even short ones that stand only 3 feet high, serve as important transition points from the garden to the outside world or from one part of the garden to another. They define boundaries while linking the two areas together. For that reason, gates and pathways tend to go together in a landscape design.

Don't confine your gates to the perimeter of your property. Use them within your garden as well, to divide space visually and to mark the boundaries between different areas or garden rooms.

Gates come in a seemingly endless variety of styles and sizes. Massive wrought-iron gates mark the entrances to many large Victorian parks and private estates. Painted, slatted gates set in white picket fences tend to belong with small, intimate cottages or traditional country homes. The gate to a vegetable plot at the bottom of the garden might be rough-hewn, in keeping with an untreated wooden fence designed to keep out foraging wildlife. Japanese moon gates have cutout circles symbolic of the full moon. These circles may be open or filled in with a fretted design of wood or iron to add visual interest and increase security.

Formal front yards, above, require a distinctive-looking entrance. The metalwork shown here works well with the formal brick wall and posts topped with decorative urns.

Hanging a Gate

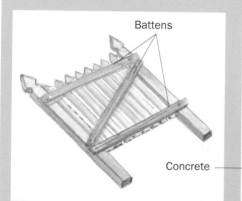

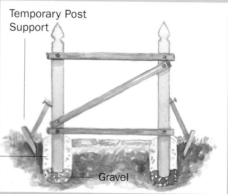

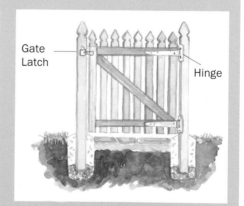

Step One: Space the Posts. Lay the gate on the ground, and position the posts on each side, allowing enough space for the hinges and latch. Make sure the tops and bottoms of the posts are even. Nail temporary battens onto the posts as shown. (The bottom batten should be at the bottom of the gate.)

Step Two: Set the Posts. Dig postholes. Set the posts on a gravel bed, making sure the bottom batten is 3 inches off the ground and that the posts are plumb and level. Secure the posts temporarily with braces and stakes, and then fill the holes with concrete. Check again for plumb and level before the concrete sets.

Step Three: Hang the Gate. When the concrete has completely cured, remove the braces and battens, attach the hinges (with the gate attached) to the post, and then attach the latch. The job is easier if one person holds the gate in position while the other person drills the screw holes and attaches the hardware.

Choose your gates to fit the style of your garden, but don't be afraid to have fun. For example, use a terra-cotta color to blend with a Spanish-style house, or set a light-colored gate set against a dark backdrop of heavy foliage.

Informal designs, above, put visitors at ease. This type of fence and gate is a good way to welcome visitors to a rear or side yard. It also helps support tall plants.

This distinctive gate, far left, is attached to a house of similar style. Look to the facade of the house and the landscaping style of the front yard when selecting a fence and gate style.

Gates, left, don't always need a fence. Here a decorative metal gate forms part of an arbor that is set in a hedge. This gate opens to a field beyond the garden.

The simple lattice design, above, of this fence is both appealing and practical. It not only encloses the garden but also serves as a trellis for climbing plants. A fence builder can create a custom design for you, or you can buy sections of fencing at home centers and fence specialty retailers.

This arbor and trellis, left, can serve as a destination in a large garden. You might find this type of structure in a front yard, but only in a very informal garden setting. Many large arbors contain a bench as part of the design. For interest, try placing a tall arbor in a rear or side yard that can be seen from the street.

Designing a Trellis

Trellises were a key element in Renaissance gardens and continued in popularity through the eighteenth century. Trellises enjoyed a resurgence of popularity in the late-nineteenth century, but never to the extent of earlier times. Trellises can lend an air of magic and mystery to a garden. Generally, we think of trellises in terms of the prefabricated sheets of diamond- or square-grid lattice and the fan-shaped supports for training climbers, both of which are readily available at home and garden centers in both wood and plastic. Lacking a pattern book, most gardeners are unaware of the incredible variety of designs, patterns, and optical illusions that can be created with trellises.

A trellis screen is a wonderfully airy way to achieve privacy or to partition off a space. The lath slats of lattice interrupt the view without totally obscuring it, creating the effect of a transparent curtain. Left bare, the pretty design of diamonds or squares makes an attractive effect. Covered in vines or decorated with hanging baskets, a trellis screen is enchanting.

The art of *treillage*, as the French call it, is not limited to screens. You can cover a bare wall or unattractive fence with a trellis pattern. Arrange the trellis pieces to create an optical illusion of an archway in the wall. Paint a realistic

Typical Trellis Designs

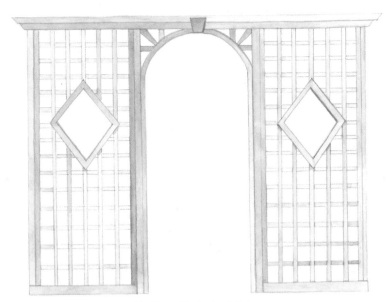

Trellis with Arched Entry

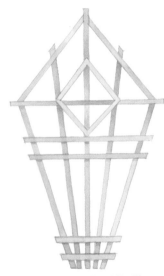

Traditional Wood Trellis

Wire Trellis

mural of the make-believe garden space beyond. Use a trellis for the walls of a gazebo to provide enclosure without being claustrophobic. Put a trellis screen with a pleasing, intricate pattern at the end of a walkway as a focal point.

Closely spaced horizontal slats, left, topped with decorative beams combine to form a handsome trellis and arbor that forms a border in this garden. The slats on the structure provide some privacy without impeding air flow into the garden. Decorative posts and beams add interest when seen from the street.

Plan #131027

Dimensions: 62'4" W x 53'6" D
Levels: 1.5
Square Footage: 2,567
Main Level Sq. Ft.: 2,017
Upper Level Sq. Ft.: 550
Bedrooms: 4
Bathrooms: 3
Foundation: Crawl space, slab, or basement
Materials List Available: Yes
Price Category: F

This home, as shown in the photograph, may differ from the actual blueprints. For more detailed information, please check the floor plans carefully.

Images provided by designer/architect.

The features of this home are so good that you may have trouble imagining all of them at once.

Features:

• Great Room: Imagine a stepped ceiling, corner fireplace, built-media center, and wall of windows with a glass door to the backyard—in one room.

• Dining Room: A stepped ceiling and server with a sink add to the elegance of this formal room.

• Breakfast Room: Eat at the bar this room shares with the island kitchen, and admire the

12-ft. cathedral ceiling and bayed group of 8- and 9-ft. windows. Or go through the sliding glass door to the covered side porch.

• Master Suite: The bedroom has a tray ceiling and cozy sitting area, and a whirlpool tub, shower, and walk-in closet are in the skylighted bath.

• Optional Study: The private bath in bedroom 2 makes it ideal for a study or home office.

Breakfast Nook

Rear View

Great Room

Main Level Floor Plan

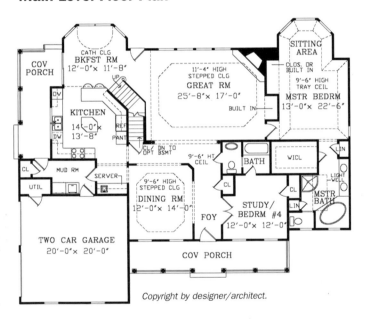

COV PORCH

CATH CLG
BKFST RM
12'-0" x 11'-8"

UP

DW

KITCHEN
14'-0" x 13'-8"

REF

PANT

DV

CL

MUD RM

SERVER

UTIL

TWO CAR GARAGE
20'-0" x 20'-0"

9'-6" HIGH STEPPED CLG
DINING RM
12'-0" x 14'-0"

FOY

11'-4" HIGH STEPPED CLG
GREAT RM
25'-8" x 17'-0"

BUILT IN

CL / DN TO OPT BSMT

9'-6" HT CEIL

BATH

CL

STUDY/ BEDRM #4
12'-0" x 12'-0"

COV PORCH

SITTING AREA

CLOS. OR BUILT IN

9'-6" HIGH TRAY CEIL
MSTR BEDRM
13'-0" x 22'-6"

WICL

LIN

LIGHT WELL

CL

MSTR BATH

LIN

Copyright by designer/architect.

Upper Level Floor Plan

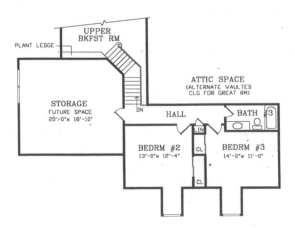

PLANT LEDGE

UPPER BKFST RM

STORAGE
FUTURE SPACE
20'-0" x 18'-10"

DN

HALL

ATTIC SPACE
(ALTERNATE VAULTED CLG FOR GREAT RM)

BATH #3

LIN

BEDRM #2
13'-0" x 12'-4"

CL

CL

BEDRM #3
14'-0" x 11'-0"

CL

Painting Tips

As with any skill, there is a right and a wrong way to paint. There is a right way to hold a brush, a right way to maneuver a roller, a right way to spray a wall, etc. Follow these basic professional tips:

Brushing vs. Rolling. Some painters insist that only a brush-painted job looks right. However, most painters will "cut in" the edges with a brush, and then finish the main body of a wall or ceiling using a roller. Brushing alone can be time-consuming, and it is typically reserved for architectural woodwork.

Using the Right Brush. Use the largest brush with which you are comfortable. Professional painters seldom pick up anything smaller than a 4-inch brush. Most homeowners will achieve good results using a 4-inch brush for "cutting in" and for large surfaces, and an angled 2½- to 3-inch sash brush for trim around windows and doors. Be sure, also, to use brushes that are appropriate for the type of paint being applied. Oil-based paints require a natural bristle (also called "China bristles"), while water-based paints are applied with a synthetic bristle brush.

Handling a Brush. Many people grip a paintbrush as if they were shaking someone's hand. It is better to grip a brush more like a pencil, with the fingers and thumb wrapped around the metal ferrule. This grip provides the hand and wrist with a wider range of motion and therefore greater speed and precision. If your hand cramps, switch hands or switch temporarily to the handshake grip.

Wiping Rags. Before you begin painting, put a dust rag in your pocket. This is helpful for clearing away cobwebs and dust before painting. It is also handy for wiping off paint drips before they have a chance to dry.

Paint Hooks. When working on a ladder, use a good-quality paint hook to secure the paint bucket to your ladder. Avoid makeshift hooks made with wire or coat hangers. Paint hooks are inexpensive and available at virtually all paint and hardware stores.

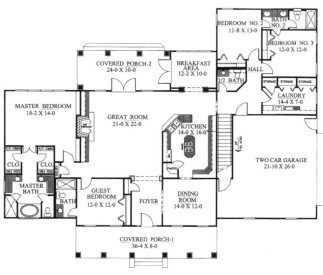

Plan #191028

Dimensions: 80' W x 63' D

Levels: 1

Square Footage: 2,669

Bedrooms: 4

Bathrooms: 3½

Foundation: Slab or basement

Materials List Available: No

Price Category: F

Images provided by designer/architect.

Copyright by designer/architect.

Plan #191029

Dimensions: 78' W x 67' D

Levels: 1

Square Footage: 2,726

Bedrooms: 4

Bathrooms: 3½

Foundation: Crawl space, slab, or basement

Materials List Available: No

Price Category: F

Images provided by designer/architect.

Copyright by designer/architect.

Main Level Floor Plan

Three Car Garage 23'9" x 32'4"

Master Bedroom 15' x 15'

Porch

Breakfast 11'2" x 12'10"

Great Room 17' x 25'

Bath

Bath

Kitchen 11'2" x 11'9"

Laun. 8'6" x 7'6"

Foyer

Dining Room or Study 11'2" x 11'

Bedroom 13' x 11'

Bedroom 12'9" x 13'

Porch

Images provided by designer/architect.

Plan #161072

Dimensions: 80' W x 74' D

Levels: 1

Square Footage: 2,183

Bedrooms: 3

Bathrooms: 3

Foundation: Basement

Materials List Available: Yes

Price Category: D

Upper Level Floor Plan

Bonus Room 15' x 15'

Great Room Below

Kitchen Below

Copyright by designer/architect.

Main Level Floor Plan

81'0"

49'10"

PATIO

3-CAR GARAGE 23' x 31'

UTIL

BRKFST. 12' x 11'

LIVING 21' x 16'

MASTER SUITE 17' x 16'

KITCHEN 13' x 14'

LOGGIA

PWDR

MASTER BATH

DINING 12' x 14'

FOYER

LIBRARY 12' x 17'

PORCH

Plan #331004

Dimensions: 81' W x 49'10" D

Levels: 2

Square Footage: 3,125

Main Level Sq. Ft.: 2,147

Upper Level Sq. Ft.: 978

Bedrooms: 4

Bathrooms: 3½

Foundation: Crawl space, slab, or basement

Materials List Available: No

Price Category: G

Images provided by designer/architect.

This home, as shown in the photograph, may differ from the actual blueprints. For more detailed information, please check the floor plans carefully.

Upper Level Floor Plan

BEDRM 3 15' x 12'

BONUS 15' x 14'

BATH

BALCONY

BEDRM 2 14' x 11'

BEDRM 4 12' x 13'

BATH

Copyright by designer/architect.

Images provided by designer/architect.

Plan #181151

Dimensions: 50' W x 46' D

Levels: 2

Square Footage: 2,283

Main Level Sq. Ft.: 1,274

Second Level Sq. Ft.: 1,009

Bedrooms: 3

Bathrooms: 2½

Foundation: Basement

Materials List Available: Yes

Price Category: F

Multiple porches, stately columns, and arched multi-paned windows adorn this country home.

Features:

- Ceiling Height: 8 ft. unless otherwise noted.

- Great Room: The second-floor mezzanine overlooks this great room. With its soaring ceiling, this dramatic room is the centerpiece of a spacious and flowing design that is just as suited to entertaining as it is to family life.

- Dining Area: Guests will naturally flow into this dining area when it is time to eat. After dinner they can step directly out onto the porch to enjoy coffee and dessert when the weather is fair.

- Kitchen: This efficient and well-designed kitchen has double sinks and offers a separate eating area for those impromptu family meals.

- Master Suite: This master retreat has a walk-in closet and its own sumptuous bath.

- Home Office: Whether you work at home or just need a place for the family computer and keeping track of family finances, this home office fills the bill.

Main Level Floor Plan

Upper Level Floor Plan

Copyright by designer/architect.

Plan #351003

Dimensions: 64' W x 45'10" D

Levels: 1

Square Footage: 1,751

Bedrooms: 3

Bathrooms: 2

Foundation: Crawl space, slab, or basement

Materials List Available: Yes

Price Category: D

Images provided by designer/architect.

This beautiful three-bedroom brick house with a covered porch is perfect for today's family.

Features:

- **Great Room:** This gathering room features a tray ceiling, a gas fireplace, and built-in cabinets.

- **Kitchen:** This island kitchen with a raised bar is open to the great room and eating area.

- **Master Suite:** This primary bedroom features a vaulted ceiling and large walk-in closet. The private bath boasts a double vanity, corner tub, and walk-in closet.

- **Bedrooms:** Two additional bedrooms are located on the other side of the home from the master suite and share a common bathroom.

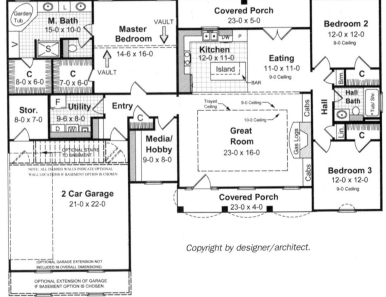

Copyright by designer/architect.

Plan #131030

Dimensions: 51' W x 41'10" D

Levels: 2

Square Footage: 2,470

Main Level Sq. Ft.: 1,290

Upper Level Sq. Ft.: 1,180

Bedrooms: 4

Bathrooms: 2½

Foundation: Crawl space, slab, basement, or walkout

Materials List Available: Yes

Price Category: F

This home, as shown in the photograph, may differ from the actual blueprints. For more detailed information, please check the floor plans carefully.

Images provided by designer/architect.

If high ceilings and spacious rooms make you happy, you'll love this gorgeous home.

Features:

• Family Room: An 18-ft. vaulted ceiling that's open to the balcony above, a corner fireplace, and a wall of windows make this room feel special.

• Dining Room: This formal room, which flows into the living room, also opens to the front porch and optional backyard deck.

• Kitchen: A bright breakfast room joins with this kitchen and opens to the backyard deck.

• Master Suite: You'll smile when you see the 11-ft. vaulted ceiling, stunning arched window, and two walk-in closets in the bedroom. A skylight lets natural light into the private bath, with its spa tub, separate shower, and dual-sink vanity.

• Bedrooms: To reach these three charming bedrooms, you'll admire the view into the family room below as you walk along the balcony hall.

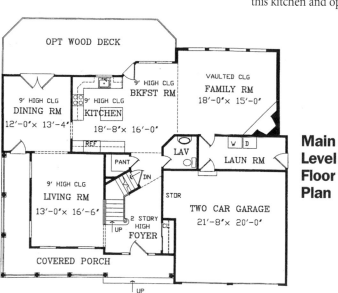

Main Level Floor Plan

Upper Level Floor Plan

Copyright by designer/architect.

Images provided by designer/architect.

Plan #181085

Dimensions: 56'4" W x 44' D
Levels: 2
Square Footage: 2,183
Main Level Sq. Ft.: 1,232
Second Level Sq. Ft.: 951
Bedrooms: 3
Bathrooms: 2½
Foundation: Basement
Materials List Available: Yes
Price Category: E

This country home features an inviting front porch and a layout designed for modern living.

CAD FILE AVAILABLE

Features:

- Ceiling Height: 8 ft.
- Solarium: Sunlight streams through the windows of this solarium at the front of the house.
- Living Room: Walk through French doors, and you will enter this inviting living room. Family and friends will be drawn to the corner fireplace.
- Formal Dining Room: Usher your guests directly from the living room into this formal dining room. The kitchen is located on the other side of the dining room for convenient service.

- Kitchen: This generously sized kitchen is a delight, it offers a center island, separate eat-in area, and access to the back deck.
- Bonus Room: This room just off the entry hall can become a family room, a bedroom, or an office.
- Master Suite: Curl up by the corner fireplace in this master retreat, with its walk-in closet and lavish bath with separate shower and tub.

Main Level Floor Plan

Upper Level Floor Plan

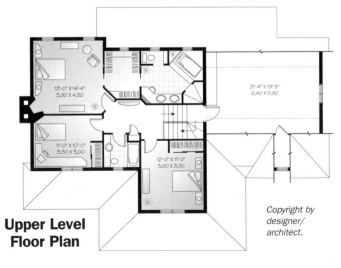

Copyright by designer/ architect.

Plan #131002

Dimensions: 70'1" W x 60'7" D
Levels: 1
Square Footage: 1,709
Bedrooms: 3
Bathrooms: 2½
Foundation: Crawl space, slab, or basement
Materials List Available: Yes
Price Category: D

Images provided by designer/architect.

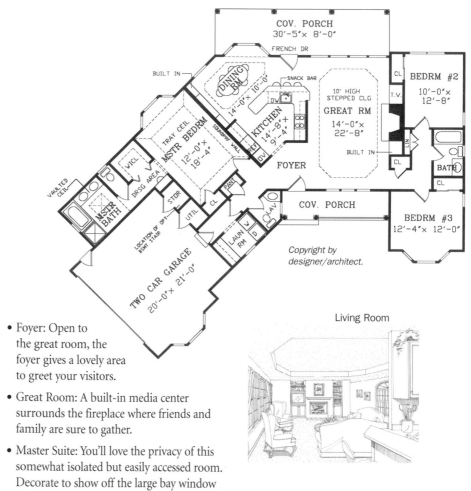

Copyright by designer/architect.

Rear View

Living Room

You'll love the way this angled ranch brings out the best in a corner lot or on a slope.

Features:

- Ceiling Height: 8 ft.

- Front Porch: Hang baskets of plants from the roof of this porch, which is just the right size for a couple of rockers and a side table.

- Dining Room: Well-placed windows flood this room with sunlight during the day and a built-in cabinet gives ample storage space for all your china, linens, and collectables.

- Foyer: Open to the great room, the foyer gives a lovely area to greet your visitors.

- Great Room: A built-in media center surrounds the fireplace where friends and family are sure to gather.

- Master Suite: You'll love the privacy of this somewhat isolated but easily accessed room. Decorate to show off the large bay window and tray ceiling, and enjoy the luxury of a separate toilet room.

Plan #121047

Dimensions: 67'8" W x 57' D

Levels: 1.5

Square Footage: 3,072

Main Level Sq. Ft.: 2,116

Upper Level Sq. Ft.: 956

Bedrooms: 4

Bathrooms: 3½

Foundation: Slab; basement for fee

Materials List Available: Yes

Price Category: G

Images provided by designer/architect.

A long porch and a trio of roof dormers give this gracious home a sophisticated country look.

Features:

- Ceiling Height: 8 ft. unless otherwise noted.
- Balcony: This balcony overlooks the entry and the staircase hall.
- Dining Room: Columns and a cased opening lend elegance, making this the perfect venue for stylish dinner parties.

- Family Room: A cathedral ceiling gives this room a light and airy feel. The handsome fireplace framed by windows is sure to become a favorite family gathering place.
- Master Bedroom: This architecturally distinctive bedroom features a bayed sitting area and a tray ceiling.
- Bedrooms: One of the bedrooms enjoys a private bath, making it a perfect guest room. Other bedrooms feature walk-in closets.

CAD FILE AVAILABLE

Main Level Floor Plan

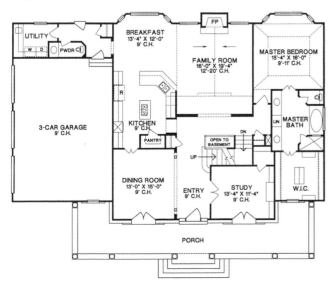

Upper Level Floor Plan

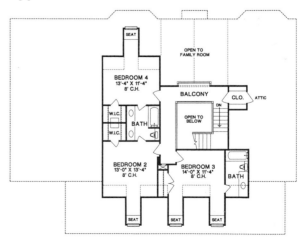

Copyright by designer/architect.

Plan #191003

Dimensions: 56' W x 42' D

Levels: 1

Square Footage: 1,785

Bedrooms: 3

Bathrooms: 3

Foundation: Crawl space, slab, or basement

Materials List Available: No

Price Category: C

Images provided by designer/architect.

Enjoy the amenities you'll find in this gracious home, with its traditional Southern appearance.

Features:

- Great Room: This expansive room is so versatile that everyone will gather here. A built-in entertainment area with desk makes a great lounging spot, and the French doors topped by transoms open onto the lovely rear porch.

- Dining Room: An arched entry to this room helps to create the open feeling in this home.

- Kitchen: Another arched entryway leads to this fabulous kitchen, which has been designed with the cook's comfort in mind. It features a downdraft range, many cabinets, a snack bar, and a sunny breakfast area, where the family is sure to gather.

- Laundry: A sink, shower, toilet area, and cabinets galore give total convenience in this room.

- Master Suite: Enjoy the walk-in closet and bath with toilet room, tub, and shower.

Plan #131043

Dimensions: 65'8" W x 43'10" D
Levels: 1.5
Square Footage: 1,945
Main Level Sq. Ft.: 1,375
Upper Level Sq. Ft.: 570
Bedrooms: 3
Bathrooms: 2½
Foundation: Crawl space, slab, or basement
Materials List Available: Yes
Price Category: E

Images provided by designer/architect.

This home will delight you with its three dormers and half-round transom windows, which give a nostalgic appearance, and its amenities and conveniences that are certainly contemporary.

Features:

- Porch: This covered porch forms the entryway.
- Great Room: Enjoy the fireplace in this large, comfortable room, which is open to the dining area. A French door here leads to the covered porch at the rear of the house.
- Kitchen: This large, country-style kitchen has a bayed nook, and oversized breakfast bar, and pass-through to the rear porch to simplify serving and make entertaining a pleasure.
- Master Suite: A tray ceiling sets an elegant tone for this room, and the bay window adds to it. The large walk-in closet is convenient, and the bath is sumptuous.
- Bedrooms: These comfortable rooms have convenient access to a bath.

Main Level Floor Plan

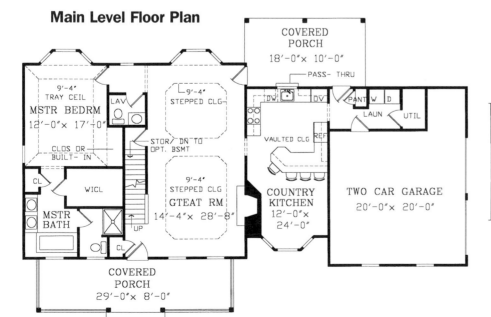

Upper Level Floor Plan

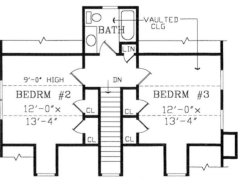

Copyright by designer/architect.

Plan #121083

Dimensions: 72' W x 45'4" D
Levels: 2
Square Footage: 2,695
Main Level Sq. Ft.: 1,881
Upper Level Sq. Ft.: 814
Bedrooms: 4
Bathrooms: 3½
Foundation: Basement
Materials List Available: Yes
Price Category: F

Images provided by designer/architect.

You'll love this home for its soaring entryway ceiling and well-designed layout.

Features:

- **Entry:** A balcony from the upper level looks down into this two-story entry, which features a decorative plant shelf.

- **Great Room:** Comfort is guaranteed in this large room, with its built-in bookcases framing a lovely fireplace and trio of transom-topped windows along one wall.

- **Living Room:** Save both this formal room and the formal dining room, both of which flank the entry, for guests and special occasions.

- **Kitchen:** This convenient work space includes a gazebo-shaped breakfast area where friends and family will gather at any time of day.

Main Level Floor Plan

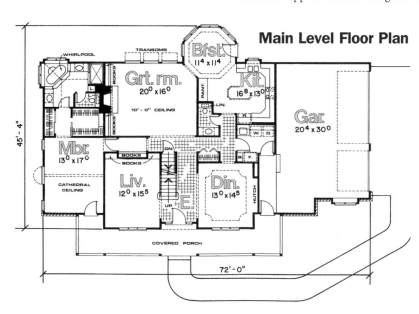

Upper Level Floor Plan

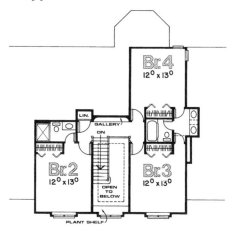

Copyright by designer/architect.

Plan #151018

Dimensions: 69' W x 69'10" D
Levels: 2
Square Footage: 2,755
Main Level Sq. Ft.: 2,406
Upper Level Sq. Ft.: 349
Bedrooms: 3
Bathrooms: 4½
Foundation: Crawl space, slab, or basement
CompleteCost List Available: Yes
Price Category: F

Images provided by designer/architect.

Treasure the countless amenities that make this home ideal for a family and welcoming to guests.

Features:

- **Great Room:** A gas fireplace and built-in shelving beg for a warm, comfortable decorating scheme.

- **Kitchen:** An island counter here opens to the breakfast room, and a swinging door leads to the dining room with its formal entry columns.

- **Laundry Room:** You'll wonder how you ever kept the laundry organized without this room and its built-in ironing board and broom closet.

- **Master Suite:** Atrium doors to the porch are a highlight of the bedroom, with its two walk-in closets, a corner whirlpool tub with glass blocks, and a separate shower.

- **Bedrooms:** These large rooms will surely promote peaceful school-day mornings for the children because each room has both a private bath and a walk-in closet.

Main Level Floor Plan

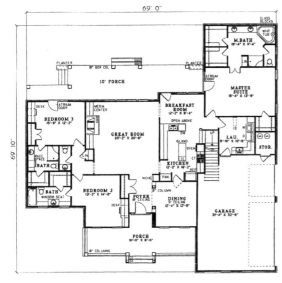

Upper Level Floor Plan

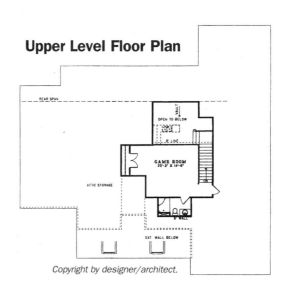

Copyright by designer/architect.

Plan #191001

Dimensions: 62' W x 72' D

Levels: 1

Square Footage: 2,156

Bedrooms: 4

Bathrooms: 3

Foundation: Crawl space, slab, or basement

Materials List Available: No

Price Category: D

This lovely home has the best of old and new — a traditional appearance combined with fabulous comforts and conveniences.

Features:

- Great Room: A tray ceiling gives stature to this expansive room, and its many windows let natural light stream into it.

- Kitchen: When you're standing at the sink in this gorgeous kitchen, you'll have a good view of the patio. But if you turn around, you'll see the island cooktop, wall oven, walk-in pantry, and snack bar, all of which make this kitchen such a pleasure.

- Master Suite: Somewhat isolated for privacy, this area is ideal for an evening or weekend retreat. Relax in the gracious bedroom or luxuriate in the spa-style bath, with its corner whirlpool tub, large shower, two sinks, and access to the walk-in closet, which measures a full 8 ft. x 10 ft.

- Mudroom: No matter whether you live where mud season is as reliable as spring thaws or where rain is a seasonal event, you'll love having a spot to confine the muddy mess.

Images provided by designer/architect.

Front View

Copyright by designer/architect.

Plan #181078

Dimensions: 58' W x 40' D

Levels: 2

Square Footage: 2,292

Main Level Sq. Ft.: 1,266

Upper Level Sq. Ft.: 1,026

Bedrooms: 4

Bathrooms: 2½

Foundation: Full basement

Materials List Available: Yes

Price Category: E

This two-story home will be a fine addition to any neighborhood.

Features:

- **Living Room:** This gathering area is open to the kitchen and will warm you with its cozy fireplace.

- **Kitchen:** This island kitchen has a raised bar that looks into the living room, and it provides access to the rear porch.

- **Master Suite:** This private area has a cozy fireplace in the sleeping area. The master bath features dual vanities, a walk-in closet, and a large tub.

- **Bedrooms:** The two additional bedrooms are located upstairs with the master suite and share the Jack-and-Jill bathroom.

Images provided by designer/architect.

This home, as shown in the photograph, may differ from the actual blueprints. For more detailed information, please check the floor plans carefully.

CAD FILE AVAILABLE

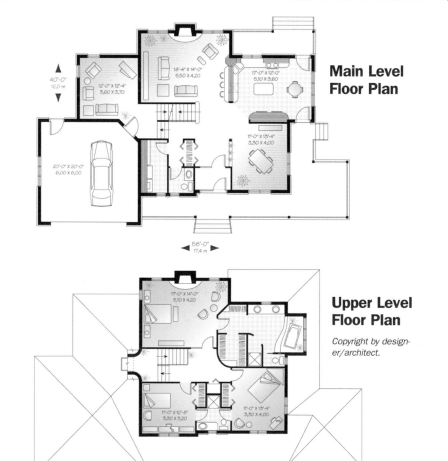

Main Level Floor Plan

Upper Level Floor Plan

Copyright by designer/architect.

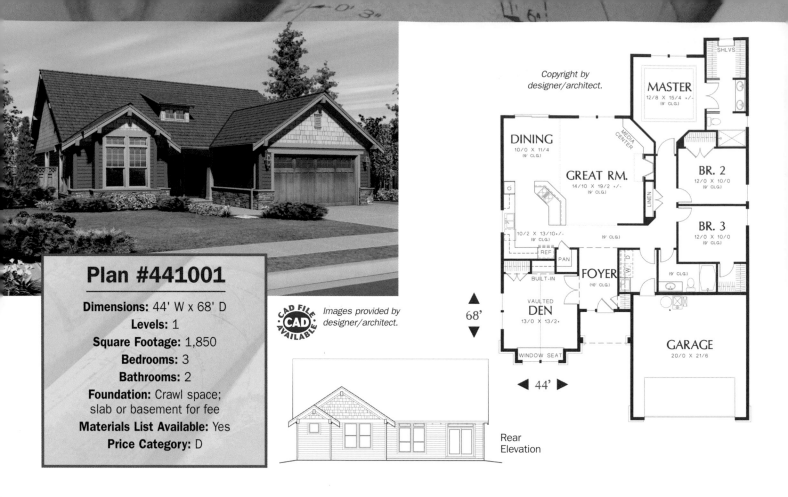

Plan #441001

Dimensions: 44' W x 68' D

Levels: 1

Square Footage: 1,850

Bedrooms: 3

Bathrooms: 2

Foundation: Crawl space; slab or basement for fee

Materials List Available: Yes

Price Category: D

Images provided by designer/architect.

Rear Elevation

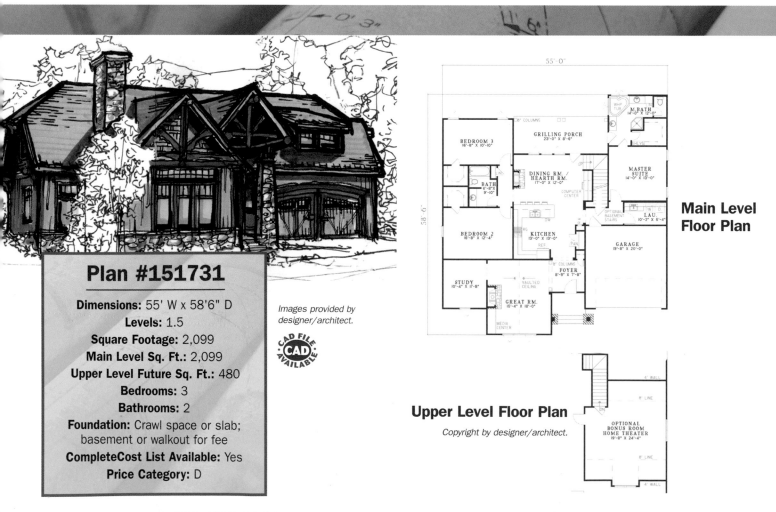

Plan #151731

Dimensions: 55' W x 58'6" D

Levels: 1.5

Square Footage: 2,099

Main Level Sq. Ft.: 2,099

Upper Level Future Sq. Ft.: 480

Bedrooms: 3

Bathrooms: 2

Foundation: Crawl space or slab; basement or walkout for fee

CompleteCost List Available: Yes

Price Category: D

Images provided by designer/architect.

Main Level Floor Plan

Upper Level Floor Plan

Copyright by designer/architect.

Plan #481097

Dimensions: 86' W x 48' D
Levels: 2
Square Footage: 2,945
Main Level Sq. Ft.: 1,650
Upper Level Sq. Ft.: 1,295
Bedrooms: 3
Bathrooms: 2½
Foundation: Walkout
Material List Available: No
Price Category: F

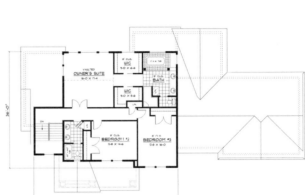

Main Level Floor Plan

Images provided by designer/architect.

Upper Level Floor Plan

Copyright by designer/architect.

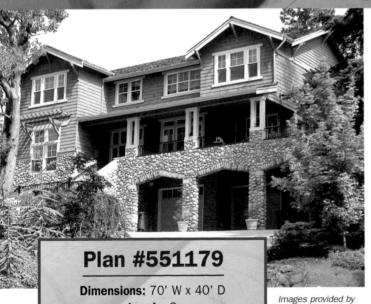

Plan #551179

Dimensions: 70' W x 40' D
Levels: 2
Square Footage: 3,900
Main Level Sq. Ft.: 1,825
Upper Level Sq. Ft.: 1,370
Bedrooms: 4
Bathrooms: 3½
Foundation: Crawl space or walkout; slab or basement for fee
Material List Available: No
Price Category: H

Images provided by designer/architect.

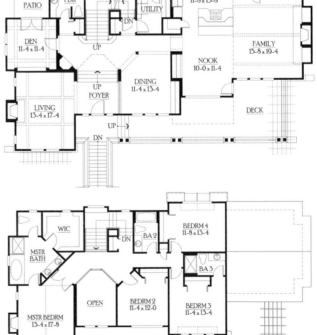

Main Level Floor Plan

Upper Level Floor Plan

Copyright by designer/architect.

Plan #441012

Dimensions: 65' W x 55' D
Levels: 1
Square Footage: 3,682
Main Level Sq. Ft.: 2,192
Basement Level Sq. Ft.: 1,490
Bedrooms: 4
Bathrooms: 4
Foundation: Walkout
Materials List Available: Yes
Price Category: H

CAD FILE AVAILABLE

Images provided by designer/architect.

Accommodating a site that slopes to the rear, this home is not only good-looking but practical.

Features:

• Den: Just off the foyer is this cozy space, complete with built-ins.

• Great Room: This vaulted gathering area features a lovely fireplace, a built-in media center, and a view of the back yard.

• Kitchen: This island kitchen is ready to handle the daily needs of your family or aid in entertaining your guests.

• Lower Level: Adding even more livability to the home, this floor contains the games room with media center and corner fireplace, two more bedrooms (each with a full bathroom), and the wide covered patio.

Rear Elevation

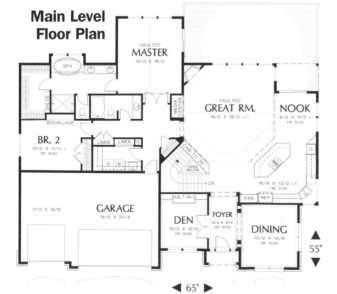

Copyright by designer/architect.

Plan #441025

Dimensions: 70' W x 100'6" D
Levels: 2
Square Footage: 3,457
Main Level Sq. Ft.: 2,222
Upper Level Sq. Ft.: 1,235
Bedrooms: 4
Bathrooms: 3 full, 2 half
Foundation: Crawl space;
slab or basement for fee
Materials List Available: Yes
Price Category: G

Classic Craftsman tradition shines through in this spectacular two-story home.

Features:

- Great Room: This open room features two sets of double doors to the rear yard, a fireplace, and a built-in media center.

- Kitchen: Casual dining takes place in the breakfast nook, which is open to this island kitchen and leads to a vaulted porch.

- Master Suites: One master suite is found on the first floor. It glows with appointments, from double-door access to the rear yard to a fine bath with spa tub, separate shower, and double sinks. The second master suite, on the second floor, holds a window seat and a private bath with spa tub.

- Bedrooms: Two additional bedrooms (or a bedroom and a study) share a full bathroom with private vanities for each room.

- Garage: This four-car garage connects to the main house at a laundry/mud room with a half-bath, coat closet, built-in bench, and washer/dryer space. Extra room in the garage can be used as a workshop or for storage space.

Images provided by designer/architect.

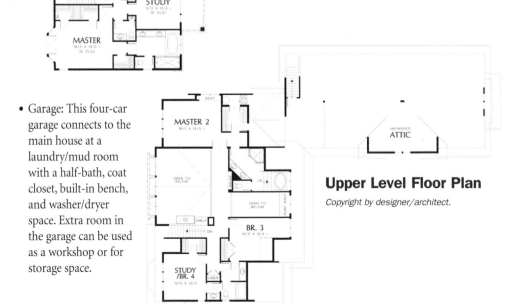

Main Level Floor Plan

Upper Level Floor Plan

Copyright by designer/architect.

Plan #151530

Dimensions: 38'10" W x 70'4" D
Levels: 2
Square Footage: 2,146
Main Level Sq. Ft.: 1,654
Upper Level Sq. Ft.: 492
Bedrooms: 3
Bathrooms: 2½
Foundation: Crawl space or slab
CompleteCost List Available: Yes
Price Category: D

Images provided by designer/architect.

Gables, columns, and architectural detailing give this home a warm feeling reminiscent of your grandmother's house.

CAD FILE AVAILABLE

Features:

- **Foyer:** The cozy porch gently welcomes you into this column-lined foyer, which separates the formal dining room from the large great room with fireplace.

- **Kitchen:** This kitchen with breakfast room is centrally located and looks out at the lovely courtyard patio, which is perfect for entertaining.

- **Master Suite:** Your perfect hideaway awaits you in this spacious suite, with its large walk-in closet and master bath packed with amenities.

- **Upper Level:** The upstairs has two bedrooms, each with private access to the full bathroom, as well as future bonus space when desired.

Main Level Floor Plan
Copyright by designer/architect.

Upper Level Floor Plan

Front View

Plan #441005

Dimensions: 50' W x 59' D
Levels: 1
Square Footage: 1,800
Bedrooms: 3
Bathrooms: 2
Foundation: Crawl space; slab or basement for fee
Materials List Available: Yes
Price Category: D

Images provided by designer/architect.

This home looks as if it's a quaint little abode—with its board-and-batten siding, cedar shingle detailing, and column-covered porch—but even a quick peek inside will prove that there is much more to this plan than meets the eye.

CAD FILE AVAILABLE

Features:

- **Foyer:** This entry area rises to a 9-ft.-high ceiling. On one side is a washer-dryer alcove with a closet across the way; on the other is another large storage area. Just down the hallway is a third closet.

- **Kitchen:** This kitchen features a center island, built-in desk/work center, and pantry. This area and the dining area also boast 9-ft.-high ceilings and are open to a vaulted great room with corner fireplace.

- **Dining Room:** Sliding doors in this area lead to a covered side porch, so you can enjoy outside dining.

- **Master Suite:** This suite has a vaulted ceiling. The master bath is wonderfully appointed with a separate shower, spa tub, and dual sinks.

- **Bedrooms:** Three bedrooms (or two plus an office) are found on the right side of the plan.

Copyright by designer/architect.

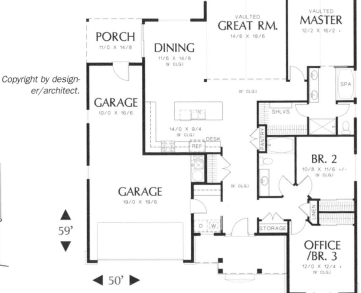

Rear Elevation

Plan #441035

Dimensions: 50' W x 56' D

Levels: 2

Square Footage: 2,196

Main Level Sq. Ft.: 1,658

Upper Level Sq. Ft.: 538

Bedrooms: 4

Bathrooms: 2½

Foundation: Crawl space; slab or basement available for fee

Materials List Available: Yes

Price Category: D

Images provided by designer/architect.

This home's stone-and-cedar-shingle facade is delightfully complemented by French Country detailing, dormer windows, and shutters at the large arched window and its second-story sister.

Features:

- Great Room: Containing a fireplace and double doors to the rear yard, this large room is further enhanced by a vaulted ceiling.
- Kitchen: This cooking center has an attached nook with corner windows overlooking the backyard.
- Master Suite: This suite is well designed with a vaulted ceiling and Palladian window. Its bath sports a spa tub.
- Bonus Space: This huge space, located on the second level, provides for a future bedroom, game room, or home office. Two dormer windows grace it.
- Garage: A service hall, with laundry alcove, opens to this garage. There is space enough here for three cars or two and a workshop.

Rear Elevation

Main Level Floor Plan

Upper Level Floor Plan

Copyright by designer/architect.

Plan #551132

Dimensions: 42' W x 52'6" D
Levels: 2
Square Footage: 2,520
Main Level Sq. Ft.: 1,365
Upper Level Sq. Ft.: 1,155
Bedrooms: 3
Bathrooms: 2½
Foundation: Crawl space, slab or walkout
Material List Available: No
Price Category: E

Images provided by designer/architect.

The exterior of this Craftsman-style home is unmatched. Slanted gables and varying textures make the house a stylish addition to any neighborhood.

Features:

- Entry: Cross the threshold through a formal entryway and foyer, and enjoy the view of the open living and dining rooms.

- Family Room: Snuggle by the fire in this comfortable family room.

- Den: Located off of the kitchen, this quaint room is the perfect accent for making a large home cozier. Use the den as an area for homework or a place where unsightly computer cords and electronics can be concealed.

- Master Suite: This bedroom features a vaulted ceiling and walk-in closet. Enter into a luxurious spa-like bathroom, with a whirlpool tub and his and her sinks. Storage space is ample, and a loft overlooks the lower level for a dramatic effect.

- Garage: A three-car garage is great for keeping cars out of the elements.

Copyright by designer/architect.

Main Level Floor Plan

Upper Level Floor Plan

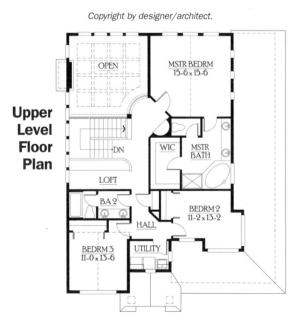

Main Level Floor Plan

◄ 67' ►   ▲
          68'
          ▼

Plan #441033

Dimensions: 67' W x 68' D

Levels: 2

Square Footage: 2,986

Main Level Sq. Ft.: 2,162

Upper Level Sq. Ft.: 824

Bedrooms: 3

Bathrooms: 2½

Foundation: Crawl space; slab or basement for fee

Materials List Available: Yes

Price Category: F

Images provided by designer/architect.

This home, as shown in the photograph, may differ from the actual blueprints. For more detailed information, please check the floor plans carefully.

CAD FILE AVAILABLE — **CAD**

Rear Elevation

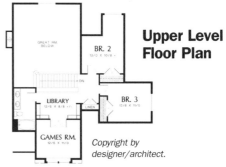

Upper Level Floor Plan

Copyright by designer/architect.

Plan #161224

Dimensions: 87'4" W x 57'4" D

Levels: 1

Square Footage: 2,796

Bedrooms: 2

Bathrooms: 2½

Foundation: Walkout

Material List Available: Yes

Price Category: F

Images provided by designer/architect.

Copyright by designer/architect.

Rear View

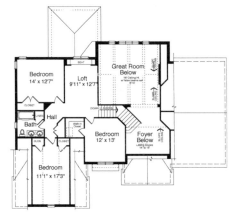

Main Level Floor Plan

Copyright by designer/architect.

Covered Porch 14' x 14'

Laun.

Breakfast 11'10" x 9'9"

Great Room 18'2 x 18'2

Master Bedroom 16'2" x 14'

Hall

Bath

Kitchen 14'7" x 12'

Dining Room 12' x 13'

Foyer

Bath

Dressing

WALK-IN CLOSET

Garage 20' x 21'

Porch

Plan #161153

Dimensions: 62'7" W x 49' D

Levels: 2

Square Footage: 2,824

Main Level Sq. Ft.: 1,864

Upper Level Sq. Ft.: 960

Bedrooms: 4

Bathrooms: 2 full, 2 half

Foundation: Basement; walkout for fee

Material List Available: Yes

Price Category: F

Images provided by designer/architect.

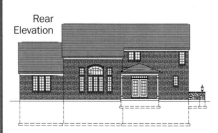

Rear Elevation

Upper Level Floor Plan

Bedroom 14' x 12'7"

SEAT

Great Room Below 14' Ceiling Ht. w/ false beams opt. at 9' Ht.

Loft 9'11" x 12'7"

Bath

Hall

DOWN

Bedroom 12' x 13'

Foyer Below

Bedroom 11'1" x 17'3"

Main Level Floor Plan

GREAT RM 21' X 18'

DINING 21' X 10'

KITCHEN 15' X 14'

STUDY 11' X 13'

MUD RM

PORCH

GARAGE 40' X 24'

Plan #271094

Dimensions: 71' W x 70' D

Levels: 2

Square Footage: 3,242

Main Level Sq. Ft.: 1,552

Upper Level Sq. Ft.: 1,690

Bedrooms: 5

Bathrooms: 2½

Foundation: Full basement

Materials List Available: No

Price Category: G

Images provided by designer/architect.

CAD FILE AVAILABLE

Upper Level Floor Plan

BED RM 10' X 14'

BED RM 10' X 14'

BATH

OWNER'S SUITE 14' X 18'

LAUN

BATH

WIC

BATH

BED RM 11' X 13'

BED RM 11' X 13'

Copyright by designer/architect.

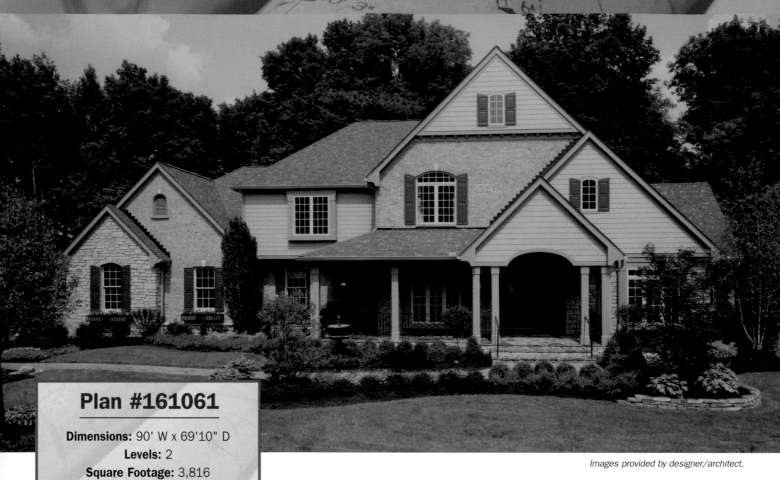

Plan #161061

Dimensions: 90' W x 69'10" D

Levels: 2

Square Footage: 3,816

Main Level Sq. Ft.: 2,725

Upper Level Sq. Ft.: 1,091

Bedrooms: 4

Bathrooms: 3½

Foundation: Basement, walkout basement

Materials List Available: No

Price Category: H

Images provided by designer/architect.

Luxurious amenities make living in this spacious home a true pleasure for the whole family.

Features:

- **Great Room:** A fireplace, flanking built-in shelves, a balcony above, and three lovely windows create a luxurious room that's always comfortable.

- **Hearth Room:** Another fireplace with surrounding built-ins and double doors to the outside deck (with its own fireplace) highlight this room.

- **Kitchen:** A butler's pantry, laundry room, and mudroom with a window seat and two walk-in closets complement this large kitchen.

- **Library:** Situated for privacy and quiet, this spacious room with a large window area may be reached from the master bedroom as well as the foyer.

- **Master Suite:** A sloped ceiling and windows on three walls create a lovely bedroom, and the huge walk-in closet, dressing room, and luxurious bath add up to total comfort.

Main Level Floor Plan

Upper Level Floor Plan

Copyright by designer/architect.

Rear Elevation

Right Side
Elevation

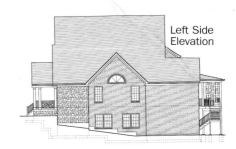

Left Side
Elevation

Great Room

Hearth Room

Kitchen

Dining Room

Library

Plan #441004

Dimensions: 55' W x 48' D

Levels: 1

Square Footage: 1,728

Bedrooms: 2

Bathrooms: 2

Foundation: Crawl space;
slab or basement available for fee

Materials List Available: Yes

Price Category: C

CAD FILE AVAILABLE

Images provided by designer/architect.

Empty nesters and first-time homeowners will adore the comfort within this charming home. Rooms benefit from the many windows, which welcome light into the home.

Features:

- Great Room: This vaulted room is equipped with a media center and fireplace. Windows span across the back of the room and the adjoining dining room, extending the perceived area and offering access to the covered patio.

- Kitchen: Taking advantage of corner space, this kitchen provides ample cabinets and countertops to store goods and prepare meals. Every chef will appreciate the extra space afforded by the pantry.

- Master Suite: This luxurious escape has a large sleeping area with views of the backyard. The master bath features a spa tub, dual vanities, and a walk-in closet.

- Garage: This front-loading two-car garage has a shop area located in the rear.

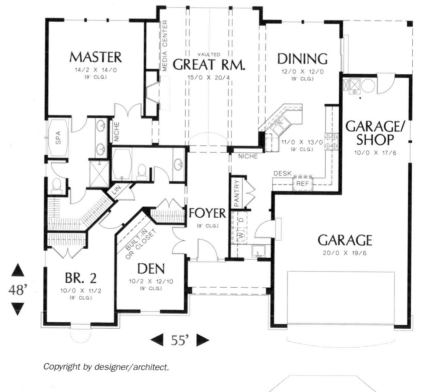

Copyright by designer/architect.

Rear
Elevation

Plan #211075

Dimensions: 80' W x 84' D
Levels: 2
Square Footage: 3,568
Main Level Sq. Ft.: 2,330
Upper Level Sq. Ft.: 1,238
Bedrooms: 4
Bathrooms: 3½
Foundation: Crawl space
Materials List Available: Yes
Price Category: H

Images provided by designer/architect.

The porte-cochere—or covered passage over a driveway—announces the quality and beauty of this spacious country home.

Features:

- **Front Porch:** Spot groups of potted plants on this 779-sq.-ft. porch, and add a glider and some rocking chairs to take advantage of its comfort.

- **Family Room:** Let this family room become the heart of the home. With a fireplace to make it cozy and a wet bar for easy serving, it's a natural for entertaining.

- **Game Room:** Expect a crowd in this room, no matter what the weather.

- **Kitchen:** A cooktop island and a pantry are just two features of this fully appointed kitchen.

- **Master Suite:** The bedroom is as luxurious as you'd expect, but the quarter-circle raised tub in the master bath might surprise you. Two walk-in closets and two vanities add a practical touch.

Main Level Floor Plan

Upper Level Floor Plan

Copyright by designer/architect.

Main Level Floor Plan

34'-0"
10,2 m

15'-0" x 15'-6"
3,80 x 4,30

12'-4" x 11'-4"
3,70 x 3,40

12'-0" x 14'-4"
3,60 x 4,30

20'-4" x 24'-6"
6,10 x 7,40

17'-0" x 16'-0"
5,10 x 4,80

7'-8" x 15'-0"
2,30 x 4,50

6'-0" x 9'-0"
2,40 x 2,70

68'-0"
20,4 m

Images provided by designer/architect.

CAD FILE AVAILABLE
CAD

Plan #181137

Dimensions: 68' W x 34' D

Levels: 2

Square Footage: 2,353

Main Level Sq. Ft.: 1,281

Upper Level Sq. Ft.: 1,072

Bedrooms: 3

Bathrooms: 2½

Foundation: Full basement

Materials List Available: Yes

Price Category: E

Upper Level Floor Plan

10'-8" x 11'-4"
3,20 x 3,40

17'-0" x 14'-0"
5,10 x 4,20

11'-0" x 15'-0"
3,30 x 3,80

10'-0" x 13'-0"
3,00 x 3,90

Copyright by designer/architect.

Plan #441008

Dimensions: 60' W x 50' D

Levels: 1

Square Footage: 2,001

Bedrooms: 3

Bathrooms: 2

Foundation: Crawl space; slab or basement available for fee

Materials List Available: Yes

Price Category: D

Images provided by designer/architect.

CAD FILE AVAILABLE
CAD

SPA

VAULTED
MASTER
16/6 X 13/0

DINING
12/8 X 14/0
(9' CLG.)

MEDIA CENTER

GARAGE/SHOP
11/6 X 15/6

VAULTED
GREAT RM.
17/6 X 20/0

DESK
REF

FOYER
(9' CLG.)

OPT. DESK OR CLOSET

GARAGE
19/0 X 22/0

NICHE

DEN
10/0 X 13/2
(9' CLG.)

50'

BR. 3
11/8 X 12/2
(9' CLG.)

BR. 2
10/0 X 13/2
(9' CLG.)

60'

Copyright by designer/architect.

Rear Elevation

Main Level Floor Plan

Copyright by designer/architect.

Upper Level Floor Plan

Plan #161080

Dimensions: 67'4" W x 59'6" D

Levels: 2

Square Footage: 2,759

Main Level Sq. Ft.: 2,007

Upper Level Sq. Ft.: 752

Bedrooms: 4

Bathrooms: 3½

Foundation: Basement or walkout

Material List Available: Yes

Price Category: F

Images provided by designer/architect.

Rear Elevation

Main Level Floor Plan

Upper Level Floor Plan

Copyright by designer/architect.

Plan #661210

Dimensions: 91'4" W x 77'4" D

Levels: 2

Square Footage: 3,338

Main Level Sq. Ft.: 2,854

Upper Level Sq. Ft.: 484

Bedrooms: 4

Bathrooms: 3½

Foundation: Slab

Material List Available: No

Price Category: G

CAD FILE AVAILABLE

Main Level Floor Plan

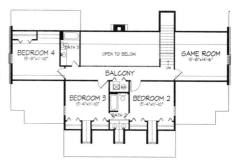

Images provided by designer/architect.

Upper Level Floor Plan

Copyright by designer/architect.

Plan #271098

Dimensions: 68'10" W x 81'5" D

Levels: 2

Square Footage: 3,382

Main Level Sq. Ft.: 2,136

Upper Level Sq. Ft.: 1,246

Bedrooms: 4

Bathrooms: 3½

Foundation: Slab

Materials List Available: No

Price Category: G

Plan #191017

Dimensions: 78' W x 51' D

Levels: 1

Square Footage: 2,605

Bedrooms: 4

Bathrooms: 2½

Foundation: Crawl space, slab, or basement

Materials List Available: No

Price Category: F

Images provided by designer/architect.

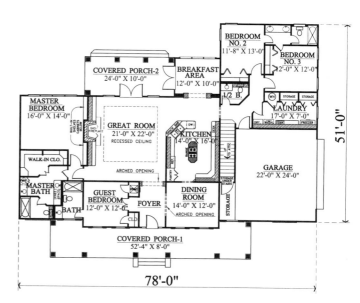

Copyright by designer/architect.

Main Level Floor Plan

Lower Level Floor Plan

Copyright by designer/architect.

Plan #441013

Dimensions: 69' W x 59' D
Levels: 2
Square Footage: 3,317
Main Level Sq. Ft.: 2,657
Lower Level Sq. Ft.: 660
Bedrooms: 4
Bathrooms: 3½
Foundation: Slab
Materials List Available: Yes
Price Category: G

Images provided by designer/architect.

CAD FILE AVAILABLE

Plan #191037

Dimensions: 57'4" W x 65' D
Levels: 1
Square Footage: 1,575
Bedrooms: 3
Bathrooms: 2
Foundation: Crawl space, slab
Materials List Available: No
Price Category: C

Images provided by designer/architect.

Copyright by designer/architect.

Plan #441003

Dimensions: 50' W x 48' D
Levels: 1
Square Footage: 1,580
Bedrooms: 3
Bathrooms: 2½
Foundation: Crawl space;
slab or basement available for fee
Materials List Available: Yes
Price Category: C

Images provided by designer/architect.

CAD FILE CAD AVAILABLE

Craftsman styling with modern floor planning—that's the advantage of this cozy design. Covered porches at front and back enhance both the look and the livability of the plan.

Features:

- **Great Room:** This vaulted entertaining area boasts a corner fireplace and a built-in media center. The area is open to the kitchen and the dining area.

- **Kitchen:** This large, open island kitchen will please the chef in the family. The raised bar is open to the dining area and the great room.

- **Master Suite:** Look for luxurious amenities such as double sinks and a separate tub and shower in the master bath. The master bedroom has a vaulted ceiling and a walk-in closet with built-in shelves.

- **Bedrooms:** Two secondary bedrooms are located away from the master suite. Each has a large closet and access to a common bathroom.

PORCH

DINING
11/2 X 12/8
(9' CLG.)

SHELVES

VAULTED
MASTER
12/8 X 15/2

VAULTED
GREAT RM.
16/8 X 17/0

BUILT-INS

11/4 X 12/10

REF.

W D

MEDIA

LIN. LIN.

FOYER
(10' CLG.)

BR. 3/
DEN
10/6 X 11/4
(9' CLG.)

GARAGE
20/6 X 21/0

48'

BR. 2
11/0 X 10/0
(9' CLG.)

PORCH

◀ 50' ▶

Copyright by designer/architect.

Rear Elevation

Plan #181081

Dimensions: 58' W x 33' D
Levels: 2
Square Footage: 2,350
Main Level Sq. Ft.: 1,107
Second Level Sq. Ft.: 1,243
Bedrooms: 3
Bathrooms: 2½
Foundation: Basement
Materials List Available: Yes
Price Category: F

Images provided by designer/architect.

This traditional country home features a wrap-around porch and a second-floor balcony.

Features:

- Ceiling Height: 8 ft. unless otherwise noted.

- Family Room: Double French doors and a fireplace in this inviting front room enhance the beauty and warmth of the home's open floor plan.

- Kitchen: You'll love working in this bright and convenient kitchen. The breakfast bar is the perfect place to gather for informal meals.

- Master Suite: You'll look forward to retiring to this elegant upstairs suite at the end of a busy day. The suite features a private bath with separate shower and tub, as well as dual vanities.

- Secondary Bedrooms: Two family bedrooms share a full bath with a third room that opens onto the balcony.

- Basement: An unfinished full basement provides plenty of storage and the potential to add additional finished living space.

Main Level Floor Plan

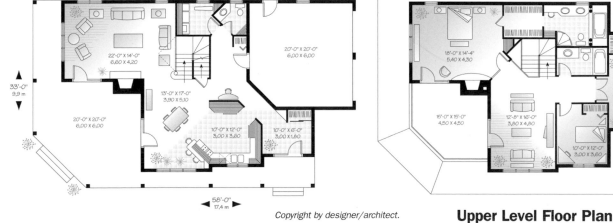

Copyright by designer/architect.

Upper Level Floor Plan

Plan #191012

Dimensions: 60' W x 76' D

Levels: 1

Square Footage: 2,123

Bedrooms: 3

Bathrooms: 2½

Foundation: Crawl space or slab

Materials List Available: No

Price Category: D

Images provided by designer/architect.

The wraparound porch adds to the charm of this home.

Features:

- Porches: The front wraparound porch will be the perfect spot to greet neighbors as they stroll by. The rear porch is a private place to relax and enjoy a beautiful day.

- Great Room: This large gathering area features a 10-ft.-high ceiling and large windows, which offer a view of the backyard. There is even room for a formal dining table.

- Master Suite: Located on the opposite side of the home from the secondary bedrooms, this retreat offers a large sleeping area. The master bath will pamper you with an oversize shower, a tub, and dual vanities.

- Secondary Bedrooms: Two similarly sized bedrooms have ample closet space and share a full bathroom.

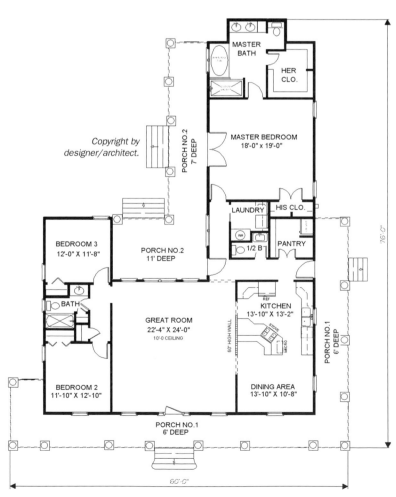

Copyright by designer/architect.

Plan #441010

Dimensions: 108'6" W x 59' D

Levels: 1

Square Footage: 2,973

Bedrooms: 4

Bathrooms: 4½

Foundation: Crawl space; slab or basement available for fee

Materials List Available: Yes

Price Category: F

Bordering on estate-sized, this plan borrows elements from Norman, Mediterranean, and English architecture.

Images provided by designer/architect.

Features:

- **Great Room:** This gathering area features a large bay window and a fireplace flanked with built-ins. The vaulted ceiling adds to the large feel of the area.

- **Kitchen:** This large island kitchen features a walk-in pantry and a built-in desk. The breakfast nook has access to the patio.

- **Master Suite:** This retreat features a vaulted ceiling in the sleeping area and access to the patio. The master bath boasts dual vanities, a stand-up shower, a spa tub, and a very large walk-in closet.

- **Bedrooms:** Two family bedrooms, each with its own private bathroom, have large closets.

CAD FILE AVAILABLE

Copyright by designer/architect.

Rear Elevation

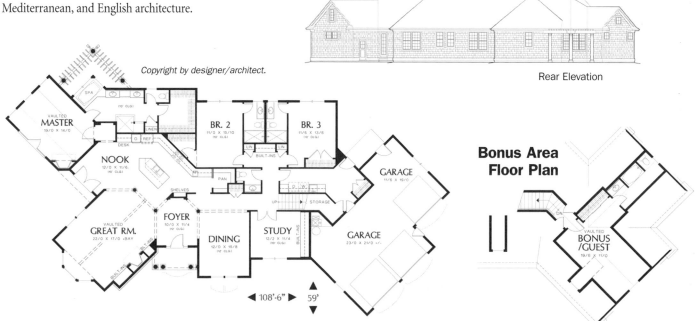

Bonus Area Floor Plan

Plan #131003

Dimensions: 60' W x 39'10" D
Levels: 1
Square Footage: 1,466
Bedrooms: 3
Bathrooms: 2
Foundation: Crawl space, slab, or basement
Materials List Available: Yes
Price Category: C

This home, as shown in the photograph, may differ from the actual blueprints. For more detailed information, please check the floor plans carefully.

Victorian styling adds elegance to this compact and easy-to-maintain ranch design.

Images provided by designer/architect.

Features:

- Ceiling Height: 8 ft.
- Foyer: Bridging between the front door and the great room, this foyer is a surprise feature.
- Great Room: A 10-ft. ceiling adds to the spacious feeling of this room, while the corner fireplace gives it an intimate feeling. Sliding glass doors at the rear of the room open to the backyard.
- Dining Room: This formal room adjoins the great room, allowing guests and family to flow between the rooms.
- Breakfast Room: Turrets add a Victorian feeling to this room that's just off the kitchen and overlooks the front porch.
- Master Suite: Privacy is assured in this suite, which is separated from the main part of the house. A separate toilet room and large walk-in closet add convenience to its beauty.

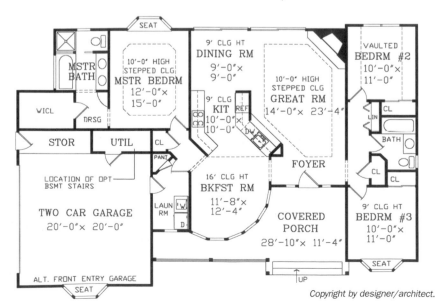

Copyright by designer/architect.

Front View

Foyer/Kitchen/Breakfast Room

Breakfast Room

Great Room

Great Room

design ideas for   CREATIVE HOMEOWNER®

DECORATIVE
Concrete & Stone

| products | | inspiration | | materials |

Ellen Frankel and Mervyn Kaufman

This article was reprinted from *Design Ideas
for Decorative Concrete & Stone* (Creative
Homeowner 2006).

Using Granite in Kitchens

Granite is as hardy as your kitchen's heaviest iron frypan. It resists nicks, scratches, and scorching, and its beauty is legendary, making it the perfect surface for kitchens. Some granites are porous, however; they must be dutifully sealed, and when used on the floor they can be slippery when wet. A range of finishes would enable you to easily adapt this stone to any home need. *Polished* is a high-gloss finish that makes a particularly powerful color statement. *Brushed* creates a smooth surface with a timeless, worn character. *Flamed*, ideal for floors, is roughened, the result of high heat. *Honed* presents a smooth-as-satin finish.

In this kitchen, above, the sleek countertop fits well with the modern design and trendy appliances. What looks like a granite slab cut to accommodate two undermount sinks is actually a series of tiles pressed so close together that the grout is virtually invisible. Be sure your contractor uses grout and mortar designed for use with granite tiles.

Granite counters, reflect natural sunlight, ceiling lights, and the high-intensity task lighting supplied by an arrangement of pendant fixtures, opposite, left and below. For food-prep areas, make sure the installer applies a nontoxic sealer. It will make the area easier to clean, prevent stains, and ensure that you can safely cut on the counter, although it is best to use a cutting board.

order direct: 1-800-523-6789

In planning her kitchen, opposite and above left, the owner told her designer, "All I want is a classic white kitchen." What she got was a white-painted bead-board backsplash, white recessed-panel cabinets, and white ogee-edged granite countertops.

In what appears a seamless granite installation, above right, this kitchen countertop was created from tightly placed tiles placed directly over a suitable substrate, creating a sleek countertop.

Granite with a large ogee edge, left, tops an island that has cupboards and drawers on two sides. The countertop, cut from one stone slab, extends over classic pilasters at the corners.

Black granite counters, right, plus brushed-nickel fittings and cabinet hardware lend understated elegance to this contemporary kitchen.

For maximum light and the most efficient layout, below, a professional chef added a wall of windows and black granite to top twin islands, creating separate food-prep areas that are a snap to clean up.

The owners of a Mediterranean-style home, opposite top, wanted to add some intimacy around the snack island so they set the granite-topped island into an arch between the kitchen and dining room.

Adding a sculptural shape to the geometry of this space, opposite bottom, a custom-designed range hood spills light onto a cooktop set into a Black Absolute granite surface, which also forms the backsplash.

order direct: 1-800-523-6789

SMARTtip

Fast Fixes

Recently imported materials now make it possible to have the look plus the indestructible surface of granite without using large slabs.

You can upgrade almost any surface by the application of special tiles over a prepared substrate. These tiles are set so close together that the result resembles a single slab of granite.

The beauty of such installations is that the work can occur quickly, so you can enjoy the benefits shared by all users of granite. If the job is done skillfully, few people can tell the difference between a granite slab and tiles.

order direct: 1-800-523-6789

In a splash of versatility, this granite countertop, opposite and below, has roughened irregularity on its forward edge and on the top edge of the backsplash.

A rare form of granite with dramatic marble-like veining is used on counters and backsplashes, and as trim around this kitchen's single window, above and right. Note that at the far end of the island, above, granite in a free-form shape panels parts of two sides of an angled wall.

In a simple yet elegant kitchen, above right, with tile walls and flooring, the granite countertop flanks a pure-white farm sink.

**Main Level
Floor Plan**

Images provided by designer/architect.

**Upper Level
Floor Plan**

Copyright by designer/architect.

Plan #151030

Dimensions: 59' W x 73' D

Levels: 2

Square Footage: 2,802

Main Level Sq. Ft.: 2,058

Upper Level Sq. Ft.: 744

Bonus Room Sq. Ft.: 493

Bedrooms: 3

Bathrooms: 3½

Foundation: Crawl space, slab; basement for fee

CompleteCost List Available: Yes

Price Category: F

**Main Level
Floor Plan**

Images provided by designer/architect.

**Upper Level
Floor Plan**

Copyright by designer/architect.

Plan #181061

Dimensions: 56' W x 53'2" D

Levels: 2

Square Footage: 2,111

Main Level Sq. Ft.: 1,545

Upper Level Sq. Ft.: 566

Bedrooms: 2

Bathrooms: 2½

Foundation: Crawl space, basement

Materials List Available: Yes

Price Category: D

Plan #271076

Dimensions: 69' W x 57' D

Levels: 1

Square Footage: 2,188

Bedrooms: 2-4

Bathrooms: 1½-2½

Foundation: Daylight basement

Materials List Available: No

Price Category: D

Images provided by designer/architect.

CAD FILE AVAILABLE

Optional Basement Level Floor Plan

Copyright by designer/architect.

Plan #441007

Dimensions: 70' W x 64' D

Levels: 1

Square Footage: 2,197

Bedrooms: 4

Bathrooms: 2½

Foundation: Crawl space

Materials List Available: Yes

Price Category: D

Images provided by designer/architect.

CAD FILE AVAILABLE

Copyright by designer/architect.

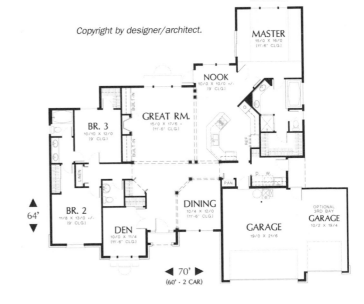

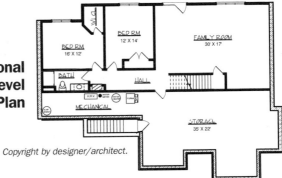

Rear Elevation

Plan #131081

Dimensions: 106'4" W x 75'10" D

Levels: 1

Square Footage: 3,301

Bedrooms: 5

Bathrooms: 3½

Foundation: Walkout

Material List Available: Yes

Price Category: L

Images provided by designer/architect.

Coming home to this luxurious and spacious one-story home will be a joy.

Features:

• **Great Room:** This great room is filled with natural light, thanks to the expansive windows that surround the room. The vaulted ceiling adds to the dramatic architecture, making it a stunning place to entertain.

• **Kitchen:** This bright and airy kitchen features generous counter and cabinet space. A center island serves as a dining spot for everyday meals or a place to serve hors d'oeuvres and

drinks when entertaining. The attached breakfast area is a great place to start your mornings.

• **Gazebo and Outdoor Kitchen:** A gracious gazebo and outdoor kitchen area will be the envy of your friends and neighbors. This generous outdoor area expands your entertaining and dining space during warm weather months.

• **Master Suite:** Stretch out in this spacious master suite, featuring a large master bedroom area and bath with his and her sinks and tub.

Optional Lower Level Floor Plan

Copyright by designer/architect.

Plan #661191

Dimensions: 58'8" W x 68' D
Levels: 2
Square Footage: 2,998
Main Level Sq. Ft.: 2,227
Upper Level Sq. Ft.: 771
Bedrooms: 4
Bathrooms: 4
Foundation: Slab
Material List Available: No
Price Category: F

A soaring, two-story ceiling and dramatic staircase help create the "wow factor" in the grand entryway of this home.

This home, as shown in the photograph, may differ from the actual blueprints. For more detailed information, please check the floor plans carefully.

Images provided by designer/architect.

Features:

- **Family Room:** This open, airy space is wonderful for entertaining guests or enjoying a movie with the family. Close proximity to the kitchen makes getting a quick snack even easier.

- **Kitchen:** This gourmet kitchen offers easy access to everything the family cook requires. A large pantry and plentiful counter space are just two of the special amenities.

- **Rear Patio:** This versatile covered patio at the back of the house is great for entertaining guests or watching the kids play in the back-yard. It is conveniently accessed through the family room and kitchen, creating a wonderful flow during large get-togethers.

- **Master Suite:** You'll love to escape to this luxurious master suite, made complete with his and her sinks, walk-in closet, and large tub.

Main Level Floor Plan

Copyright by designer/architect.

Upper Level Floor Plan

Plan #121049

Dimensions: 82' W x 60'8" D
Levels: 2
Square Footage: 3,335
Main Level Sq. Ft.: 2,054
Upper Level Sq. Ft.: 1,281
Bedrooms: 4
Bathrooms: 3½
Foundation: Slab; basement for fee
Materials List Available: Yes
Price Category: G

This charming European-style home creates a welcoming environment with its covered porch, two-story foyer, and attractive accommodations.

CAD FILE AVAILABLE

Features:

- **Living Room:** Bask in the quiet glow of abundant natural light; cozy up to the smoldering fireplace; or gather with the family in this large, relaxing area.

- **Kitchen:** This design creates a great balance between workspace and play space. The kitchen surrounds the household chef with workspace without feeling closed-in.

Copyright by designer/ architect.

A breakfast bar opens into the large breakfast area, making life a little simpler in the mornings.

- **Master Suite:** This spacious room is yours for the styling, a private space that features a walk-in closet and full bath, which includes his and her sinks, a standing shower, and a large tub.

- **Second Floor:** "Go to your room" sounds much better when that room is separated by a story. Identically sized bedrooms with ample closet space save you from family squabbles. The second floor has everything you need, with a full bathroom and computer loft.

Images provided by designer/architect.

Upper Level Floor Plan

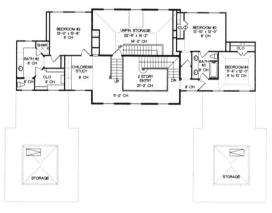

Third Floor Bedroom Floor Plan

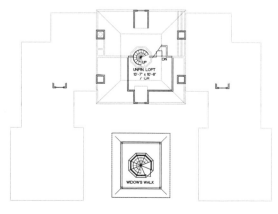

Main Level Floor Plan

Plan #161035

Dimensions: 75' W x 64'11" D
Levels: 1.5
Square Footage: 3,688
Main Level Sq. Ft.: 2,702
Upper Level Sq. Ft.: 986
Bedrooms: 4
Bathrooms: 3½
Foundation: Basement
Materials List Available: No
Price Category: H

Images provided by designer/architect.

You'll appreciate the style of the stone, brick, and cedar shake exterior of this contemporary home.

Features:

• Hearth Room: Positioned for an easy flow for guests and family, this hearth room features a bank of windows that integrate it with the yard.

• Breakfast Room: Move through the sliding doors here to the rear porch on sunny days.

• Kitchen: Outfitted for a gourmet cook, this kitchen is also ideal for friends and family who can perch at the island or serve themselves at the bar.

• Master Suite: A stepped ceiling, crown moldings, and boxed window make the bedroom easy to decorate, while the two walk-in closets, lavish dressing area, and tub in the bath make this area comfortable and luxurious.

Main Level Floor Plan

Upper Level Floor Plan

Copyright by designer/architect.

Plan #131033

Dimensions: 84'10" W x 48' D
Levels: 1.5
Square Footage: 2,813
Main Level Sq. Ft.: 1,890
Upper Level Sq. Ft.: 923
Bedrooms: 5
Bathrooms: 3½
Foundation: Crawl space, slab, or basement
Materials List Available: Yes
Price Category: G

Contemporary styling, luxurious amenities, and the classics that make a house a home are all available here.

Features:

- **Family Room:** A sloped ceiling with skylight and a railed overlook to make this large space totally up to date.

- **Living Room:** Sunken for comfort and with a cathedral ceiling for style, this room features a fireplace flanked by windows and sliding glass doors.

- **Master Suite:** Unwind in this room, with its cathedral ceiling, with a skylight, walk-in closet, and private access to the den.

- **Upper Level:** A bridge overlooks the living room and foyer and leads through the family room to three bedrooms and a bath.

- **Optional Guest Suite:** 500 sq. ft. above the master suite and den provides total comfort.

Images provided by designer/architect.

Main Level Floor Plan

Copyright by designer/architect.

Upper Level Floor Plan

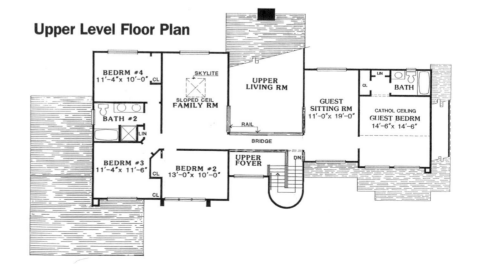

Plan #151001

Dimensions: 70' W x 88'2" D

Levels: 1

Square Footage: 3,124

Bedrooms: 4

Bathrooms: 3½

Foundation: Crawl space, slab

CompleteCost List Available: Yes

Price Category: G

This home, as shown in the photograph, may differ from the actual blue-prints. For more detailed information, please check the floor plans carefully.

Images provided by designer/architect.

From the double front doors to sleek arches, columns, and a gallery with arched openings to the bedrooms, you'll love this elegant home.

Features:

- **Grand Room:** With a 13-ft. pan ceiling and column entry, this room opens to the rear covered porch as well as through French doors to the bay-windowed morning room that, in turn, leads to the gathering room.

- **Gathering Room:** A majestic fireplace, built-in entertainment center, and book shelves give comfort and ease.

- **Kitchen:** A double oven, built-in desk, and a work island add up to a design for efficiency.

- **Master Suite:** Enjoy the practicality of walk-in closets, the comfort of a private sitting area, and the convenience of an adjacent study or nursery. The bath features a step-up whirlpool tub and separate shower.

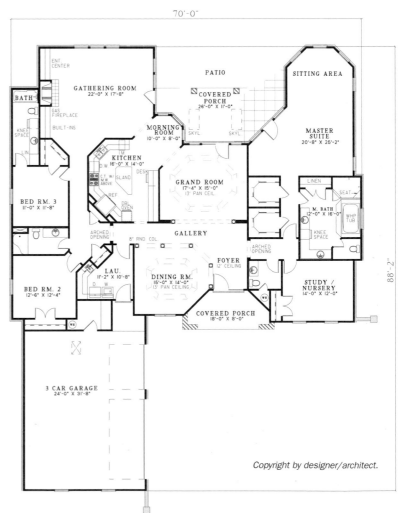

Copyright by designer/architect.

Plan #101019

Dimensions: 58'4" W x 55'2" D

Levels: 2

Square Footage: 2,954

Main Level Sq. Ft. 2,093

Upper Level Sq. Ft. 861

Bedrooms: 4

Bathrooms: 3½

Foundation: Basement

Materials List Available: No

Price Category: F

Images provided by designer/architect.

This luxurious home features a spectacular open floor plan and a brick exterior.

Features:

- Ceiling Height: 9 ft. unless otherwise noted.

- Foyer: This inviting two-story foyer, which vaults to 18 ft., will greet guests with an impressive "welcome."

- Dining Room: To the right of the foyer is this spacious dining room surrounded by decorative columns.

- Family Room: There's plenty of room for all kinds of family activities in this enormous room, with its soaring two-story ceiling.

- Master Suite: This sumptuous retreat boasts a tray ceiling. Optional pocket doors provide direct access to the study. The master bath features his and her vanities and a large walk-in closet.

- Breakfast Area: Perfect for informal family meals, this bayed breakfast area has real flair.

- Secondary Bedrooms: Upstairs are three large bedrooms with 8-ft. ceilings. One has a private bath.

CAD FILE AVAILABLE

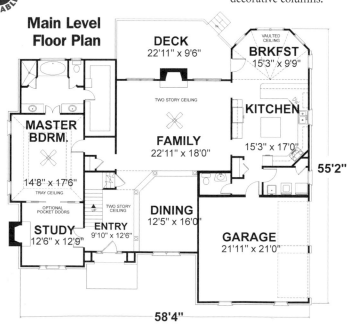

Main Level Floor Plan

DECK 22'11" x 9'6"

BRKFST 15'3" x 9'9" VAULTED CEILING

KITCHEN 15'3" x 17'0"

MASTER BDRM. 14'8" x 17'6" TRAY CEILING

FAMILY 22'11" x 18'0" TWO STORY CEILING

STUDY 12'6" x 12'9" OPTIONAL POCKET DOORS

ENTRY 9'10" x 12'6" TWO STORY CEILING

DINING 12'5" x 16'0"

GARAGE 21'11" x 21'0"

55'2"

58'4"

Upper Level Floor Plan

OPEN BELOW

BEDRM 4 13'0" x 11'6"

OPEN BELOW

BEDRM 2 12'5" x 12'5"

PLANT SHELF

BEDRM 3 11'3" x 17'1"

Copyright by designer/architect.

Plan #331005

Dimensions: 85'11" W x 55'7" D

Levels: 2

Square Footage: 3,585

Main Level Sq. Ft.: 2,691

Upper Level Sq. Ft.: 894

Bedrooms: 4

Bathrooms: 3½

Foundation: Crawl space, slab, or basement

Materials List Available: No

Price Category: H

Images provided by designer/architect.

You'll love the stately, traditional exterior design and the contemporary, casual interior layout as they are combined in this elegant home.

Features:

- **Foyer:** The highlight of this spacious area is the curved stairway to the balcony overhead.

- **Family Room:** The two-story ceiling and second-floor balcony overlooking this room add to its spacious feeling, but you can decorate around the fireplace to create a cozy, intimate area.

- **Study:** Use this versatile room as a guest room, home office or media room.

- **Kitchen:** Designed for the modern cook, this kitchen features a step-saving design, an island for added work space, and ample storage space.

- **Master Suite:** Step out to the rear deck from the bedroom to admire the moonlit scenery or bask in the morning sun. The luxurious bath makes an ideal place to relax in privacy.

Rear View

Copyright by designer/architect.

Main Level Floor Plan

Upper Level Floor Plan

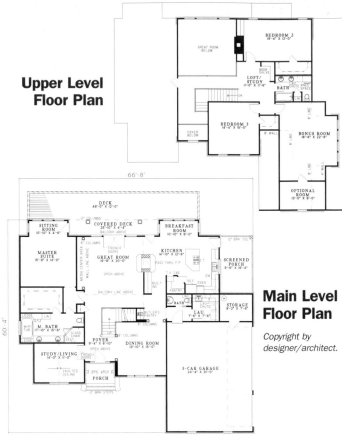

Plan #151121

Dimensions: 66'8" W x 60'4" D

Levels: 2

Square Footage: 3,108

Main Level Sq. Ft.: 2,107

Upper Level Sq. Ft.: 1,001

Bedrooms: 3

Bathrooms: 2½

Foundation: Crawl space, slab; basement option for fee

CompleteCost List Available: Yes

Price Category: G

Images provided by designer/architect.

CAD FILE AVAILABLE

This home, as shown in the photograph, may differ from the actual blueprints. For more detailed information, please check the floor plans carefully.

Upper Level Floor Plan

Main Level Floor Plan

Copyright by designer/architect.

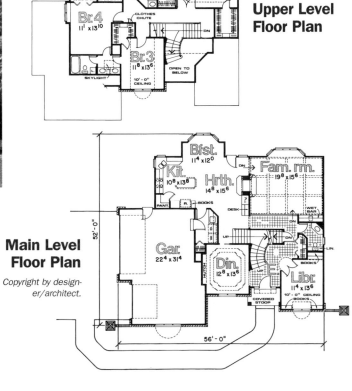

Plan #121061

Dimensions: 56' W x 52' D

Levels: 2

Square Footage: 3,025

Main Level Sq. Ft.: 1,583

Upper Level Sq. Ft.: 1,442

Bedrooms: 4

Bathrooms: 3½

Foundation: Basement

Materials List Available: Yes

Price Category: G

Images provided by designer/architect.

CAD FILE AVAILABLE

Upper Level Floor Plan

Main Level Floor Plan

Copyright by designer/architect.

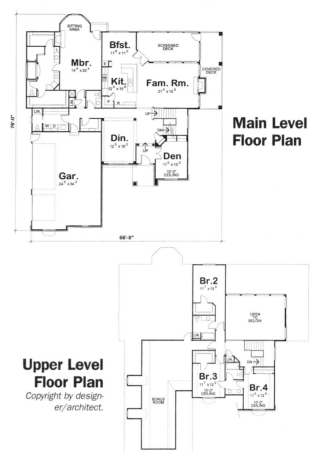

Main Level Floor Plan

Upper Level Floor Plan

Copyright by designer/architect.

Images provided by designer/architect.

Plan #121026

Dimensions: 66'8" W x 76' D
Levels: 2
Square Footage: 3,926
Main Level Sq. Ft.: 2,351
Upper Level Sq. Ft.: 1,575
Bedrooms: 4
Bathrooms: 3 full, 2 half
Foundation: Basement
Materials List Available: Yes
Price Category: H

Plan #661218

Dimensions: 73'2" W x 73'4" D
Levels: 1
Square Footage: 2,397
Bedrooms: 3
Bathrooms: 2½
Foundation: Slab
Material List Available: No
Price Category: E

Images provided by designer/architect.

CAD FILE AVAILABLE

Copyright by designer/architect.

Plan #121025

Dimensions: 60' W x 59'4" D
Levels: 2
Square Footage: 2,562
Main Level Sq. Ft.: 1,875
Upper Level Square Footage: 687
Bedrooms: 4
Bathrooms: 2½
Foundation: Basement; slab for fee
Materials List Available: Yes
Price Category: E

Images provided by designer/architect.

Dramatic arches are the reoccurring architectural theme in this distinctive home.

Features:

• Ceiling Height: 8 ft. unless otherwise noted.

• Foyer: This is a grand two-story entrance. Plants will thrive on the plant shelf thanks to light streaming through the arched window.

• Great Room: The foyer flows into the great room through dramatic 15-ft.-high arched openings.

• Kitchen: An island is the centerpiece of this highly functional kitchen that includes a separate breakfast area.

• Office: French doors open into this versatile office that features a 10-ft. ceiling and transom-topped windows.

• Master Suite: The master suite features a volume ceiling, built-in dresser, and two closets. You'll unwind in the beautiful corner whirlpool bath with its elegant window treatment.

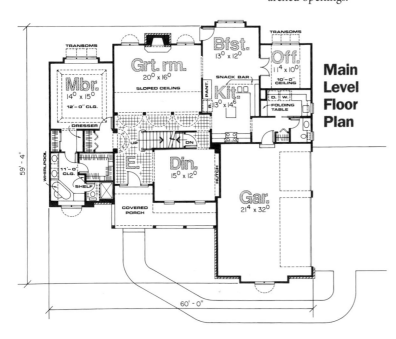

Main Level Floor Plan

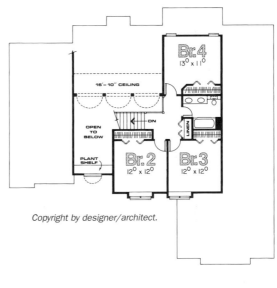

Upper Level Floor Plan

Copyright by designer/architect.

Plan #121029

Dimensions: 58'8" W x 54' D
Levels: 1.5
Square Footage: 2,576
Main Level Sq. Ft.: 1,735
Upper Level Sq. Ft.: 841
Bedrooms: 4
Bathrooms: 2½
Foundation: Basement
Materials List Available: Yes
Price Category: E

Images provided by designer/architect.

This gracious home is designed with the contemporary lifestyle in mind.

Features:

• Ceiling Height: 8 ft. unless otherwise noted.

• Great Room: This room features a fireplace and entertainment center. It's equally suited for family gatherings and formal entertaining.

• Breakfast Area: The fireplace is two-sided so it shares its warmth with this breakfast area — the perfect spot for informal family meals.

• Master Suite: Halfway up the staircase you'll find double-doors into this truly distinctive suite featuring a barrel-vault ceiling, built-in bookcases, and his and her walk-in closets. Unwind at the end of the day by stretching out in the oval whirlpool tub.

• Computer Loft: This loft overlooks the great room. It is designed as a home office with a built-in desk for your computer.

• Garage: Two bays provide plenty of storage in addition to parking space.

CAD FILE AVAILABLE

Main Level Floor Plan

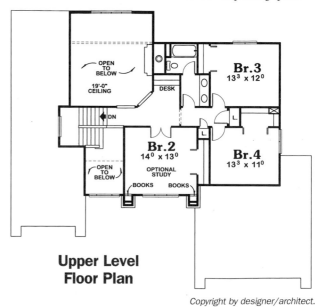

Upper Level Floor Plan

Copyright by designer/architect.

Plan #221023

Dimensions: 90'3" W x 65'8" D

Levels: 2

Square Footage: 3,511

Main Level Sq. Ft.: 1,931

Upper Level Sq. Ft.: 1,580

Bedrooms: 4

Bathrooms: 3½

Foundation: Basement

Materials List Available: No

Price Category: H

Images provided by designer/architect.

The curb appeal of this traditional two-story home, with its brick-and-stucco facade, is well matched by the luxuriousness you'll find inside.

 CAD FILE AVAILABLE

Features:

- Ceiling Height: 9 ft.

- Family Room: This large room is open to the kitchen and the dining nook, making it an ideal spot in which to entertain.

- Living Room: The high ceiling in this room contributes to its somewhat formal feeling, and the fireplace and built-in bookcase allow you to decorate for a classic atmosphere.

- Master Suite: The bedroom in this suite has a luxurious feeling, partially because of the double French doors that are flanked by niches for displaying small art pieces or collectables. The bathroom here is unusually large and features a walk-in closet.

- Upper Level: You'll find four bedrooms, three bathrooms, and a large bonus room to use as a study or play room on this floor.

Rear View

Main Level Floor Plan

Upper Level Floor Plan

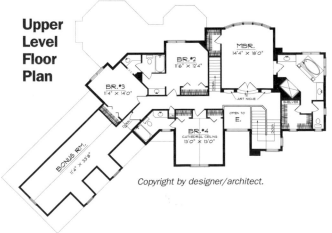

Copyright by designer/architect.

Plan #371092

Dimensions: 71'6" W x 70'8" D
Levels: 2
Square Footage: 3,836
Main Level Sq. Ft.: 2,981
Upper Level Sq. Ft.: 855
Bedrooms: 5
Bathrooms: 4
Foundation: Slab
Materials List Available: No
Price Category: H

This grand home has an arched covered entry and great styling that would make this home a focal point of the neighborhood.

CAD FILE AVAILABLE

Features:

- **Family Room:** This large gathering area boasts a fireplace flanked by a built-in media center. Large windows flood the room with natural light, and there is access to the rear porch.

- **Kitchen:** This large island kitchen has a raised bar and is open to the family room. Its walk-in pantry has plenty of room for supplies.

- **Master Suite:** This retreat features a stepped ceiling and a see-through fireplace to the master bath, which has a large walk-in closet, dual vanities, a glass shower, and a marble tub.

- **Secondary Bedrooms:** Bedrooms 2 and 3 are located on the main level and share a common bathroom. Bedrooms 4 and 5 are located on the upper level and share a Jack-and-Jill bathroom.

Images provided by designer/architect.

Front View

Copyright by designer/architect.

Main Level Floor Plan

Upper Level Floor Plan

Plan #651049

Dimensions: 66' W x 60' D
Levels: 2
Square Footage: 3,769
Main Level Sq. Ft.: 2,249
Upper Level Sq. Ft.: 1,520
Bedrooms: 4
Bathrooms: 3½
Foundation: Slab
Material List Available: No
Price Category: H

This home is filled with special architectural details that make it both beautiful and unique.

CAD FILE AVAILABLE

Images provided by designer/architect.

Features:

- Hearth Room: Located off of the breakfast room, this hearth room features a fireplace, making it a warm and homey spot to curl up with your favorite book.

- Kitchen: The home chef will love this gourmet kitchen, which features a walk-in pantry and easy access to both the breakfast room and dining room.

- Master Suite: Amenities come in pairs in this glorious master suite, including two walk-in closets and his and her sinks. Additional features include a graciously sized bedroom area, tub, and coffered ceilings.

- Rec. Room: On the upstairs level, this recreation room will keep the kids occupied for hours. This flexible room can also be a spot for entertaining guests.

Rear Elevation

Main Level Floor Plan

Upper Level Floor Plan

Plan #651050

Dimensions: 53' W x 75' D
Levels: 2
Square Footage: 3,178
Main Level Sq. Ft.: 2,193
Upper Level Sq. Ft.: 985
Bedrooms: 3
Bathrooms: 3
Foundation: Slab
Material List Available: No
Price Category: G

This European-style home combines Old World elegance with modern convenience.

Images provided by designer/architect.

Features:

- **Great Room:** Entertain all of your guests in this beautiful great room, which opens dramatically to the second floor.

- **Kitchen:** This spacious kitchen boasts tons of counter space and easy access to a pantry and utility closet. The attached breakfast area features large windows that fill the space with light while you enjoy your morning coffee.

- **Master Suite:** You'll have all the space you've ever dreamed of in this master suite, including a luxurious master bath with two large walk-in closets and his and her sinks.

- **Garage:** This two-car garage conveniently connects to the house near the utility closet and pantry, making both grocery trips and repair jobs quicker and easier.

CAD FILE AVAILABLE

Main Level Floor Plan

Upper Level Floor Plan

Copyright by designer/architect.

Plan #481036

Dimensions: 84'8" W x 82'4" D

Levels: 1

Square Footage: 4,258

Main Level Sq. Ft.: 2,440

Lower Level Sq. Ft.: 1,818

Bedrooms: 4

Bathrooms: 3½

Foundation: Walkout

Material List Available: No

Price Category: I

Images provided by designer/architect.

Old-world style with a modern floor plan makes this home perfect for you.

Features:

- Great Room: With a 12-ft.-high ceiling and a glowing fireplace, this room welcomes you home. Relax with your family, or entertain your friends.

- Study: Located off the foyer, this room would make a perfect home office; clients can come and go without disturbing the family.

- Master Suite: Unwind in this private space,

and enjoy its many conveniences. The full master bath includes a standing shower, his and her sinks, a large tub, and a spacious walk-in closet.

- Garage: This large storage space has room for three full-size cars and includes a convenient sink. The stairs to the storage area in the basement will help keep things organized.

Main Level Floor Plan

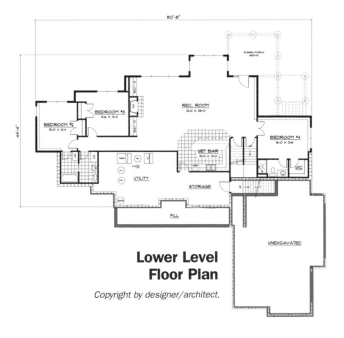

Lower Level Floor Plan

Copyright by designer/architect.

Plan #161036

Dimensions: 74'10" W x 65' D
Levels: 2
Square Footage: 3,664
Main Level Sq. Ft.: 2,497
Upper Level Sq. Ft.: 1,167
Bedrooms: 4
Bathrooms: 2½
Foundation: Basement
Materials List Available: No
Price Category: H

Images provided by designer/architect.

The traditional European brick-and-stone facade on the exterior of this comfortable home will thrill you and make your guests feel welcome.

Features:

- **Pub:** The beamed ceiling lends a casual feeling to this pub and informal dining area between the kitchen and the great room.
- **Dining Room:** Columns set off this formal dining room, from which you can see the fireplace in the expansive great room.
- **Library:** Close to the master suite, this room lends itself to quiet reading or work.
- **Master Suite:** The ceiling treatment makes the bedroom luxurious, while the tub, double-bowl vanity, and large walk-in closet make the bath a pleasure.
- **Upper Level:** Each of the three bedrooms features a large closet and easy access to a convenient bathroom.

Main Level Floor Plan

Upper Level Floor Plan

Copyright by designer/architect.

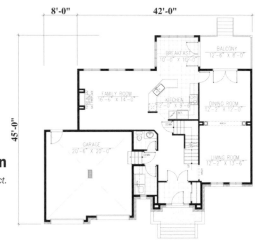

Upper Level Floor Plan

Images provided by designer/architect.

Plan #571102

Dimensions: 50' W x 45' D

Levels: 2

Square Footage: 2,260

Main Level Sq. Ft.: 1,166

Upper Level Sq. Ft.: 1,094

Bedrooms: 3

Bathrooms: 2½

Foundation: Basement

Material List Available: Yes

Price Category: E

Main Level Floor Plan

Copyright by designer/architect.

Main Level Floor Plan

Plan #481035

Dimensions: 99' W x 64' D

Levels: 2

Square Footage: 3,204

Main Level Sq. Ft.: 1,701

Upper Level Sq. Ft.: 1,503

Bedrooms: 3

Bathrooms: 2½

Foundation: Walkout

Material List Available: No

Price Category: G

Images provided by designer/architect.

Upper Level Floor Plan

Copyright by designer/architect.

Plan #661211

Dimensions: 80' W x 68'4" D
Levels: 2
Square Footage: 3,339
Main Level Sq. Ft.: 2,898
Upper Level Sq. Ft.: 441
Bedrooms: 4
Bathrooms: 4
Foundation: Slab
Material List Available: No
Price Category: G

Images provided by designer/architect.

Main Level Floor Plan

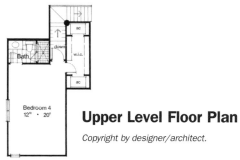

Upper Level Floor Plan

Copyright by designer/architect.

Upper Level Floor Plan

Plan #651047

Dimensions: 64' W x 71' D
Levels: 2
Square Footage: 2,669
Main Level Sq. Ft.: 2,057
Upper Level Sq. Ft.: 612
Bedrooms: 3
Bathrooms: 2½
Foundation: Slab
Material List Available: No
Price Category: F

Images provided by designer/architect.

Main Level Floor Plan

Copyright by designer/architect.

Plan #481034

Dimensions: 84'8" W x 77'8" D

Levels: 2

Square Footage: 2,830

Main Level Sq. Ft.: 1,673

Upper Level Sq. Ft.: 1,157

Bedrooms: 3

Bathrooms: 2½

Foundation: Walkout

Materials List Available: No

Price Category: F

This European-influenced two-story home has stone accents and wide board siding.

Images provided by designer/architect.

Features:

- **Great Room:** The fireplace, flanked by built-in cabinets, is the focal point of this gathering area. Because the area is located just off the foyer, your guests can easily enter this area.

- **Dining Room:** This formal dining area features a built-in cabinet and a 9-ft,-high ceiling. The triple window has a view of the front yard.

- **Kitchen:** This large island kitchen is a bonus in any home. Open to the dinette and the great room, the area has a light and open feeling. The built-in pantry is ready to store all of your supplies.

- **Master Suite:** Occupying most of the upper level, this retreat boasts a vaulted ceiling in the sleeping area and a large walk-in closet. The master bath features his and her vanities and a large stall shower.

Rear View

Main Level Floor Plan

Upper Level Floor Plan

Copyright by designer/architect.

Plan #481090

Dimensions: 72'6" W x 65'8" D
Levels: 2
Square Footage: 2,896
Main Level Sq. Ft.: 1,713
Upper Level Sq. Ft.: 1,183
Bedrooms: 3
Bathrooms: 2½
Foundation: Walkout
Material List Available: No
Price Category: F

Images provided by designer/architect.

Turn this European-style house into a home. With an ample amount of space, your family will have plenty of room to grow.

Features:

- Porch: This front porch welcomes visitors and provides a sanctuary for an afternoon nap in the warm weather.

- Dining Room: This formal dining room is a luxurious center for entertaining with class.

- Kitchen: This large kitchen with its central island is an ideal setup for the master chef. Enjoy a relaxed meal in the kitchen or in the adjoining dinette, which features 9-ft. ceilings.

- Master Suite: An impressive second level features this master suite with vaulted ceilings and a gorgeous full bath, which includes a tub, his and her sinks, and large walk-in closet.

- Garage: This garage offers you the option of storage for your cars or other home accessories.

Main Level Floor Plan

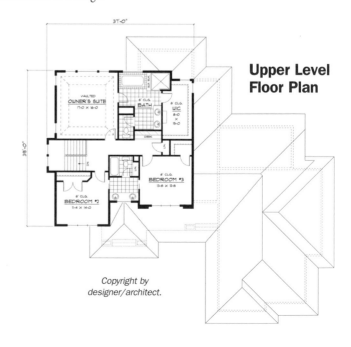

Upper Level Floor Plan

Copyright by designer/architect.

Main Level Floor Plan

Copyright by designer/architect.

Plan #571066

Dimensions: 50' W x 36' D

Levels: 2

Square Footage: 3,484

Main Level Sq. Ft.: 1,741

Upper Level Sq. Ft.: 1,743

Bedrooms: 3

Bathrooms: 2½

Foundation: Basement

Material List Available: Yes

Price Category: H

Images provided by designer/architect.

Rear Elevation

Upper Level Floor Plan

Main Level Floor Plan

Plan #181253

Dimensions: 68' W x 50' D

Levels: 2

Square Footage: 3,614

Main Level Sq. Ft.: 1,909

Upper Level Sq. Ft.: 1,705

Bedrooms: 4

Bathrooms: 3½

Foundation: Basement; crawl space or slab for fee

Material List Available: Yes

Price Category: H

Images provided by designer/architect.

Upper Level Floor Plan

Copyright by designer/architect.

Plan #131084

Dimensions: 57'10" W x 56'2" D

Levels: 2

Square Footage: 3,309

Main Level Sq. Ft.: 2,104

Upper Level Sq. Ft.: 1,205

Bedrooms: 4

Bathrooms: 3½

Foundation: Crawl space, slab, or basement

Material List Available: Yes

Price Category: K

Images provided by designer/architect.

Main Level Floor Plan

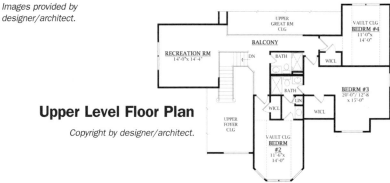

Upper Level Floor Plan

Copyright by designer/architect.

Plan #181640

Dimensions: 50' W x 43' D

Levels: 2

Square Footage: 3,002

Main Level Sq. Ft.: 1,554

Upper Level Sq. Ft.: 1,448

Bedrooms: 3

Bathrooms: 2½

Foundation: Slab or basement; crawl space for fee

Material List Available: Yes

Price Category: G

Images provided by designer/architect.

Main Level Floor Plan

Upper Level Floor Plan

Copyright by designer/architect.

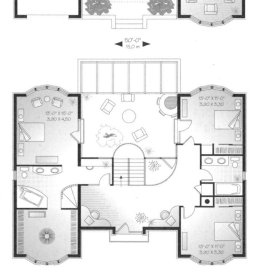

Plan #121067

Dimensions: 56' W x 59'4" D
Levels: 1.5
Square Footage: 2,708
Main Level Sq. Ft.: 1,860
Upper Level Sq. Ft.: 848
Bedrooms: 4
Bathrooms: 3½
Foundation: Basement
Materials List Available: Yes
Price Category: F

Images provided by designer/architect.

You'll love this home because it is such a perfect setting for a family and still has room for guests.

Features:

- **Family Room:** Expect everyone to gather in this room, near the built-in entertainment centers that flank the lovely fireplace.

- **Living Room:** The other side of the see-through fireplace looks out into this living room, making it an equally welcoming spot in chilly weather.

- **Kitchen:** This room has a large center island, a corner pantry, and a built-in desk. It also features a breakfast area where friends and family will congregate all day long.

- **Master Suite:** Enjoy the oversized walk-in closet and bath with a bayed whirlpool tub, double vanity, and separate shower.

Main Level Floor Plan

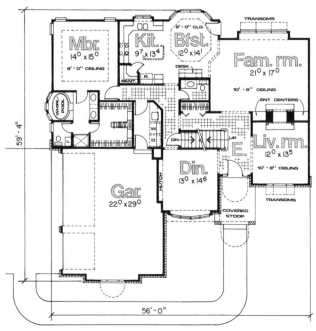

Upper Level Floor Plan

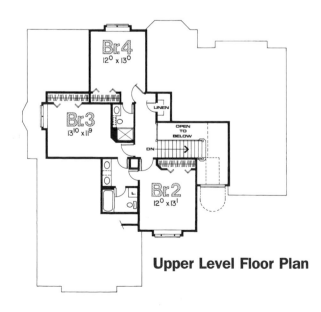

Copyright by designer/architect.

Plan #121081

Dimensions: 76'8" W x 68' D

Levels: 1.5

Square Footage: 3,623

Main Level Sq. Ft.: 2,603

Upper Level Sq. Ft.: 1,020

Bedrooms: 4

Bathrooms: 4½

Foundation: Basement

Materials List Available: Yes

Price Category: H

This home, as shown in the photograph, may differ from the actual blueprints. For more detailed information, please check the floor plans carefully.

Images provided by designer/architect.

You'll love this impressive home if you're looking for a perfect spot for entertaining as well as a home for comfortable family living.

Features:

- **Entry:** Walk into this grand two-story entryway through double doors, and be greeted by the sight of a graceful curved staircase.

- **Great Room:** This two-story room features stacked windows, a fireplace flanked by an entertainment center, a bookcase, and a wet bar.

- **Dining Room:** A corner column adds formality to this room, which is just off the entryway for the convenience of your guests.

- **Hearth Room:** Connected to the great room by a lovely set of French doors, this room features another fireplace as well as a convenient pantry.

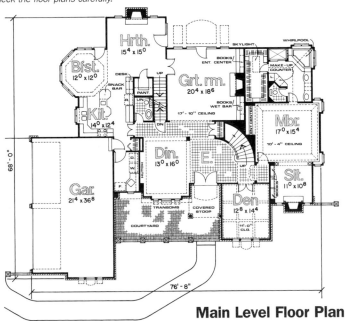

Main Level Floor Plan

Upper Level Floor Plan

Copyright by designer/architect.

Plan #441024

Dimensions: 90'6" W x 84' D

Levels: 2

Square Footage: 3,517

Main Level Sq. Ft.: 2,698

Upper Level Sq. Ft.: 819

Bedrooms: 3

Bathrooms: 3½

Foundation: Crawl space; slab or basement available for fee

Materials List Available: Yes

Price Category: H

You'll feel like royalty every time you pull into the driveway of this European-styled manor house.

Images provided by designer/architect.

Features:

- Kitchen: This gourmet chef's center hosts an island with a vegetable sink. The arched opening above the primary sink provides a view of the fireplace and entertainment center in the great room. A walk-in food pantry and a butler's pantry are situated between this space and the dining room.

- Master Suite: Located on the main level, this private retreat boasts a large sleeping area and a sitting area. The grand master bath features a large walk-in closet, dual vanities, a large tub, and a shower.

- Bedrooms: Two secondary bedrooms are located on the upper level, and each has its own bathroom.

- Laundry Room: This utility room houses cabinets, a folding counter, and an ironing board.

- Garage: This large three-car garage has room for storage. Family members entering the home from this area will find a coat closet and a place to stash briefcases and backpacks.

Main Level Floor Plan

Upper Level Floor Plan

Copyright by designer/architect.

Plan #121018

Dimensions: 95'9" W x 70'2" D
Levels: 2
Square Footage: 3,950
Main Level Sq. Ft.: 2,839
Upper Level Sq. Ft.: 1,111
Bedrooms: 4
Bathrooms: 4 full, 2 half
Foundation: Basement
Materials List Available: Yes
Price Category: H

Images provided by designer/architect.

A spectacular two-story entry with a floating curved staircase welcomes you home.

Features:

- Ceiling Height: 8 ft. except as noted.

- Den: To the left of the entry, French doors lead to a spacious and stylish den featuring a spider-beamed ceiling.

- Living Room: The volume ceiling, transom windows, and large fireplace evoke a gracious traditional style.

- Gathering Rooms: There is plenty of space for large-group entertaining in the gathering rooms that also feature fireplaces and transom windows.

- Master Suite: Here is the height of luxurious living. The suite features an oversized walk-in closet, tiered ceilings, and a sitting room with fireplace. The pampering bath has a corner whirlpool and shower.

- Garage: An angle minimizes the appearance of the four-car garage.

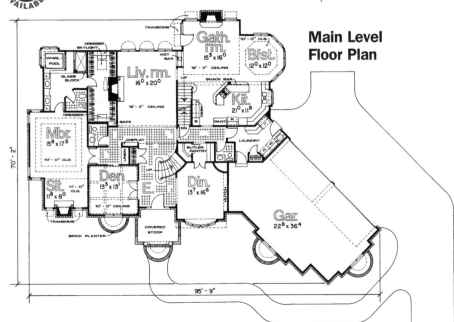

Main Level Floor Plan

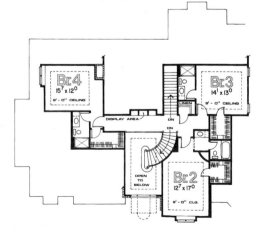

Upper Level Floor Plan

Copyright by designer/architect.

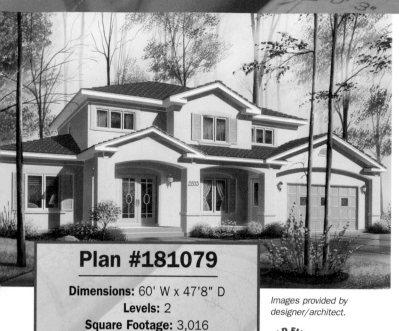

**Main
Level
Floor
Plan**

Plan #181079

Dimensions: 60' W x 47'8" D
Levels: 2
Square Footage: 3,016
Main Level Sq. Ft.: 1,716
Upper Level Sq. Ft.: 1,300
Bedrooms: 6
Bathrooms: 4½
Foundation: Crawl space
Materials List Available: Yes
Price Category: G

Images provided by
designer/architect.

CAD FILE
CAD
AVAILABLE

**Upper Level
Floor Plan**

Copyright by design-
er/architect.

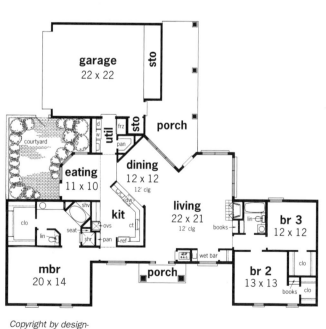

Plan #211049

Dimensions: 73' W x 66' D
Levels: 1
Square Footage: 2,023
Bedrooms: 3
Bathrooms: 2
Foundation: Slab
Materials List Available: Yes
Price Category: D

Images provided by design-
er/architect.

CAD FILE
CAD
AVAILABLE

Copyright by design-
er/architect.

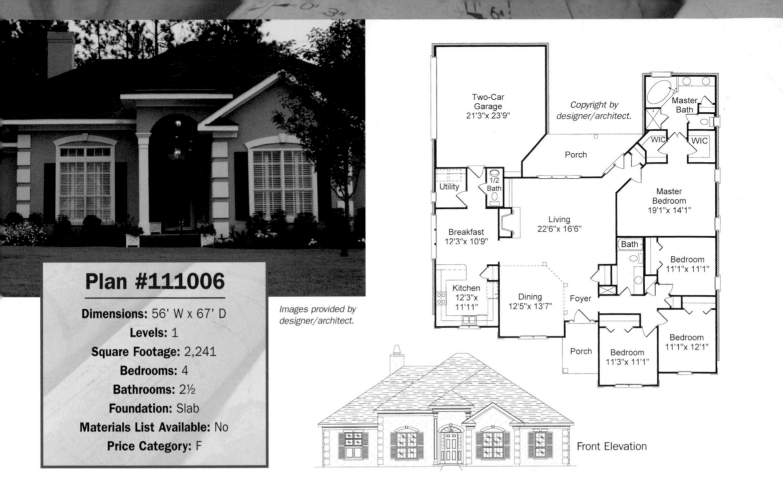

Plan #111006

Dimensions: 56' W x 67' D

Levels: 1

Square Footage: 2,241

Bedrooms: 4

Bathrooms: 2½

Foundation: Slab

Materials List Available: No

Price Category: F

Images provided by designer/architect.

Front Elevation

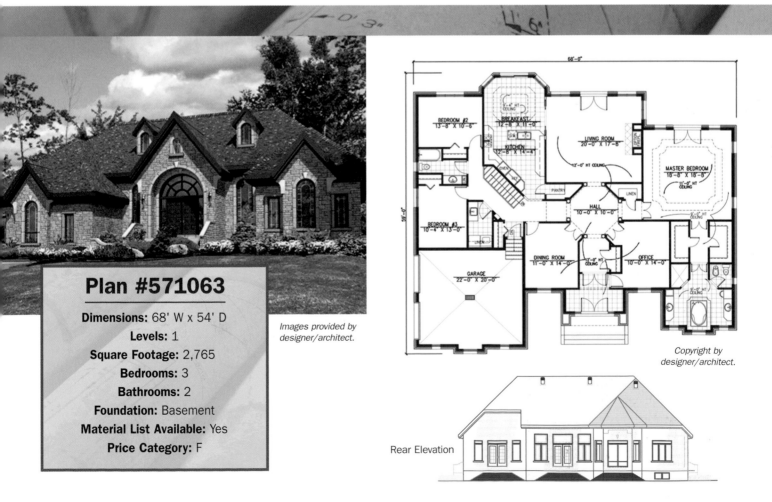

Plan #571063

Dimensions: 68' W x 54' D

Levels: 1

Square Footage: 2,765

Bedrooms: 3

Bathrooms: 2

Foundation: Basement

Material List Available: Yes

Price Category: F

Images provided by designer/architect.

Copyright by designer/architect.

Rear Elevation

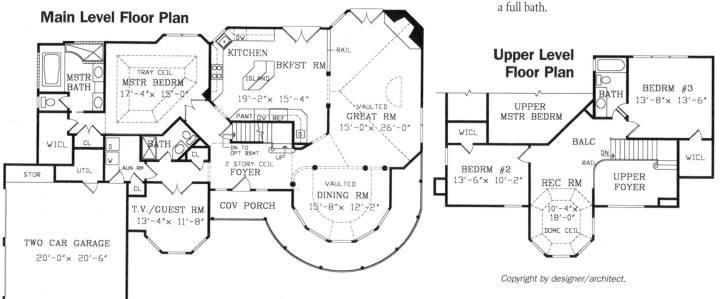

Plan #131028

Dimensions: 69'2" W x 50'2" D
Levels: 1.5
Square Footage: 2,696
Main Level Sq. Ft.: 1,960
Upper Level Sq. Ft.: 736
Bedrooms: 4
Bathrooms: 3
Foundation: Crawl space, slab, or basement
Materials List Available: Yes
Price Category: F

Images provided by designer/architect.

Imagine owning a home with Victorian styling and a dramatic, contemporary interior design.

Features:

- **Foyer:** Enter from the curved covered porch into this foyer with its 17-ft. ceiling.

- **Great Room:** A vaulted ceiling sets the tone for this large room, where friends and family are sure to congregate.

- **Dining Room:** A 14-ft. ceiling here accentuates the rounded shape of this room.

- **Kitchen:** From the angled corner sink to the angled island with a snack bar, this room has character. A pantry adds convenience.

- **Master Suite:** A 13-ft. tray ceiling exudes elegance, and the bath features a tub and designer shower.

- **Upper Level:** The balcony hall leads to a turreted recreation room, two bedrooms, and a full bath.

Main Level Floor Plan

Upper Level Floor Plan

Copyright by designer/architect.

Rear View

Entry

Dining Room

Kitchen View to Great Room

Great Room

This article was reprinted from *Ultimate Guide to Basements, Attics, and Garages* (Creative Homeowner 2006).

The Ultimate Garage

For years, most homeowners have used their garages for parking cars and storing stuff that doesn't fit anywhere else or is overflow from other parts of the house. Or they have taken that valuable floor space and turned it into another master suite or family room.

Rather than using your garage as a scaled-down storage unit or new living space that looks like the rest of the house, consider making it into a high-end recreational space that is improved but at the same time more garage-like. If you like working on cars, why not create a state-of-the-art car-restoration studio? Maybe you'd prefer a furniture-making shop that will be the envy of every craftsman in town, or a big home gym.

Part of what's driving this change is the availability of new storage products designed specifically for the garage. But simple common sense plays a bigger role. Most two-car garages occupy about 500 square feet of space, and that's space that already has a foundation under it, a floor in it, walls around it, a roof over it, and very easy access for big and heavy items through the overhead doors. In these times of high real estate costs, you can't find 500 nearly habitable square feet for less money anywhere.

A total garage makeover, above, costs some money, especially if you choose high-end cabinets and flooring. But the results look great, create accessible storage for all the essentials, and even leave room for the cars, at least for the time being.

Modular storage systems, below, that include both cabinets and wall-hung options can accommodate just about everything that most people need to store.

Storage Systems

If you want to make the most out of the garage space you have, then you have to figure out how much space is actually available. It's no good to create a plan that calls for your expensive garden tractor to be banished suddenly to the elements, when you know you want to keep it inside.

Start by waiting for a few days of good weather. Then place everything you want to keep in the garage in the driveway. Start putting things into the garage, starting with the biggest (your cars, if you plan to keep them inside) and moving down in size. You'll quickly see this as the zero-sum game that it is. For every box of old lawn ornaments you keep, that's one less piece of exercise equipment for your new home gym or power tool for your workshop. In this case, being ruthless is a virtue. Either get rid of nonessentials or find a new place to store them.

Once the essentials are back in place, you have defined the true available space with which you have to work. Now is the time to start looking for storage systems. You'll find two basic options: a cabinet-based system and a wall-hung system. Both are designed to make the most out of vertical storage.

The main difference between the two is the amount of floor space each occupies. For example, the typical base cabinet will measure about 24 inches deep, which makes it hard to fit alongside a car and still have room to open the cabinet or the car door. On the other hand, the average perforated hardboard wall system projects only a few inches into the room.

Because of their different virtues, a combination of the two basic systems makes sense for filling the needs of most people.

Perforated hardboard, above, is the granddaddy of all wall storage systems. The material contains holes into which you put metal hooks. It works as well today as it did 50 years ago.

Some storage systems, above, blend cabinets with traditional open shelving. This shelving is very versatile and avoids the expense of cabinet doors.

Modular cabinet systems, like those shown above, make for very flexible storage, particularly when mounted on casters. The layout can change easily when your needs change.

Many ceiling-mounted storage units, above, are available. Some have doors like this one, others are open. Large specialty units can even fit above overhead garage doors.

Cabinet Systems

A good cabinet system is best defined by how it works, not by how it looks. If you have specialty items that are difficult to store, like some sporting goods, make sure that you find a cabinet that will handle the job. Probably the best—and the most expensive—way to get a good cabinet system is to have a cabinet dealer outfit your garage for you. However, you can do the same thing by figuring out what cabinet sizes you need and then buying knockdown units at a home center.

Another option is to buy one of the new modular garage storage systems. These systems have a big selection of different base and wall cabinets, often with a caster-mounting option so you can easily reposition the units when your needs change. Some of these manufacturers also offer wall-hung storage systems that complement their cabinets.

When looking at different cabinet lines, be sure to check for specialty units that hang from the ceiling. Some are just simple boxes with clever hanging hardware.

SMARTtip

Increasing Your Mobility

Not everything in a garage is best stored permanently against a wall. Woodworking equipment and exercise machines are just two kinds of hardware that come to mind. These things need more space when they're being used and need much less when they're not. The logical solution is to mount them on casters so they're easy to move.

Sometimes the base of heavy-duty tools comes with holes for installing casters, but usually you'll have to create some way to mount them. This can take some time and often a lot of creativity. But once things are rolling you'll be happy you made the effort.

Casters come in different sizes and with different mounting hardware. Some simply swivel while others swivel and can be locked in place. Because you'll almost always need four casters for anything you want to move, it's a good idea to put a combination of two swivel and two locking casters on each item. This yields good maneuverability and locking capability, and at less cost than putting locking casters on each corner.

But others are designed to make use of the entire space above your garage doors.

Wall Systems

Traditional perforated hardboard is still going strong today because it's inexpensive, easy to install, and works well. But now consumers have a lot of other choices.

The most basic alternative is a shelving system that hangs from standards attached to the wall. One popular version of this is the steel-wire systems originally designed for organizing closets. With a wide variety of shelves, drawers, and compartments, you should be able to store most of what you need.

Another alternative is a slat-wall storage system. These slotted plastic panels are screwed directly to the garage wall, and then hooks are placed in the slots to support just about whatever you have. The system is very flexible and can easily change as your storage requirements change.

Steel-grid systems are also available. The open-grid panels are attached to the wall, and hooks and brackets are clipped onto the grid. The grids themselves are pretty inexpensive. But as with most of the wall storage systems, the cost of the hooks and brackets can add up quickly.

Easy-to-install and inexpensive, above, steel-wire storage systems, originally de-signed for closets and kitchens, work just as well in the garage.

Wall-hung metal shelving, below, is a quick and clean way to get stuff off the floor. Most systems have wall-mounted standards and adjustable shelf brackets.

Flooring Options

Most garage floors are made of concrete, which is a wonderful building material. It's hard and durable, and it can carry a tremendous amount of weight without breaking. In other words, it's perfect for garage floors. When properly installed, the only problems concrete will give you are cosmetic: it stains easily, and it's uncomfortable—standing on concrete for a long time hurts your feet and legs. Even when concrete is clean, though, some people find its appearance boring. In recent years, these people have been drawn to a number of different flooring treatments that make concrete look as good as it works.

Upgrading Concrete

The most common way to improve your concrete floor is to paint it. Until the last few years, this choice was often disappointing. The paint didn't bond well to the concrete and was damaged when hot tires were parked on it. But new garage floor paints, available at home centers, are designed to work much better. One good system has two parts. First you apply an epoxy paint; then you sprinkle colored paint chips over the fresh surface. When the floor dries, the chips provide extra traction to make the concrete much less slippery.

The high-end garage-conversion people tend to favor floor coverings rather than coatings. One popular option is floor pads. These come in rolls, often 6 feet wide, that are installed in much the same way as

Garage floors, right, have requirements that differ from other floors in your home. Standard paints won't hold up, but speciality finishes can provide an attractive, durable floor.

Specialty floor paint, far right, creates a clean, attractive surface for any garage floor. Proper preparation is essential for the paint to bond successfully to the concrete.

sheet acrylic flooring, though no adhesive is used. The material floats on the floor, and any seams are taped together. Many colors and textures are available.

Plastic floor tiles are another high-end option. They usually come in 12-inch interlocking squares and require no adhesive or tape. You lay out, measure, and cut these tiles much as you would vinyl tiles for the bathroom or kitchen. The tiles will take longer to install than the roll pads, but the work is easier and the tiles are thicker than the pads, so you'll get more cushioning if that's important to you.

Neither the pads nor the tiles are cheap, especially if you cover the entire floor of a two-car garage. Expect to pay at least $1,000 to do the job yourself. But then, nothing can change the look of your garage as dramatically as a bright red or yellow floor.

Garage Mechanicals

If you plan to use your garage a lot during cold weather, you will want some heat; and if you want heat, you're going to want insulation unless you've got money to burn. Some newer garages are built with insulation in place and finished with dry-

Brightly colored floor tiles, above, laid in a clever pattern make a strong design statement. No one could confuse this floor with a boring concrete slab.

wall, but many garages aren't. Make the space more livable by adding insulation and weather stripping the door.

Choosing your heat source can be complicated because so many different options are available. If your garage is attached to your house and your furnace has the extra capacity, a heating contractor can often run a heat duct from your house to the garage.

SMARTtip

Keeping Your Floor Clean

Your new floor may look great when you're done installing it, but a short trip on a muddy road or a day spent driving on salty winter highways can make it look pretty bad once you get home. If you are fortunate enough to have a floor drain, you can just wait until your cars drip dry and then hose down the floor and let the drain take the dirty water away.

On a coated or uncoated floor without a drain, a 3-foot-wide floor squeegee is a great help. Hose down the floor; then use the squeegee to push the water out through the garage door openings. The squeegee also works for grooved floor pads, but not as well on modular floor tiles. Traditional tools, a floor mop and bucket, are required for those.

You also have space-heating options. Probably the most practical choice is an electric-resistance heater, either a standard model or a convection unit that includes a fan to circulate the warmed air quicker. These heaters have no open flame, so they can't ignite flammable fumes that might be present in your garage. And they put no combustion by-products (carbon monoxide and water vapor) into the air. But in most areas, electricity is more expensive than natural gas or heating oil. Space heaters using other fuels are available in many different designs—most are vented; some are ventless. A local heating equipment supplier can explain your options.

Ventilation

Your garage ventilation needs are directly proportional to how much your activities foul the air. In warm climates, opening the overhead doors and using a floor fan to keep fresh air moving through should do the trick. But if

Ventilation and lighting, left, can help make what was once a dank, uninviting space livable and inviting.

you keep your garage heated, you'll need active ventilation.

You'll probably find more ventilation options than heating options if you really need to clean a lot of air. The most common solution is to install an electric exhaust fan in the garage wall or on the roof. These units are rated by how much air they can move per minute (abbreviated as cfm, cubic feet of air per minute). The air they remove is replaced by fresh air coming into the building from air leaks.

If your garage is tightly constructed, you'll need to supply fresh air in another way. Some people just open a window when the fan is on. But air-to-air heat exchangers are a high-end alternative. These electric units draw warm, dusty air from the garage and dump it outside. At the same time, they pull cool, fresh air from outside into the garage. When these air streams pass each other (confined to separate tubes), the outgoing air preheats the incoming air.

Lighting

It may require work to pick a good heater and ventilator, but lighting for

Concrete floors, above, are durable, but they require much maintenance to keep them looking good.

Fluorescent fixtures, above, are inexpensive. Newer models offer truer color renderings than older types.

Hanging pendant lights, opposite, are a good way to provide task lighting for counters and worktables.

SMARTtip

Garage Safety

The following safety checklist is worth reviewing for those who plan to spend a lot of time in their garages. It was compiled by the Home Safety Council (homesafetycouncil.org), a nonprofit, industry-supported group created to help prevent injuries in the home.

1 Organize all items in designated, easy-to-reach places so that large piles don't accumulate.

2 Store shovels, rakes, lawn chairs, bikes, and other sharp and large objects on the wall to prevent trips and falls.

3 Clear floors and steps of clutter, grease, and spills.

4 Keep children's playthings in one area and within their reach to prevent kids from exploring potentially dangerous areas.

5 Light your garage brightly with maximum safe wattage as designated by light fixtures.

6 Protect light bulbs near work areas with substantial guards to reduce risk of breakage and fire.

7 Light stairs brightly, and install on both sides secure handrails or banisters that extend the entire length of the stairs.

8 Make sure poisonous products, such as pesticides, automotive fluids, lighter fluid, paint thinner, antifreeze, and turpentine, have child-resistant caps, are clearly labeled, and are stored either on a high shelf or in a locked cabinet.

9 Do not use barbecue grills and electric generators inside the garage, as they emit carbon monoxide (CO) and pose a fire hazard.

10 Install a smoke alarm and CO detector in the garage.

11 Never leave cars running inside a closed or open garage to prevent CO poisoning.

12 Store gasoline in small quantities only and in a proper, tightly sealed container labeled "gasoline."

13 Do not keep gasoline in a garage with an appliance that contains a pilot light.

14 Mount a fire extinguisher and stocked first-aid kit in the garage, and make sure every family member knows where they are and how to use them.

15 Store pool chemicals according to the manufacturers' directions to prevent combustion and potential poisoning exposures.

16 Do not overload outlets, and make sure the electrical ratings on extension cords have been checked to ensure they are carrying no more than their proper loads.

17 Lock electrical supply boxes to prevent children from opening them.

18 Clean the garage of dust, cobwebs, and trash, which can interfere with the electrical system.

19 Properly secure shelving units to the wall; make sure they are not overloaded; and store heavier items closest to the ground.

20 Keep a sturdy step stool within easy reach to aid in reaching items stored high off the ground.

the garage is much easier. Simply put, it's hard to beat overhead fluorescent lighting for general room illumination. These units provide good light, are easy to install, and are cheap to run. Higher-end models are often sold without bulbs. Of course buying the bulbs lets you choose the bulb wattage (typically from 20 to 40 watts) and color temperature to match your needs.

Task lighting can be accomplished the old fashioned way, with small shop lights installed just where you need them. Some wall storage systems also have light fixtures that mount in the panel slots.

Plan #151031

Dimensions: 60'2" W x 60'2" D
Levels: 2
Square Footage: 3,130
Main Level Sq. Ft.: 1,600
Upper Level Sq. Ft.: 1,530
Bedrooms: 3
Bathrooms: 3½
Foundation: Crawl space, slab, or walkout
CompleteCost List Available: Yes
Price Category: F

If you love traditional Southern plantation homes, you'll want this house with its wraparound porches that are graced with boxed columns.

Features:

- Great Room: Use the gas fireplace for warmth in this comfortable room, which is open to the kitchen.

- Living Room: 8-in. columns add formality as you enter this living and dining room.

- Kitchen: You'll love the island bar with a sink. An elevator here can take you to the other floors.

- Master Suite: A gas fireplace warms this area, and the bath is luxurious.

- Bedrooms: Each has a private bath and built-in bookshelves for easy organizing.

- Optional Features: Choose a 2,559-sq.-ft. basement and add a kitchen to it, or finish the 1,744-sq.-ft. bonus room and add a spiral staircase and a bath.

Images provided by designer/architect.

Main Level Floor Plan

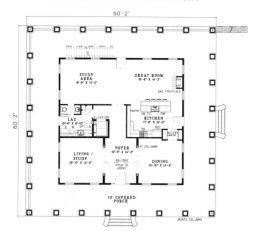

Upper Level Floor Plan

Copyright by designer/architect.

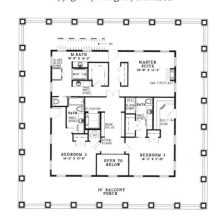

Lower Level Floor Plan

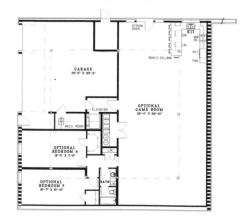

Optional Upper Level Floor Plan

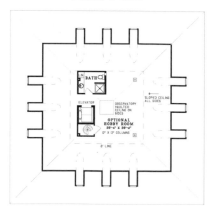

Plan #271095

Dimensions: 70' W x 74'4" D
Levels: 2
Square Footage: 3,220
Main Level Sq. Ft.: 2,040
Upper Level Sq. Ft.: 1,180
Bedrooms: 3
Bathrooms: 3½
Foundation: Crawl space, slab
Materials List Available: No
Price Category: G

Images provided by designer/architect.

Triple dormers add a touch of charm to this upscale country-style home.

Features:

• Porch: A columned porch gives a warm welcome to visiting relatives and friends.

• Dining Room: Columns define this formal dining room, which is perfect for all of your entertaining needs.

• Family Room: This two-story high family room is warmed by a fireplace and

brightened by lots of windows.

• Kitchen: With a nice serving bar, a menu desk and a good-sized pantry, this open kitchen will be the envy of any cooking enthusiast.

• Master Suite: Double doors introduce this suite, where a spacious sitting room is superseded only by the sumptuous master bath.

• Secondary Bedrooms: On the upper level, each bedroom boasts its own private bath.

Family Room

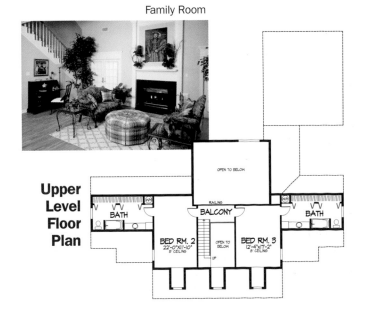

Plan #101013

Dimensions: 72' W x 66' D

Levels: 1

Square Footage: 2,564

Bedrooms: 3

Bathrooms: 2½

Foundation: Basement; crawl space or slab for fee

Materials List Available: Yes

Price Category: F

Images provided by designer/architect.

This exciting design combines a striking classic exterior with a highly functional floor plan.

CAD FILE AVAILABLE

Features:

- Ceiling Height: 9 ft. unless otherwise noted.

- Family Room: This warm and inviting room measures 18 ft. x 22 ft. It features a 14-ft. ceiling and a rear wall of windows. French doors lead to an enormous deck.

- Kitchen: This unique angled kitchen is open to the hearth room and eating areas, all of which enjoy vaulted ceilings and are surrounded by windows. The hearth room has a TV niche.

- Master Suite: This 19-ft. x 18-ft. master suite is truly sumptuous, with its 12-ft. ceiling, sitting area, two walk-in closets, and full-featured bath.

- Secondary Bedrooms: Each of the secondary bedrooms measures 11 ft. x 14 ft. and has direct access to a shared bath.

- Bonus Room: Just beyond the entry are stairs leading to this bonus room, which measures approximately 12 ft. x 21 ft.—plenty of room for storage or future expansion.

Master Bedroom

Copyright by designer/architect.

Plan #101009

Dimensions: 70'2" W x 59' D
Levels: 1
Square Footage: 2,097
Bedrooms: 3
Bathrooms: 3
Foundation: Crawl space, slab, or basement
Materials List Available: Yes
Price Category: E

Images provided by designer/architect.

Round columns enhance this country porch design, which will nestle into any neighborhood.

Features:

• Ceiling Height: 9 ft. unless otherwise noted.

• Family Room: This large family room seems even more spacious, thanks to the vaulted ceiling. It's the perfect spot for all kinds of family activities.

• Dining Room: This elegant dining room is adorned with a decorative round column and a tray ceiling.

• Kitchen: You'll love the convenience of this enormous 14-ft.-3-in. x 22-ft.-6-in. country kitchen, which is open to the family room.

• Screened Porch: A French door leads to this breezy porch, with its vaulted ceiling.

• Master Suite: This sumptuous suite includes a double tray ceiling, a sitting area, a large walk-in closet, and a luxurious bath.

• Patio or Deck: This area is accessible from both the screened porch and master suite.

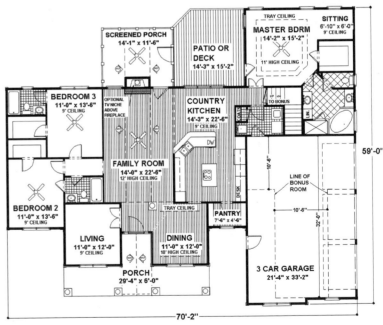

Copyright by designer/architect.

SMARTtip

Single-Level Decks

A single-level deck can use a strong vertical element, such as a pergola or a gazebo, to make it interesting. A simple and less-expensive option is a potted conical shrub or a clematis growing on a trellis.

Plan #121063

Dimensions: 84' W x 52' D
Levels: 1.5
Square Footage: 3,473
Main Level Sq. Ft.: 2,500
Upper Level Sq. Ft.: 973
Bedrooms: 4
Bathrooms: 3½
Foundation: Basement; crawl space or slab for fee
Materials List Available: Yes
Price Category: G

Images provided by designer/architect.

Enjoy the many amenities in this well-designed and gracious home.

Features:

• **Entry:** A large sparkling window and a tapering split staircase distinguish this lovely entryway.

• **Great Room:** This spacious great room will be the heart of your new home. It has a 14-ft. spider-beamed window that serves to highlight its built-in bookcase, built-in entertainment center, raised hearth fireplace,

wet bar, and lovely arched windows topped with transoms.

• **Kitchen:** Anyone who walks into this kitchen will realize that it's designed for both convenience and efficiency.

• **Master Suite:** The tiered ceiling in the bedroom gives an elegant touch, and the bay window adds to it. The two large walk-in closets and the spacious bath, with columns setting off the whirlpool tub and two vanities, complete this dream of a suite.

Main Level Floor Plan

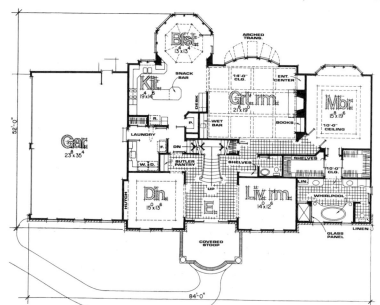

Upper Level Floor Plan

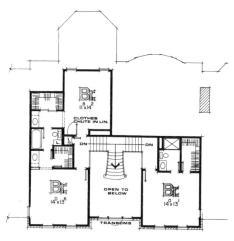

Copyright by designer/architect.

Plan #101006

Dimensions: 63' W x 58' D
Levels: 1
Square Footage: 1,982
Bedrooms: 3
Bathrooms: 2½
Foundation: Crawl space, slab, basement, or walkout
Materials List Available: Yes
Price Category: D

Images provided by designer/architect.

Radius-top windows and siding accented with wood shingles give this home a distinctive look.

Features:

• Ceiling Height: 9 ft. unless otherwise noted.

• Family Room: This room is perfect for all kinds of informal family activities. A vaulted ceiling adds to its sense of spaciousness.

• Dining Room: This room, with its tray ceiling, is designed for elegant dining.

• Porch: When the weather gets warm, you'll enjoy stepping out onto this large screened porch to catch a breeze.

• Master Suite: You'll love ending your day and getting up in the morning to this exquisite master suite, with its vaulted ceiling, sitting area, and large walk-in closet.

• Bonus Room: Just off the kitchen are stairs leading to this enormous bonus room, offering more than 330 sq. ft. of future expansion space.

Copyright by designer/architect.

SMARTtip

Art in Pools

The tiled walls and floor of a pool make great canvases for art, so incorporate a serious or whimsical design. Also, make the stairs wide and shallow to form a wading area for kids.

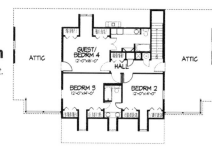

Main Level Floor Plan

Images provided by designer/architect.

Plan #271096

Dimensions: 66' W x 90' D

Levels: 2

Square footage: 3,190

Main Level Sq. Ft.: 2,152

Upper Level Sq. Ft.: 1,038

Bedrooms: 4

Bathrooms: 3½

Foundation: Crawl space

Materials List Available: No

Price Category: G

Upper Level Floor Plan

Copyright by designer/architect.

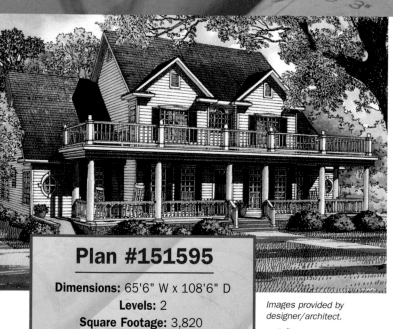

Main Level Floor Plan

Upper Level Floor Plan

Copyright by designer/architect.

Plan #151595

Dimensions: 65'6" W x 108'6" D

Levels: 2

Square Footage: 3,820

Main Level Sq. Ft.: 2,484

Upper Level Sq. Ft.: 1,336

Bedrooms: 4

Bathrooms: 3½

Foundation: Crawl space or slab; basement or walkout for fee

CompleteCost List Available: Yes

Price Category: H

Images provided by designer/architect.

Main Level Floor Plan

Copyright by designer/architect.

Plan #311042

Dimensions: 87' W x 64'2" D
Levels: 1.5
Square Footage: 3,910
Main Level Sq. Ft.: 3,613
Upper Level Sq. Ft.: 297
Bedrooms: 4
Bathrooms: 3 full, 2 half
Foundation: Crawl space, slab, or basement
Material List Available: Yes
Price Category: H

Images provided by designer/architect.

Rear Elevation

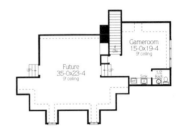

Upper Level Floor Plan

Plan #111015

Dimensions: 64' W x 58' D
Levels: 1
Square Footage: 2,208
Bedrooms: 4
Bathrooms: 2
Foundation: Slab
Materials List Available: No
Price Category: F

Images provided by designer/architect.

Copyright by designer/architect.

Plan #101022

Dimensions: 66'2" W x 62' D

Levels: 1

Square Footage: 1,992

Bedrooms: 3

Bathrooms: 3

Foundation: Crawl space, slab, or basement

Materials List Available: Yes

Price Category: D

Images provided by designer/architect.

The exterior of this lovely home is traditional, but the unusually shaped rooms and amenities are contemporary.

Features:

- **Foyer:** This two-story foyer is open to the family room, but columns divide it from the dining room.

- **Family Room:** A gas fireplace and TV niche, flanked by doors to the covered porch, sit at the rear of this seven-sided, spacious room.

- **Breakfast Room:** Set off from the family room by columns, this area shares a snack bar with the kitchen and has windows looking over the porch.

- **Bedroom 3:** Use this room as a living room if you wish, and transform the guest room to a media room or a family bedroom.

- **Master Suite:** The bedroom features a tray ceiling, has his and her dressing areas, and opens to the porch. The bath has a large corner tub, separate shower, linen closet, and two vanities.

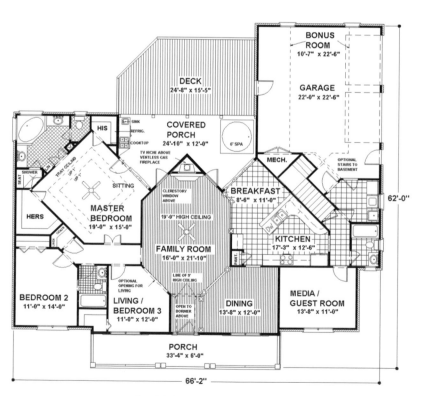

Copyright by designer/architect.

Plan #101005

Dimensions: 63' W x 57'2" D

Levels: 1

Square Footage: 1,992

Bedrooms: 3

Bathrooms: 2½

Foundation: Crawl space, slab, or basement

Materials List Available: Yes

Price Category: D

Images provided by designer/architect.

Rear View

This midsized ranch is accented with Palladian windows and inviting front porch.

Features:

- Ceiling Height: 9 ft. unless otherwise noted.

- Special Ceilings: Tray or vaulted ceilings adorn the living room, family room, dining room, and master suite.

- Kitchen: This bright and airy kitchen is designed to be a pleasure in which to work. It shares a big bay window with the contiguous breakfast room.

- Breakfast Room: The light streaming in from the bay window makes this the perfect place to linger with coffee and the Sunday paper.

- Master Suite: This lovely suite is exceptional, with its sitting area and direct access to the deck, as well as a full-featured bath, and spacious walk-in closet.

- Secondary Bedrooms: The other bedrooms each measure about 13 ft. x 11 ft. They have walk-in closets and share a "Jack-and-Jill" bath.

Copyright by designer/architect.

Plan #151014

Dimensions: 70'2" W x 51'4" D

Levels: 1.5

Square Footage: 2,698

Main Level Sq. Ft.: 1,813

Upper Level Sq. Ft.: 885

Bedrooms: 5

Bathrooms: 3

Foundation: Crawl space, slab; basement for fee

CompleteCost List Available: Yes

Price Category: F

Images provided by designer/architect.

A comfortable front porch welcomes you into this home that features a balcony over the great room, a study, and a kitchen designed for gourmet cooks.

CAD FILE AVAILABLE

Features:

- Ceiling Height: 9 ft.
- Front Porch: Stately 12-in.-wide pillars form the entryway.
- Foyer: Open to upper story.
- Great Room: A fireplace, vaulted 9-ft. ceiling, and balcony from the second floor add character to this lovely room.
- Dining Room: Open to the kitchen for convenience.
- Kitchen: A large walk-in pantry, well-designed work areas, and eat-in bar make this room a treasure.
- Breakfast Room: Enjoy this spot that opens to both the kitchen and a large covered porch at the rear of the house.
- Study: This quiet room has French doors leading to the yard.
- Master Suite: This spacious area has cozy window seats as well as his and her walk-in closets. The master bathroom is fitted with a whirlpool tub, a glass shower, and his and her sinks.

Upper Level Floor Plan

Main Level Floor Plan

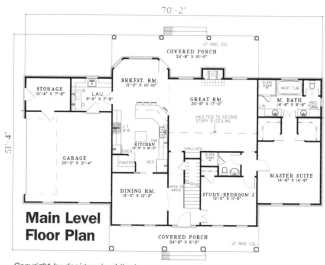

Copyright by designer/architect.

Plan #101004

Dimensions: 55'8" W x 56'6" D

Levels: 1

Square Footage: 1,787

Bedrooms: 3

Bathrooms: 2

Foundation: Crawl space, slab, or basement

Materials List Available: Yes

Price Category: D

This carefully designed ranch provides the feel and features of a much larger home.

Features:

- Ceiling Height: 9 ft. unless otherwise noted.

- Entry: Guests will step up onto the inviting front porch and into this entry, with its impressive 11-ft. ceiling.

- Dining Room: Open to the entry and to its left is this elegant dining room, perfect for entertaining or informal family gatherings.

- Family Room: This family gathering place features an 11-ft. ceiling to enhance its sense of spaciousness.

- Kitchen: This intelligently designed kitchen has an open plan. A breakfast bar and a serving bar are features that add to its convenience.

- Master Suite: This suite is loaded with amenities, including a double-step tray ceiling, direct access to the screened porch, a sitting room, deluxe bath, and his and her walk-in closets.

CAD FILE AVAILABLE

Images provided by designer/architect.

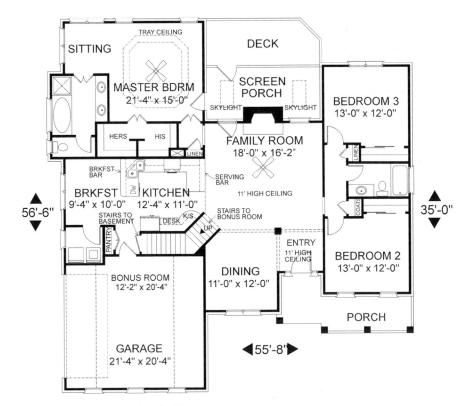

Copyright by designer/architect.

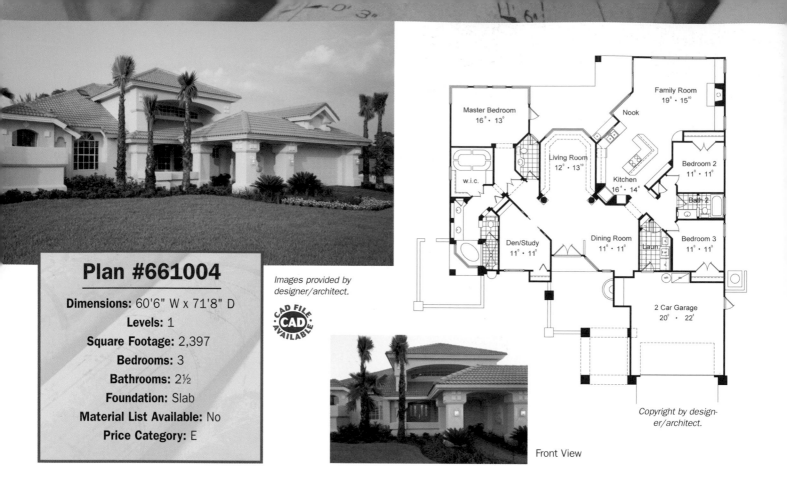

Plan #661004

Dimensions: 60'6" W x 71'8" D

Levels: 1

Square Footage: 2,397

Bedrooms: 3

Bathrooms: 2½

Foundation: Slab

Material List Available: No

Price Category: E

Images provided by designer/architect.

CAD FILE AVAILABLE

Copyright by designer/architect.

Front View

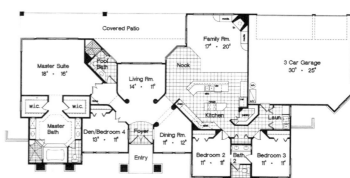

Copyright by designer/architect.

Plan #661006

Dimensions: 98'6" W x 50' D

Levels: 1

Square Footage: 2,597

Bedrooms: 4

Bathrooms: 3

Foundation: Slab

Material List Available: No

Price Category: E

Images provided by designer/architect.

CAD FILE AVAILABLE

Front View

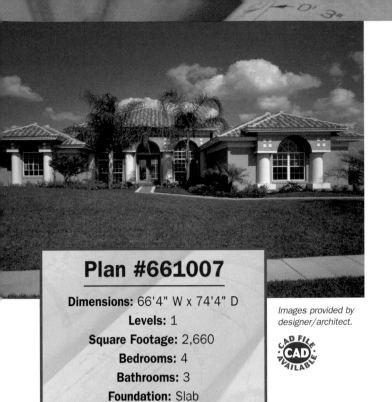

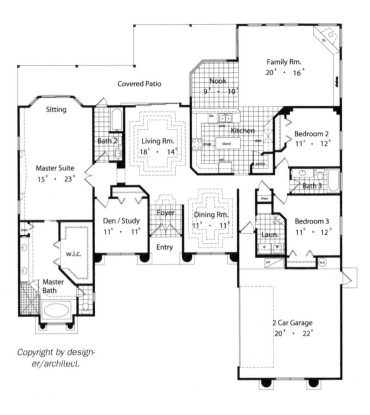

Plan #661007

Dimensions: 66'4" W x 74'4" D

Levels: 1

Square Footage: 2,660

Bedrooms: 4

Bathrooms: 3

Foundation: Slab

Material List Available: No

Price Category: F

Images provided by designer/architect.

CAD FILE AVAILABLE

Copyright by designer/architect.

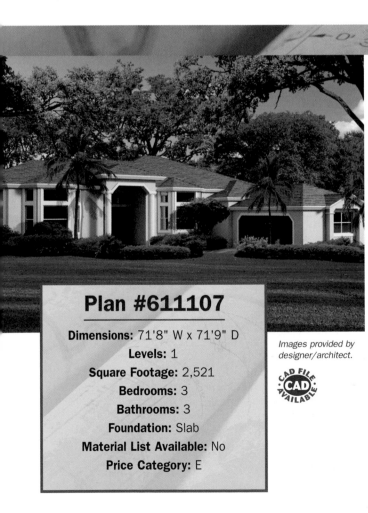

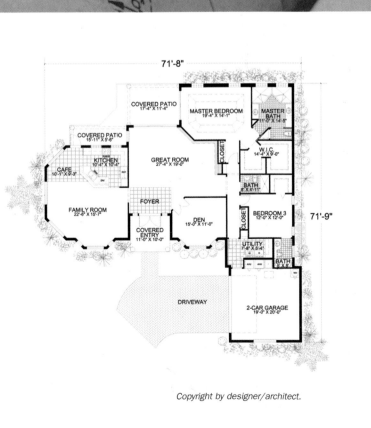

Plan #611107

Dimensions: 71'8" W x 71'9" D

Levels: 1

Square Footage: 2,521

Bedrooms: 3

Bathrooms: 3

Foundation: Slab

Material List Available: No

Price Category: E

Images provided by designer/architect.

CAD FILE AVAILABLE

Copyright by designer/architect.

Copyright by designer/architect.

Plan #221018

Dimensions: 67' W x 53' D

Levels: 1

Square Footage: 2,007

Bedrooms: 3

Bathrooms: 2

Foundation: Basement

Materials List Available: No

Price Category: D

Images provided by designer/architect.

CAD FILE AVAILABLE · CAD

Rear Elevation

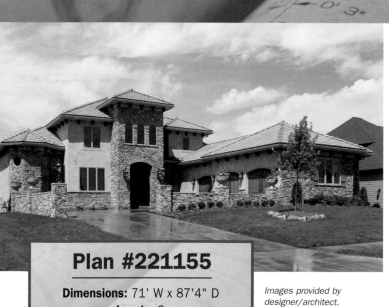

Main Level Floor Plan

Plan #221155

Dimensions: 71' W x 87'4" D

Levels: 2

Square Footage: 3,687

Square Footage: 2,567

Square Footage: 1,120

Bedrooms: 4

Bathrooms: 3½

Foundation: Walkout

Materials List Available: No

Price Category: H

Images provided by designer/architect.

CAD FILE AVAILABLE · CAD

Upper Level Floor Plan

Copyright by designer/architect.

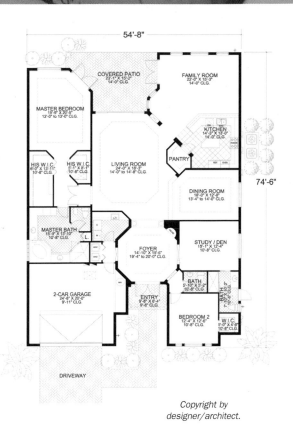

COVERED PATIO
23'-1" X 15'
14'-0" CLG.

FAMILY ROOM
22'-0" X 15'-3"
14'-0" CLG.

MASTER BEDROOM
18'-0" X 20'-5"
12'-0" to 13'-0" CLG.

KITCHEN
14'-6" X 13'-0"
14'-0" CLG.

HIS W.I.C.
6'-0" X 13'-11"
10'-8" CLG.

HIS W.I.C.
7'-1" X 8'-7"
10'-8" CLG.

LIVING ROOM
24'-0" X 16'-3"
14'-0" to 14'-8" CLG.

PANTRY

DINING ROOM
18'-0" X 12'-6"
13'-4" to 14'-0" CLG.

MASTER BATH
15'-9" X 13'-10"
10'-8" CLG.

FOYER
14'-10" X 15'-6"
19'-4" to 20'-0" CLG.

STUDY / DEN
15'-1" X 12'-4"
10'-8" CLG.

2-CAR GARAGE
24'-8" X 20'-0"
9'-11" CLG.

ENTRY
5'-6" X 6'-4"
9'-8" CLG.

BATH
5'-10" X 5'-2"
10'-8" CLG.

BEDROOM 2
12'-4" X 12'-6"
10'-8" CLG.

W.I.C.
5'-0" X 4'-8"
10'-8" CLG.

DRIVEWAY

54'-8"

74'-6"

Copyright by designer/architect.

Plan #611115

Dimensions: 54'8" W x 74'6" D

Levels: 1

Square Footage: 3,063

Bedrooms: 3

Bathrooms: 2½

Foundation: Slab

Material List Available: No

Price Category: G

Images provided by designer/architect.

CAD FILE AVAILABLE

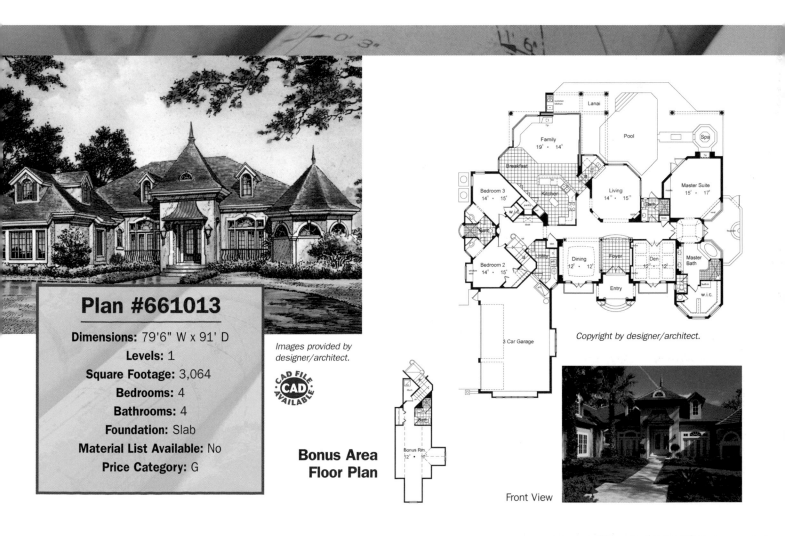

Plan #661013

Dimensions: 79'6" W x 91' D

Levels: 1

Square Footage: 3,064

Bedrooms: 4

Bathrooms: 4

Foundation: Slab

Material List Available: No

Price Category: G

Images provided by designer/architect.

CAD FILE AVAILABLE

Lanai

Family
19' · 14'

Pool

Spa

Breakfast

Living
14'² · 15'⁴

Master Suite
15' · 17'

Bedroom 3
14' · 15'

Kitchen

Bath

Bedroom 2
14' · 15'

Utility

Dining
12' · 12'

Foyer

Den
12' · 12'

Master Bath

Entry

3 Car Garage

w.i.c.

Copyright by designer/architect.

Bonus Area Floor Plan

Bonus Rm.
12' · 15'

Front View

Images provided by
designer/architect.

Copyright by
designer/architect.

Plan #661146

Dimensions: 65' W x 65'6" D

Levels: 1

Square Footage: 2,560

Bedrooms: 4

Bathrooms: 2

Foundation: Slab

Material List Available: No

Price Category: E

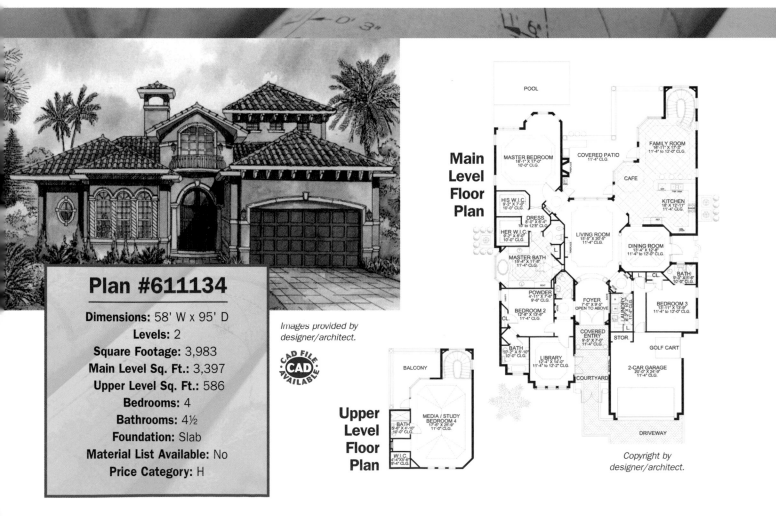

Images provided by
designer/architect.

CAD FILE AVAILABLE

Main Level Floor Plan

Upper Level Floor Plan

Copyright by
designer/architect.

Plan #611134

Dimensions: 58' W x 95' D

Levels: 2

Square Footage: 3,983

Main Level Sq. Ft.: 3,397

Upper Level Sq. Ft.: 586

Bedrooms: 4

Bathrooms: 4½

Foundation: Slab

Material List Available: No

Price Category: H

Main Level Floor Plan

w.i.c.

Bedroom 2
11⁰ · 12⁰

Bedroom 3
12⁰ · 12⁰

Covered Porch

Bath 2

Family Rm.
19⁰ · 19⁰

3 Car Garage
20⁰ · 22⁰

Nook

Laundry

Master Suite
13⁰ · 20⁰

Living Rm.
12⁰ · 13⁰

Kitchen

w.i.c.

Master
Bath

w.i.c.

Foyer

Dining Rm.
11⁰ · 14⁰

Covered Porch

Entry

Upper Level Floor Plan

Sun Room
16⁰ · 9⁰

Bath 3

Loft

Mech. Rm.

Copyright by designer/architect.

Plan #661182

Dimensions: 69' W x 70' D
Levels: 1.5
Square Footage: 3,168
Main Level Sq. Ft.: 2,729
Upper Level Sq. Ft.: 439
Bedrooms: 4
Bathrooms: 3
Foundation: Slab
Material List Available: No
Price Category: G

Images provided by designer/architect.

CAD FILE AVAILABLE

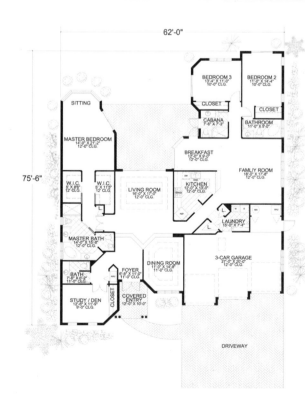

62'-0"

SITTING

BEDROOM 3
13'-4" X 11'-0"
10'-0" CLG.

BEDROOM 2
11'-0" X 14'-4"
10'-0" CLG.

CLOSET

CLOSET

MASTER BEDROOM
14'-0" X 21'-0"
12'-0" CLG.

CABANA
7'-6" X 7'-3"

BATHROOM
11'-0" X 7'-0"

75'-6"

W.I.C.
8'-X X 8'6"
12'-0"

W.I.C.
11'-0" X 11'0"
12'-0"

LIVING ROOM
16'-0" X 17'-0"
12'-0" CLG.

BREAKFAST
12'-0" X 8'-3"
12'-0" CLG.

KITCHEN
12'-0" X 13'-0"
12'-0" CLG.

FAMILY ROOM
18'-0" X 17'-6"
12'-0" CLG.

LAUNDRY
15'-0" X 7'-4"

MASTER BATH
14'-0" X 18'-0"
12'-0" CLG.

DINING ROOM
14'-0" X 14'-6"
11'-0" CLG.

3-CAR GARAGE
21'-0" X 34'-0"
12'-0" CLG.

BATH
7'-6" X 6'-2"
11'-0" CLG.

FOYER
6'-8" X 11'-2"

COVERED ENTRY
12'-0" X 10'-0"

STUDY / DEN
12'-0" X 13'-0"
9'-0" CLG.

CLOSET

DRIVEWAY

Copyright by designer/architect.

Plan #611114

Dimensions: 62' W x 75'6" D
Levels: 1
Square Footage: 2,827
Bedrooms: 4
Bathrooms: 3½
Foundation: Slab
Material List Available: No
Price Category: F

Images provided by designer/architect.

CAD FILE AVAILABLE

Plan #611038

Dimensions: 50' W x 80' D
Levels: 2
Square Footage: 3,250
Main Level Sq. Ft.: 2,268
Upper Level Sq. Ft.: 982
Bedrooms: 4
Bathrooms: 3½
Foundation: Slab
Material List Available: No
Price Category: G

Images provided by designer/architect.

Main Level Floor Plan

Upper Level Floor Plan

Copyright by designer/architect.

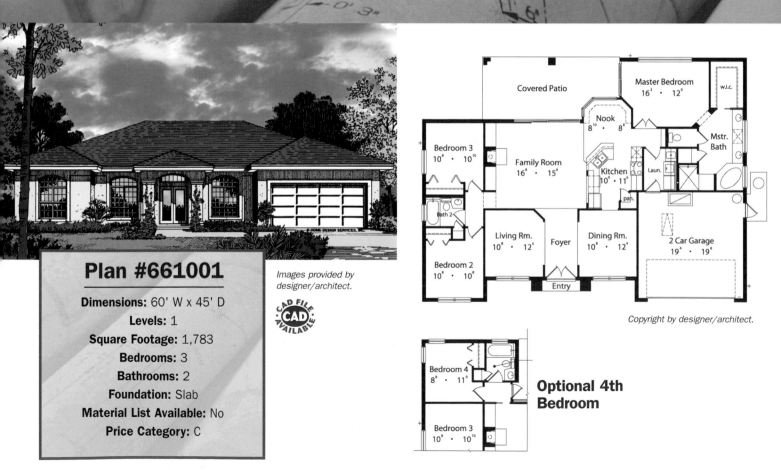

Plan #661001

Dimensions: 60' W x 45' D
Levels: 1
Square Footage: 1,783
Bedrooms: 3
Bathrooms: 2
Foundation: Slab
Material List Available: No
Price Category: C

Images provided by designer/architect.

Copyright by designer/architect.

Optional 4th Bedroom

Plan #661190

Dimensions: 82'4" W x 82'4" D

Levels: 1

Square Footage: 2,987

Bedrooms: 4

Bathrooms: 3

Foundation: Slab

Material List Available: No

Price Category: F

Images provided by designer/architect.

CAD FILE AVAILABLE

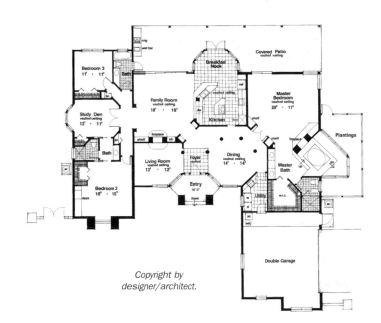

Copyright by designer/architect.

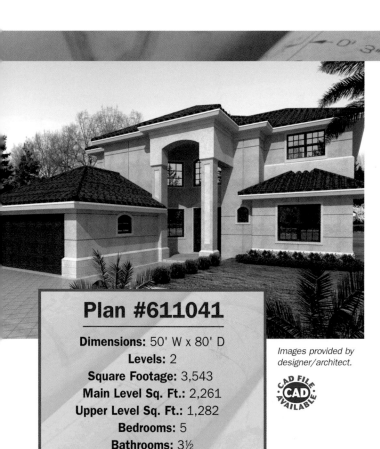

Plan #611041

Dimensions: 50' W x 80' D

Levels: 2

Square Footage: 3,543

Main Level Sq. Ft.: 2,261

Upper Level Sq. Ft.: 1,282

Bedrooms: 5

Bathrooms: 3½

Foundation: Slab

Material List Available: No

Price Category: H

Images provided by designer/architect.

CAD FILE AVAILABLE

Main Level Floor Plan

Upper Level Floor Plan

Copyright by designer/architect.

Plan #661010

Dimensions: 70' W x 74'1" D
Levels: 2
Square Footage: 2,887
Main Level Sq. Ft.: 2,212
Upper Level Sq. Ft.: 675
Bedrooms: 4
Bathrooms: 3
Foundation: Slab
Material List Available: No
Price Category: F

Images provided by designer/architect.

This house is filled with special details usually found in far more expensive homes.

CAD FILE AVAILABLE

Features:

- **Family Room:** This family room opens to the rear patio and pool through a sliding glass door wall, making it ideal for hosting a large summer gathering.

- **Kitchen:** Although easily accessible from the family room, this open kitchen is sufficiently detached from the dining area for more formal entertaining.

- **Den/Study:** This combination den/study near the master suite is situated out of the main traffic flow, meaning fewer disruptions when an important project is due. The nearby bath allows the room to double as a place for overnight guests.

- **Master Suite:** This striking master suite features direct access to the rear patio and pool, perfect for watching the sun rise or for a late-night swim. The elegant master bath includes a spacious walk-in closet, tub, and his and her sinks.

Main Level Floor Plan

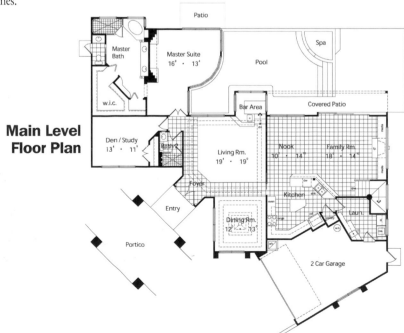

Upper Level Floor Plan

Copyright by designer/architect.

Foyer/Living Room

Family Room

Kitchen

Master Bath

Master Bedroom

Observatory

Plan #611016

Dimensions: 35' W x 66'2" D

Levels: 1

Square Footage: 1,744

Bedrooms: 3

Bathrooms: 2

Foundation: Slab

Material List Available: No

Price Category: C

Images provided by designer/architect.

CAD FILE AVAILABLE · CAD

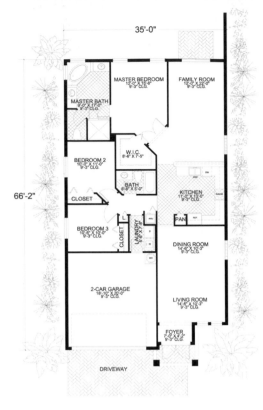

Copyright by designer/architect.

Plan #661046

Dimensions: 42' W x 55' D

Levels: 1

Square Footage: 1,750

Bedrooms: 3

Bathrooms: 2

Foundation: Slab

Material List Available: No

Price Category: C

Images provided by designer/architect.

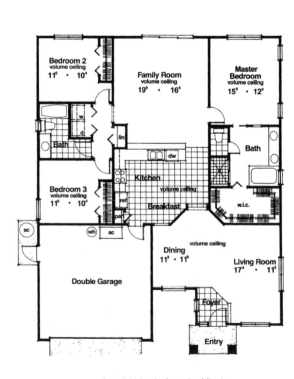

Copyright by designer/architect.

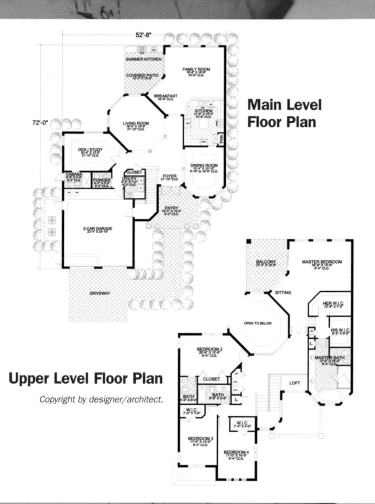

Main Level Floor Plan

Upper Level Floor Plan

Copyright by designer/architect.

Images provided by designer/architect.

CAD FILE AVAILABLE

Plan #611045

Dimensions: 52'8" W x 72' D

Levels: 2

Square Footage: 3,869

Main Level Sq. Ft.: 1,863

Upper Level Sq. Ft.: 2,006

Bedrooms: 4

Bathrooms: 3½

Foundation: Slab

Material List Available: No

Price Category: H

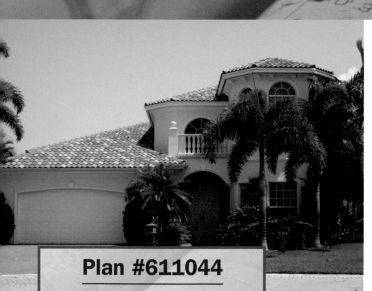

Main Level Floor Plan

Upper Level Floor Plan

Copyright by designer/architect.

Images provided by designer/architect.

CAD FILE AVAILABLE

Plan #611044

Dimensions: 54'9" W x 74'9" D

Levels: 2

Square Footage: 3,715

Main Level Sq. Ft.: 3,026

Upper Level Sq. Ft.: 689

Bedrooms: 4

Bathrooms: 3½

Foundation: Slab

Material List Available: No

Price Category: H

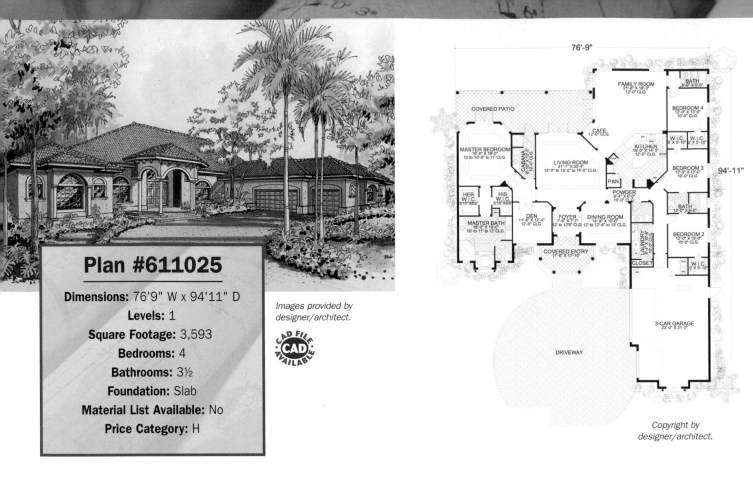

Plan #611025

Dimensions: 76'9" W x 94'11" D

Levels: 1

Square Footage: 3,593

Bedrooms: 4

Bathrooms: 3½

Foundation: Slab

Material List Available: No

Price Category: H

Images provided by designer/architect.

Copyright by designer/architect.

Plan #661014

Dimensions: 94' W x 113'6" D

Levels: 1.5

Square Footage: 3,436

Main Level Sq. Ft.: 3,146

Upper Level Sq. Ft.: 290

Bedrooms: 4

Bathrooms: 3½

Foundation: Slab

Material List Available: No

Price Category: G

Images provided by designer/architect.

Upper Level Floor Plan

Copyright by designer/architect.

Main Level Floor Plan

Optional Guest Quarters and Garage Floor Plan

Plan #611126

Dimensions: 61'11" W x 59'2" D

Levels: 2

Square Footage: 2,543

Main Level Sq. Ft.: 2,098

Upper Level Sq. Ft.: 445

Bedrooms: 4

Bathrooms: 3

Foundation: Slab

Material List Available: No

Price Category: E

Images provided by designer/architect.

Main Level Floor Plan

Upper Level Floor Plan

Copyright by designer/architect.

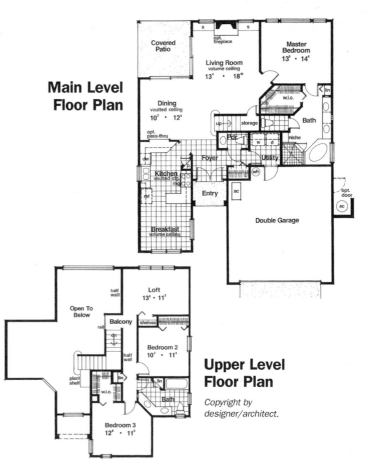

Plan #661056

Dimensions: 38' W x 53'6" D

Levels: 2

Square Footage: 1,879

Main Level Sq. Ft.: 1,230

Upper Level Sq. Ft.: 649

Bedrooms: 4

Bathrooms: 2½

Foundation: Slab

Material List Available: No

Price Category: D

Images provided by designer/architect.

Main Level Floor Plan

Upper Level Floor Plan

Copyright by designer/architect.

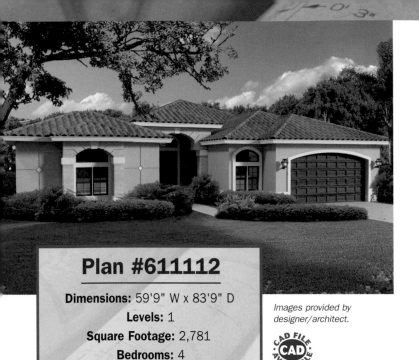

Plan #611112

Dimensions: 59'9" W x 83'9" D

Levels: 1

Square Footage: 2,781

Bedrooms: 4

Bathrooms: 3

Foundation: Slab

Material List Available: No

Price Category: F

Images provided by designer/architect.

CAD FILE AVAILABLE

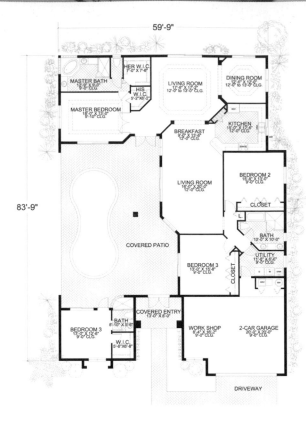

Copyright by designer/architect.

Plan #661165

Dimensions: 66'4" W x 80'8" D

Levels: 1.5

Square Footage: 2,713

Main Level Sq. Ft.: 2,713

Upper Level Future Sq. Ft.: 440

Bedrooms: 4

Bathrooms: 4

Foundation: Slab

Material List Available: No

Price Category: F

Images provided by designer/architect.

CAD FILE AVAILABLE

Main Level Floor Plan

Copyright by designer/architect.

Bonus Area Floor Plan

Plan #611036

Dimensions: 67' W x 56'8" D
Levels: 2
Square Footage: 3,110
Main Level Sq. Ft.: 2,015
Upper Level Sq. Ft.: 1,095
Bedrooms: 4
Bathrooms: 2½
Foundation: Slab
Material List Available: No
Price Category: G

Images provided by designer/architect.

CAD FILE AVAILABLE

Main Level Floor Plan

Upper Level Floor Plan

Copyright by designer/architect.

Plan #611133

Dimensions: 60' W x 76' D
Levels: 2
Square Footage: 3,497
Main Level Sq. Ft.: 2,521
Upper Level Sq. Ft.: 976
Bedrooms: 5
Bathrooms: 4
Foundation: Slab
Material List Available: No
Price Category: G

Images provided by designer/architect.

CAD FILE AVAILABLE

Main Level Floor Plan

Upper Level Floor Plan

Copyright by designer/architect.

Plan #161040

Dimensions: 63'4" W x 48' D
Levels: 2
Square Footage: 2,403
Main Level Sq. Ft.: 1,710
Upper Level Sq. Ft.: 695
Bedrooms: 4
Bathrooms: 3½
Foundation: Basement; slab for fee
Price Category: E

Designed with attention to detail, this elegant home will please the most discriminating taste.

Images provided by designer/architect.

Features:

- Great Room: The high ceiling in this room accentuates the fireplace and the rear wall of windows. A fashionable balcony overlooks the great room.

- Dining Room: This lovely formal dining room is introduced by columns and accented by a boxed window.

- Kitchen: This wonderful kitchen includes a snack bar, island, and large pantry positioned to serve the breakfast and dining rooms with equal ease.

- Master Suite: This master suite features a dressing room, private sitting area with 11-ft.

ceiling, tub, double-bowl vanity, and large walk-in closet.

- Additional Bedrooms: Three additional bedrooms complete this spectacular home.

Rear Elevation

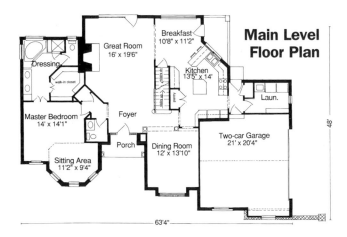

Main Level Floor Plan

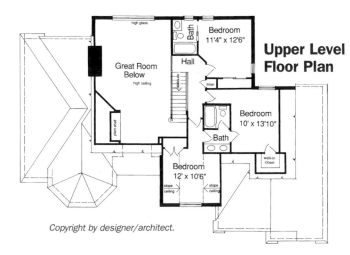

Upper Level Floor Plan

Copyright by designer/architect.

Plan #661181

Dimensions: 48' W x 74' D
Levels: 1.5
Square Footage: 2,802
Main Level Sq. Ft.: 2,293
Upper Level Sq. Ft.: 509
Bedrooms: 4
Bathrooms: 3
Foundation: Slab
Material List Available: No
Price Category: F

Images provided by designer/architect.

Features:

- **Family Room:** Conveniently located at the center of the home, this spacious family room provides a wonderful space to entertain guests or relax with the family.
- **Kitchen:** This gourmet kitchen provides plenty of cooking and storage space for the home chef. An eating bar is a versatile spot

for grabbing a quick lunch, entertaining guests, or an after-school snack.

- **Den:** This well-situated room can be used in a variety of ways. Depending on your family's needs, it can be an additional bedroom, a home office, or study.
- **Master Suite:** You'll love this large master suite with his and her sinks and walk-in closet. Direct access to the covered patio in the rear of the house is perfect for relaxing at night or waking up to see the sunrise.

CAD FILE AVAILABLE

Main Level Floor Plan

Upper Level Floor Plan

Copyright by designer/architect.

Rear View

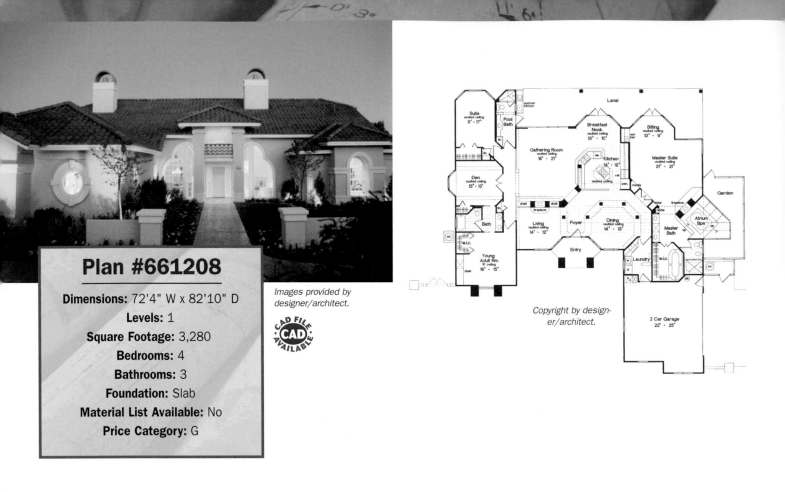

Plan #661208

Dimensions: 72'4" W x 82'10" D

Levels: 1

Square Footage: 3,280

Bedrooms: 4

Bathrooms: 3

Foundation: Slab

Material List Available: No

Price Category: G

Images provided by designer/architect.

CAD FILE AVAILABLE

Copyright by designer/architect.

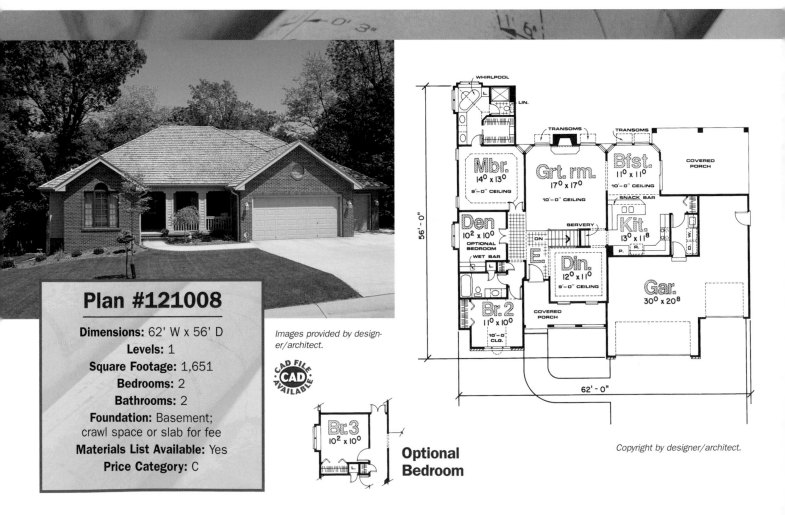

Plan #121008

Dimensions: 62' W x 56' D

Levels: 1

Square Footage: 1,651

Bedrooms: 2

Bathrooms: 2

Foundation: Basement; crawl space or slab for fee

Materials List Available: Yes

Price Category: C

Images provided by designer/architect.

CAD FILE AVAILABLE

Optional Bedroom

Copyright by designer/architect.

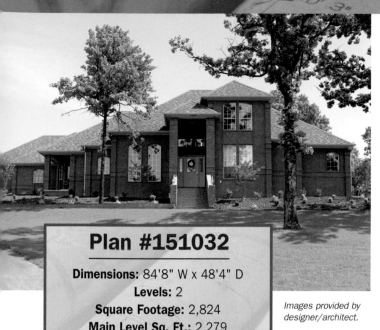

Plan #151032

Dimensions: 84'8" W x 48'4" D
Levels: 2
Square Footage: 2,824
Main Level Sq. Ft.: 2,279
Upper Level Sq. Ft.: 545
Bedrooms: 4
Bathrooms: 3
Foundation: Crawl space, slab; basement option for fee
CompleteCost List Available: Yes
Price Category: F

Images provided by designer/architect.

Upper Level Floor Plan

Copyright by designer/architect.

Main Level Floor Plan

Plan #661125

Images provided by designer/architect.

Dimensions: 60' W x 69'4" D
Levels: 1
Square Footage: 2,396
Bedrooms: 3
Bathrooms: 2½
Foundation: Slab
Material List Available: No
Price Category: E

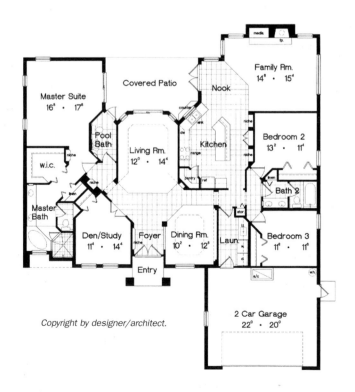

Copyright by designer/architect.

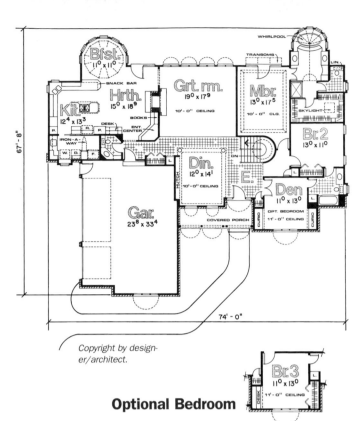

Plan #121007

Dimensions: 74' W x 67'8" D

Levels: 1

Square Footage: 2,512

Bedrooms: 3

Bathrooms: 2½

Foundation: Basement

Materials List Available: Yes

Price Category: E

Images provided by designer/architect.

Copyright by designer/architect.

Optional Bedroom

Plan #661205

Dimensions: 82'4" W x 70' D

Levels: 2

Square Footage: 3,200

Main Level Sq. Ft.: 2,531

Upper Level Sq. Ft.: 669

Bedrooms: 4

Bathrooms: 3 full, 2 half

Foundation: Slab

Material List Available: No

Price Category: G

Images provided by designer/architect.

Main Level Floor Plan

Upper Level Floor Plan

Copyright by designer/architect.

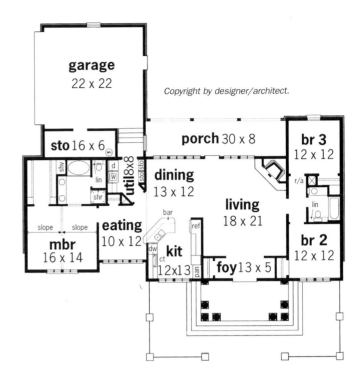

Copyright by designer/architect.

Images provided by designer/architect.

Plan #211002

Dimensions: 68' W x 62' D

Levels: 1

Square Footage: 1,792

Bedrooms: 3

Bathrooms: 2

Foundation: Crawl space

Materials List Available: Yes

Price Category: C

garage
22 x 22

sto 16 x 6

porch 30 x 8

br 3
12 x 12

util 8x8

dining
13 x 12

living
18 x 21

br 2
12 x 12

eating
10 x 12

mbr
16 x 14

kit
12 x13

foy 13 x 5

Plan #121082

Dimensions: 68'8" W x 60' D

Levels: 2

Square Footage: 2,932

Main Level Sq. Ft.: 2,084

Upper Level Sq. Ft.: 848

Bedrooms: 4

Bathrooms: 3½

Foundation: Basement

Materials List Available: Yes

Price Category: F

Main Level Floor Plan

Copyright by designer/architect.

Images provided by designer/architect.

CAD FILE AVAILABLE

Upper Level Floor Plan

Br 4
12⁰ x 13⁰

Br 2
12⁰ x 14⁰

Br 3
12⁰ x 14⁰

Grt. rm.
18⁰ x 18⁰

Hrth.
12⁷ x 15³

Bfst.
11³ x 11³

Mbr.
16³ x 14⁰

Kit.
12⁹ x 12⁸

Den
13³ x 14⁴

Din.
12⁰ x 15⁰

Gar.
21³ x 33³

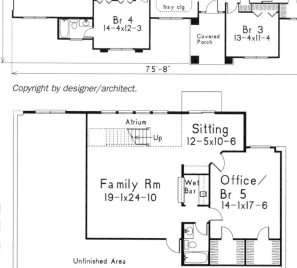

Copyright by designer/architect.

Plan #321034

Dimensions: 75'8" W x 52'6" D

Levels: 1

Square Footage: 3,508

Bedrooms: 4

Bathrooms: 3

Foundation: Basement, walkout

Material List Available: Yes

Price Category: H

Images provided by designer/architect.

Optional Basement Level Floor Plan

Plan #661073

Dimensions: 60'4" W x 56' D

Levels: 1

Square Footage: 2,041

Bedrooms: 4

Bathrooms: 2

Foundation: Slab

Material List Available: No

Price Category: D

Images provided by designer/architect.

Copyright by designer/architect.

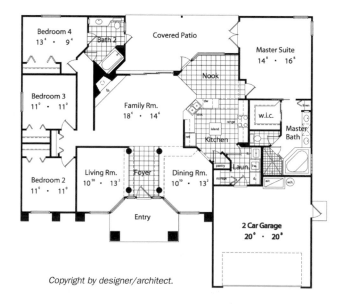

Front View

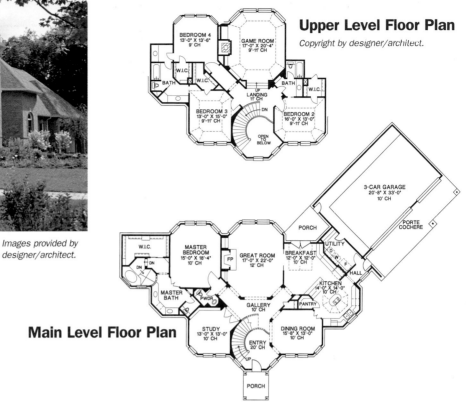

Copyright by designer/architect.

Upper Level Floor Plan

Main Level Floor Plan

Plan #121100

Dimensions: 100'10" W x 80'5" D

Levels: 2

Square Footage: 3,750

Main Level Sq. Ft.: 2,274

Upper Level Sq. Ft.: 1,476

Bedrooms: 4

Bathrooms: 3½

Foundation: Slab

Materials List Available: No

Price Category: H

Images provided by designer/architect.

Plan #661197

Dimensions: 78' W x 75'4" D

Levels: 1

Square Footage: 3,098

Bedrooms: 4

Bathrooms: 4

Foundation: Slab

Material List Available: No

Price Category: G

Images provided by designer/architect.

CAD FILE CAD AVAILABLE

Bonus Area Floor Plan

Copyright by designer/architect.

Plan #121019

Dimensions: 70' W x 60' D
Levels: 2
Square Footage: 3,775
Main Level Sq. Ft.: 1,923
Upper Level Sq. Ft.: 1,852
Bedrooms: 4
Bathrooms: 3½
Foundation: Basement; crawl space or slab for fee
Materials List Available: Yes
Price Category: H

Images provided by designer/architect.

The grand exterior presence is carried inside, beginning with the dramatic curved staircase.

Features:

• Ceiling Height: 8 ft.

• Den: French doors lead to this sophisticated den, with its bayed windows and wall of bookcases.

• Living Room: A curved wall and a series of arched windows highlight this large space.

• Formal Dining Room: This room shares the curved wall and arched windows found in the living room.

• Screened Porch: This huge space features skylights and is accessible by another French door from the dining room.

• Family Room: Family and guests alike will be drawn to this room, with its trio of arched windows and fireplace flanked by bookcases.

• Kitchen: An island adds convenience and distinction to this large, functional kitchen.

• Garage: This spacious three-bay garage provides plenty of space for cars and storage.

Main Level Floor Plan

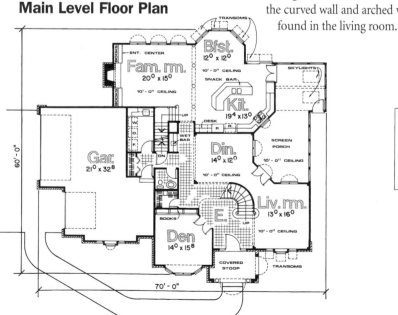

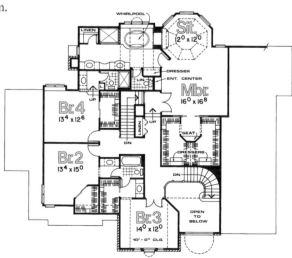

Upper Level Floor Plan

Copyright by designer/architect.

Plan #151002

Dimensions: 67' W x 66' D

Levels: 1

Square Footage: 2,444

Bedrooms: 3

Bathrooms: 2½

Foundation: Crawl space, slab, or basement

CompleteCost List Available: Yes

Price Category: F

This home, as shown in the photograph, may differ from the actual blueprints. For more detailed information, please check the floor plans carefully.

Images provided by designer/architect.

- **Kitchen:** An eat-in bar is a great place to snack, and the handy computer nook allows the kids to do their homework while you cook.

- **Breakfast Room:** Opening from the kitchen, this area gives added space for the family to gather any time.

- **Master Suite:** Featuring a 10-ft. boxed ceiling, the master bedroom also has a doorway that opens onto the covered rear porch. The master bathroom has a step-up whirlpool tub, separate shower, and twin vanities with a makeup area.

This gracious, traditional home is designed for practicality and convenience.

Features:

- **Ceiling Height:** 9 ft. except as noted below.

- **Great Room:** This room is ideal for entertaining, thanks to its lovely fireplace and French doors that open to the covered rear porch. Built-in cabinets give convenient storage space.

- **Family Room:** With access to the kitchen as well as the rear porch, this room will become your family's "headquarters."

- **Study:** Enjoy the quiet in this room with its 12-ft. ceiling and doorway to a private patio on the side of the house.

- **Dining Room:** Take advantage of the 8-in. wood columns and 12-ft. ceilings to create a formal dining area.

Copyright by designer/architect.

Plan #151057

Dimensions: 73'6" W x 80'6" D
Levels: 1
Square Footage: 2,951
Bedrooms: 4
Bathrooms: 3
Foundation: Crawl space, slab, or basement
CompleteCost List Available: Yes
Price Category: G

Images provided by designer/architect.

The stucco exterior and large windows give this ranch an elegant look.

Features:

- **Foyer:** Enter the covered porch, and walk through the beautiful front door to this large foyer with entry closet.

- **Entertaining:** The large great room has a cozy fireplace and built-ins for casual get-togethers. The formal living room, also with a fireplace, is for special entertaining.

- **Kitchen:** This large U-shaped island kitchen has a raised bar and is open to the breakfast area and the great room. A short step though the door brings you onto the rear lanai.

- **Master Suite:** This private retreat has a fireplace and a sitting area with access to the rear lanai. The master bath features dual vanities, a whirlpool tub, a glass shower, and a separate toilet room.

- **Bedrooms:** Three large bedrooms are located on the opposite side of the home to give the master suite privacy. Two bedrooms share a Jack-and-Jill bathroom. The third bedroom has access to a common bathroom.

Copyright by designer/architect.

Plan #121023

Dimensions: 85'5" W x 74'8" D

Levels: 2

Square Footage: 3,904

Main Level Sq. Ft.: 2,813

Upper Level Sq. Ft.: 1,091

Bedrooms: 4

Bathrooms: 3½

Foundation: Basement

Materials List Available: Yes

Price Category: H

CAD FILE AVAILABLE

Images provided by designer/architect.

Spacious and gracious, here are all the amenities you expect in a fine home.

Features:

• Ceiling Height: 8 ft. except as noted.

• Foyer: This magnificent entry features a graceful curved staircase with balcony above.

• Sunken Living Room: This sunken room is filled with light from a row of bowed windows. It's the perfect place for social gatherings both large and small.

• Den: French doors open into this truly distinctive den with its 11-ft. ceiling and built-in bookcases.

• Formal Dining Room: Entertain guests with style and grace in this dining room with corner column.

• Master Suite: Another set of French doors leads to this suite that features two walk-in closets, a tub flanked by vanities, and a private sitting room with built-in bookcases.

Main Level Floor Plan

Upper Level Floor Plan

Copyright by designer/architect.

Plan #211011

Dimensions: 84' W x 54' D
Levels: 1
Square Footage: 2,791
Bedrooms: 3 or 4
Bathrooms: 2
Foundation: Slab or crawl space
Materials List Available: Yes
Price Category: F

Images provided by designer/architect.

CAD FILE AVAILABLE • **CAD** •

SMARTtip

Types of Decks

Ground-level decks resemble a low platform and are best for flat locations. They can be the most economical type to build because they don't require stairs.

Raised decks can rise just a few steps up or meet the second story of a house. Lifted high on post supports, they adapt well to uneven or sloped locations.

Multilevel decks feature two or more stories and are connected by stairways or ramps. They can follow the contours of a sloped lot, unifying the deck with the outdoors.

Plenty of room plus an open, flexible floor plan make this a home that will adapt to your needs.

Features:

• Ceiling Height: 8 ft. unless otherwise noted.

• Living Room: This distinctive room features a 12-ft. ceiling and is designed so that it can also serve as a master suite with a sitting room.

• Family Room: The whole family will want to gather in this large, inviting family room.

• Morning Room: The family room blends into this sunny spot, which is perfect for informal family meals.

• Kitchen: This spacious kitchen offers a smart layout. It is also contiguous to the family room.

• Master Suite: You'll look forward to the end of the day when you can enjoy this master suite. It includes a huge, luxurious master bath with two large walk-in closets and two vanity sinks.

• Optional Bedroom: This optional fourth bedroom is located so that it can easily serve as a library, den, office, or music room.

Copyright by designer/architect.

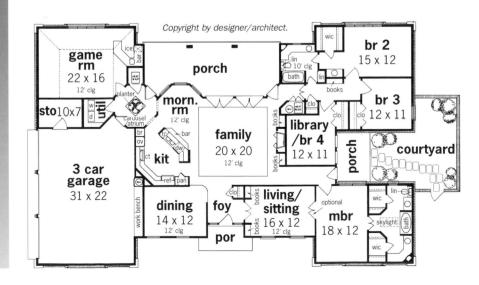

Plan #121065

Dimensions: 62' W x 55'4" D
Levels: 2
Square Footage: 3,407
Main Level Sq. Ft.: 1,719
Upper Level Sq. Ft.: 1,688
Bedrooms: 4
Bathrooms: 2½
Foundation: Basement;
crawl space for fee
Materials List Available: Yes
Price Category: G

Images provided by designer/architect.

This home, as shown in the photograph, may differ from the actual blueprints. For more detailed information, please check the floor plans carefully.

If you love contemporary design, the unusual shapes of the rooms in this home will delight you.

Features:

- Entry: You'll see a balcony from the upper level that overlooks this entryway, as well as the lovely curved staircase to this floor.

- Great Room: This room is sunken to set it apart. A fireplace, wet bar, spider-beamed ceiling, and row of arched windows give it character.

- Dining Room: Columns define this lovely octagon room, where you'll love to entertain guests or create lavish family dinners.

- Master Suite: A multi-tiered ceiling adds a note of grace, while the fireplace and private library create a real retreat. The gracious bath features a gazebo ceiling and a skylight.

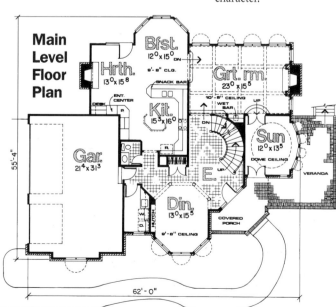

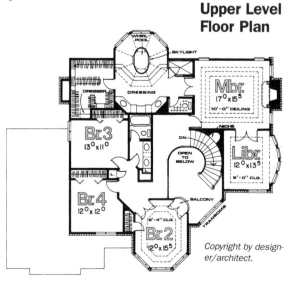

Plan #161016

Dimensions: 59'4" W x 58'8" D

Levels: 1.5

Square Footage: 2,101

Main Level Sq. Ft.: 1,626

Upper Level Sq. Ft.: 475

Bedrooms: 3

Bathrooms: 2½

Foundation: Basement; crawl space option available for fee

Materials List Available: Yes

Price Category: D

Note: Home in photo reflects a modified garage entrance.

Images provided by designer/architect.

Features:

- **Great Room:** Made for relaxing and entertaining, the great room is sunken to set it off from the rest of the house. A balcony from the second floor looks down into this spacious area, making it easy to keep track of the kids while they are playing.

- **Kitchen:** Convenience marks this well laid-out kitchen where you'll love to cook for guests and for family.

- **Master Suite:** A vaulted ceiling complements the unusual octagonal shape of the master

bedroom. Located on the first floor, this room allows some privacy from the second floor bedrooms. It is also ideal for anyone who no longer wishes to climb stairs to reach a bedroom.

Rear Elevation

You'll love the exciting roofline that sets this elegant home apart from its neighbors as well as the embellished, solid look that declares how well-designed it is—from the inside to the exterior.

CAD FILE AVAILABLE

Main Level Floor Plan

Upper Level Floor Plan

Copyright by designer/architect.

Plan #111031

Dimensions: 56' W x 53' D
Levels: 1.5
Square Footage: 2,869
Main Level Sq. Ft.: 2,152
Upper Level Sq. Ft.: 717
Bedrooms: 4
Bathrooms: 3
Foundation: Basement; slab
Materials List Available: No
Price Category: G

This home is ideal for any family, thanks to its spaciousness, beauty, and versatility.

Images provided by designer/architect.

Features:

- Ceiling Height: 9 ft.
- Front Porch: The middle of the three French doors with circle tops here opens to the foyer.
- Living Room: Archways from the foyer open to both this room and the equally large dining room.
- Family Room: Also open to the foyer, this room features a two-story sloped ceiling and a balcony from the upper level. You'll love the fireplace, with its raised brick hearth and the

two French doors with circle tops, which open to the rear porch.

- Kitchen: A center island, range with microwave, built-in desk, and dining bar that's open to the breakfast room add up to comfort and efficiency.
- Master Suite: A Palladian window and linen closet grace this suite's bedroom, and the bath has an oversized garden tub, standing shower, two walk-in closets, and double vanity.

Copyright by designer/architect.

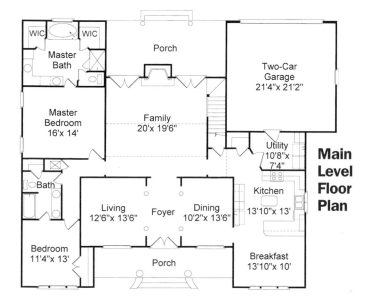

Main Level Floor Plan

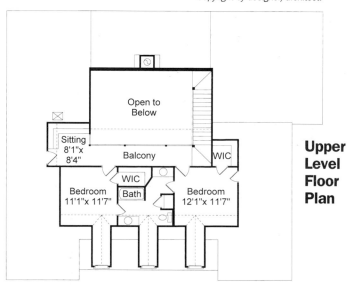

Upper Level Floor Plan

Plan #121003

Dimensions: 76' W x 55'4" D
Levels: 1
Square Footage: 2,498
Bedrooms: 4
Bathrooms: 2½
Foundation: Basement;
crawl space or slab for fee
Materials List Available: Yes
Price Category: E

Images provided by designer/architect.

Repeated arches bring style and distinction to the interior and exterior of this spacious home.

Features:

- Ceiling Height: 8 ft. except as noted.

- Den: A decorative volume ceiling helps make this spacious retreat the perfect place to relax after a long day.

- Formal Living Room: The decorative volume ceiling carries through to the living room that invites large formal gatherings.

- Formal Dining Room: There's plenty of room for all the guests to move into this gracious formal space that also features a decorative volume ceiling.

- Master Suite: Retire to this suite with its glamorous bayed whirlpool, his and her vanities, and a walk-in closet.

- Optional Sitting Room: With the addition of French doors, one of the bedrooms can be converted into a sitting room for the master suite.

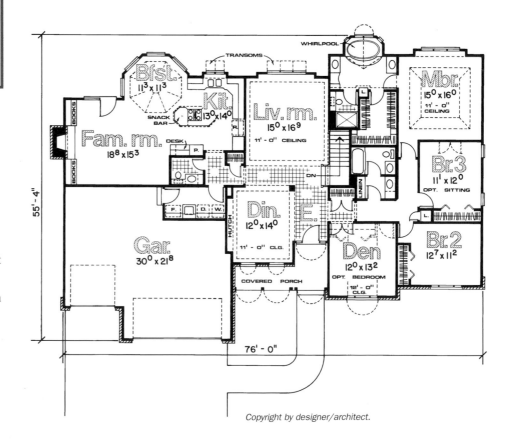

Copyright by designer/architect.

Plan #151063

Dimensions: 64' W x 60'2" D
Levels: 1
Square Footage: 2,554
Bedrooms: 4
Bathrooms: 2½
Foundation: Crawl space or slab; basement or walkout for fee
CompleteCost List Available: Yes
Price Category: E

This home boasts a beautiful arched entry on the covered porch.

Features:

- **Dining Room:** Set off by columns, this room will impress your dinner guests. The triple window gives a front-yard view while allowing natural light into the space.

- **Entertaining:** Your family and friends will love to gather in the hearth room and the great room, which share a see-through fire place. The hearth room has access to the grilling porch for outdoor entertaining.

- **Kitchen:** Centrally located, this island kitchen is open to the dining room in the front and the hearth room in the rear. It features a raised bar into the hearth room.

- **Master Suite:** This secluded retreat resides on the opposite side of the home from the secondary bedrooms. The large master bath features a whirlpool tub, two walk-in closets, and dual vanities.

This home, as shown in the photograph, may differ from the actual blueprints. For more detailed information, please check the floor plans carefully.

Images provided by designer/architect.

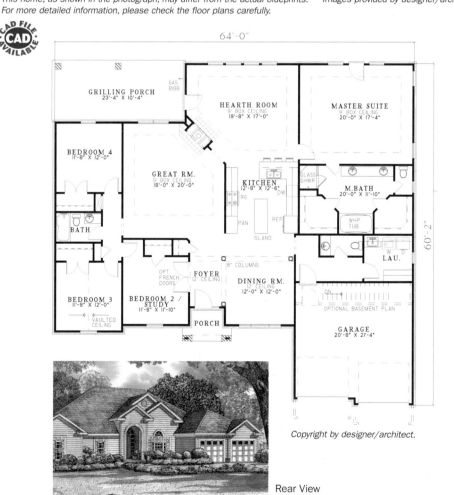

Copyright by designer/architect.

Rear View

Plan #121074

Dimensions: 68'8" W x 47'8" D

Levels: 2

Square Footage: 2,486

Main Level Sq. Ft.: 1,829

Upper Level Sq. Ft.: 657

Bedrooms: 4

Bathrooms: 2½

Foundation: Basement

Materials List Available: Yes

Price Category: E

Images provided by designer/architect.

Main Level Floor Plan

Upper Level Floor Plan

Copyright by designer/architect.

Plan #161042

Dimensions: 59'4" W x 65' D

Levels: 2

Square Footage: 2,198

Main Level Sq. Ft.: 1,706

Upper Level Sq. Ft.: 492

Bedrooms: 3

Bathrooms: 2½

Foundation: Basement

Materials List Available: Yes

Price Category: D

Images provided by designer/architect.

Main Level Floor Plan

Copyright by designer/architect

Upper Level Floor Plan

Main Level Floor Plan

SUNROOM 12'0" X 13'0"

NK. 11'0" X 8'0"

KIT. 15'0" X 14'0"

FAM. RM. 20'0" X 15'0"

VAULTED CLG.

MBR. 19'0" X 14'0"

SIT. AREA 10'0" X 8'0"

4 CAR GAR. 21'0" X 38'0"

DIN. 13'0" X 13'0"

STUDY 12'0" X 12'0"

55'-0"

79'-0"

Plan #221022

Dimensions: 79' W x 55' D

Levels: 2

Square Footage: 3,382

Main Level Sq. Ft.: 2,376

Upper Level Sq. Ft.: 1,006

Bedrooms: 4

Bathrooms: 3½

Foundation: Basement

Materials List Available: No

Price Category: G

Images provided by designer/architect.

CAD FILE AVAILABLE

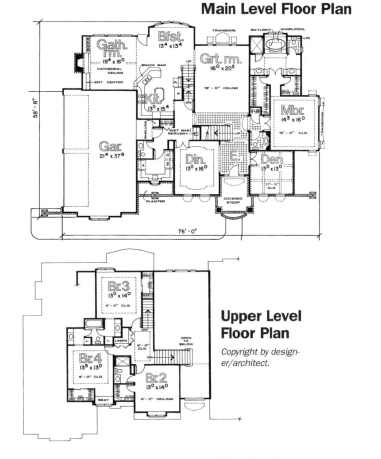

OPEN TO FAM. RM.

BR. #4 11'8" X 12'4"

BR. #2 13'4" X 12'8"

OPEN TO E.

BR. #3 11'8" X 12'6"

Upper Level Floor Plan

Copyright by designer/architect.

Main Level Floor Plan

TRANSOMS

SKYLIGHT

WHIRLPOOL

Gath. rm. 19'4 X 16'0 CATHEDRAL CEILING ENT. CENTER

Bfst. 13'4 X 13'4

SNACK BAR

Grt. rm. 16'0 X 20'5 18'-0" CEILING

Kit. 13'0 X 15'4

Mbr. 14'3 X 16'0 10'-0" CLG.

Gar. 21'4 X 37'8

WET BAR SERVERY

Din. 13'0 X 16'0

E.

Den 13'0 X 13'0

PLANTER

COVERED STOOP

58'-8"

76'-0"

Plan #121022

Dimensions: 76' W x 58'8" D

Levels: 2

Square Footage: 3,556

Main Level Sq. Ft.: 2,555

Upper Level Sq. Ft.: 1,001

Bedrooms: 4

Bathrooms: 3 full, 2 half

Foundation: Basement

Materials List Available: Yes

Price Category: H

Images provided by designer/architect.

Br. 3 13'0 X 14'0 9'-0" CLG.

Br. 4 13'5 X 13'0 9'-0" CLG.

Br. 2 13'0 X 14'0 9'-0" CEILING

OPEN TO BELOW

SEAT

LINEN

Upper Level Floor Plan

Copyright by designer/architect.

Plan #121046

Dimensions: 65'3" W x 57'1½" D
Levels: 2
Square Footage: 2,655
Main Level Sq. Ft.: 1,906
Upper Level Sq. Ft.: 749
Bedrooms: 4
Bathrooms: 2½
Foundation: Slab; basement for fee
Materials List Available: Yes
Price Category: F

CAD FILE AVAILABLE
CAD

Images provided by designer/architect.

This home beautifully blends traditional architectural detail with modern amenities.

Features:

- Ceiling Height: 8 ft. unless otherwise noted.
- Entry: This two-story entry enjoys views of the uniquely shaped study, a second-floor balcony, and the formal dining room.
- Formal Dining Room: With its elegant corner column, this dining room sets the

stage for formal entertaining as well as family gatherings.

- Kitchen: This well-appointed kitchen features a center island for efficient food preparation. It has a butler's pantry near the dining room and another pantry in the service entry.
- Breakfast Area: Here's the spot for informal family meals or lingering over coffee.
- Rear Porch: Step out through French doors in the master bedroom and the breakfast area.

Main Level Floor Plan

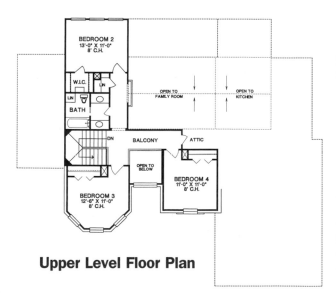

Upper Level Floor Plan

Copyright by designer/architect.

Images provided by designer/architect.

Plan #321061

Dimensions: 65'3" W x 57'1½" D
Levels: 2
Square Footage: 2,655
Main Level Sq. Ft.: 1,906
Upper Level Sq. Ft.: 749
Bedrooms: 4
Bathrooms: 2½
Foundation: Slab; basement for fee
Materials List Available: Yes
Price Category: F

You'll love the spacious interior of this gorgeous home, which is built for comfortable family living but includes amenities for gracious entertaining.

Features:

• Entry: This large entry gives a view of the handcrafted staircase to the upper floor.

• Living Room: Angled French doors open into this generously sized room with a vaulted ceiling.

• Family Room: You'll love to entertain in this huge room with a masonry fireplace, built-in entertainment area, gorgeous bay window, and well-fitted wet bar.

• Breakfast Room: A door in the bayed area opens to the outdoor patio for dining convenience.

• Kitchen: The center island provides work space and a snack bar, and the walk-in pantry is a delight.

• Master Suite: Enjoy the vaulted ceiling, two walk-in closets, and luxurious bath in this suite.

Main Level Floor Plan

Upper Level Floor Plan

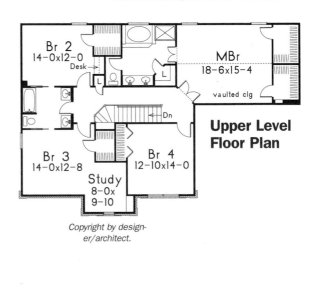

Copyright by designer/architect.

Plan #121073

Dimensions: 70' W x 52' D

Levels: 1.5

Square Footage: 2,579

Main Level Sq. Ft.: 1,933

Upper Level Sq. Ft.: 646

Bedrooms: 4

Bathrooms: 2½

Foundation: Basement

Materials List Available: Yes

Price Category: E

Images provided by designer/architect.

Luxury will surround you in this home with contemporary styling and up-to-date amenities at every turn.

Features:

• **Great Room:** This large room shares both a see-through fireplace and a wet bar with the adjacent hearth room. Transom-topped windows add both light and architectural interest to this room.

• **Den:** Transom-topped windows add visual interest to this private area.

• **Kitchen:** A center island and corner pantry add convenience to this well-planned kitchen, and a lovely ceiling treatment adds beauty to the bayed breakfast area.

• **Master Suite:** A built-in bookcase adds to the ambiance of this luxury-filled area, where you're sure to find a retreat at the end of the day.

Main Level Floor Plan

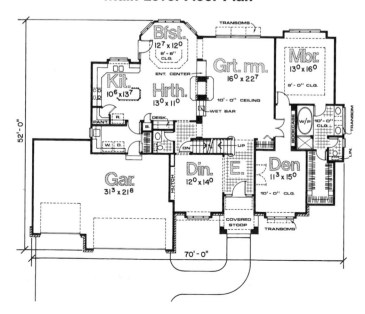

Upper Level Floor Plan

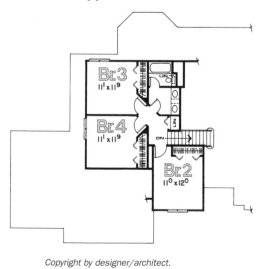

Copyright by designer/architect.

Plan #151004

Dimensions: 64'8" W x 62'1" D
Levels: 1
Square Footage: 2,107
Bedrooms: 4
Bathrooms: 2½
Foundation: Crawl space, slab, or basement
CompleteCost List Available: Yes
Price Category: E

Images provided by designer/architect.

You'll love the spacious feeling in this comfortable home designed for a family.

Features:

- **Foyer:** A 10-ft. ceiling greets you in this home.

- **Great Room:** A 10-ft. ceiling complements this large room, with its fireplace, built-in cabinets, and easy access to the rear covered porch.

- **Dining Room:** The 9-ft. boxed ceiling in this large room helps to create a beautiful formal feeling.

- **Kitchen:** The island in this kitchen is open to the breakfast room for true convenience.

- **Breakfast Room:** Morning light will stream through the bay window here.

- **Master Suite:** A 9-ft. pan ceiling adds a distinctive note to this room with access to the rear porch. In the bath, you'll find a whirlpool tub, separate shower, double vanities, and two walk-in closets.

Copyright by designer/architect.

Plan #151011

Dimensions: 59'6" W x 74'4" D
Levels: 2
Square Footage: 3,437
Main Level Sq. Ft.: 2,184
Upper Level Sq. Ft.: 1,253
Bedrooms: 5
Bathrooms: 4
Foundation: Crawl space or slab; basement or daylight basement for fee
CompleteCost List Available: Yes
Price Category: F

Images provided by designer/architect.

Beauty, comfort, and convenience are yours in this luxurious, two-level home.

Features:

- Ceiling Height: 10 ft. unless otherwise noted.

- Master Suite: The 11-ft. pan ceiling sets the tone for this secluded area, with a lovely bay window that opens onto a rear porch, a pass-through fireplace to the great room, and a sitting room.

- Great Room: The pass-through fireplace makes this spacious room a cozy spot,

while the French doors leading to a rear porch make it a perfect spot for entertaining.

- Dining Room: Gracious 8-in. columns set off the entrance to this room.

- Kitchen: An island bar provides an efficient work area that's fitted with a sink.

- Breakfast Room: Open to the kitchen, this room is defined by a bay window and a spiral staircase to the second floor.

- Laundry Room: Large enough to accommodate a folding table, this room can also be fitted with a swinging pet door.

- Play Room: French doors in the children's playroom open onto a balcony where they can continue their games.

- Bedrooms: The 9-ft. ceilings on the second story make the rooms feel bright and airy.

Copyright by designer/architect.

Main Level Floor Plan

Upper Level Floor Plan

Images provided by designer/architect.

Plan #111007

Dimensions: 72' W x 91' D

Levels: 1

Square Footage: 3,668

Bedrooms: 4

Bathrooms: 3½

Foundation: Crawl space

Materials List Available: No

Price Category: I

This Mediterranean-inspired, traditional manor home offers an enormous amount of space and every amenity you can imagine, but to do it justice, site it on a large lot with wonderful views.

Features:

- **Living Room:** With a fireplace and built-in media center, this room has the potential to become a gathering place for guests as well as family members.

- **Kitchen:** Enjoy this well-designed kitchen which will surely have you whistling as you work.

- **Breakfast Area:** Unusually large for a breakfast room, this space invites a crowd at any time of day. French doors at the back of the room open to the gracious rear porch.

- **Master Suite:** Privacy is guaranteed by the location of this spacious suite. The separate walk-in closets give plenty of storage space, and the master bath features separate vanities as well as a large corner tub.

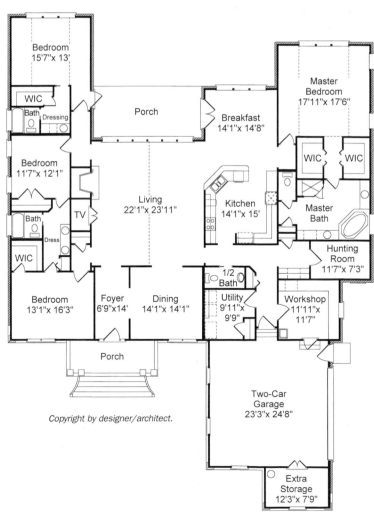

Copyright by designer/architect.

Plan #121069

Dimensions: 58' W x 59'4" D
Levels: 2
Square Footage: 2,914
Main Level Sq. Ft.: 1,583
Upper Level Sq. Ft.: 1,331
Bedrooms: 4
Bathrooms: 3½
Foundation: Basement
Materials List Available: Yes
Price Category: F

Images provided by designer/architect.

You'll love this design if you're looking for a home to complement a site with a lovely rear view.

Features:

- **Family Room:** A trio of lovely windows looks out to the back of this home.

- **Kitchen:** Designed to suit a gourmet cook, this kitchen includes a roomy pantry and an island with a snack bar.

- **Breakfast Area:** The boxed window here is perfect for houseplants or a collection of

culinary herbs. A door leads to the backyard.

- **Master Suite:** On the upper level, the bedroom features a cathedral ceiling and two walk-in closets. The bath also has a cathedral ceiling and includes dual vanities and a sunlit whirlpool tub.

Main Level Floor Plan

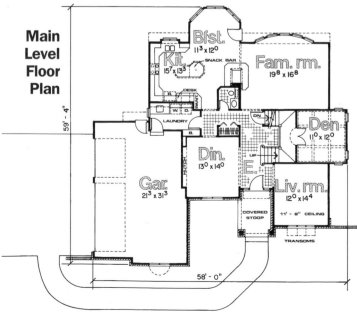

Upper Level Floor Plan

Copyright by designer/architect.

Plan #161028

Dimensions: 84'6" W x 69'4" D

Levels: 1

Square Footage: 3,570

Optional Finished Basement Sq. Ft.: 2,367

Bedrooms: 3

Bathrooms: 3½

Foundation: Basement

Materials List Available: Yes

Price Category: H

Images provided by designer/architect.

From the gabled stone-and-brick exterior to the wide-open view from the foyer, this home will meet your greatest expectations.

Features:

- Great Room/Dining Room: Columns and 13-ft. ceilings add exquisite detailing to the dining room and great room.

- Kitchen: The gourmet-equipped kitchen with an island and a snack bar merges with the cozy breakfast and hearth rooms.

- Master Suite: The luxurious master bed room pampers with a separate sitting room with a fireplace and a dressing room boasting a tub and two vanities.

- Additional: Two bedrooms include a private bath and walk-in closet. The optional finished basement solves all your recreational needs: bar, media room, billiards room, exercise room, game room, as well as an office and fourth bedroom.

Rear Elevation

Main Level Floor Plan

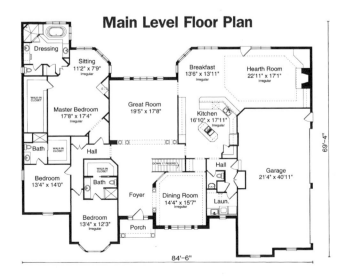

Basement Level Floor Plan

Copyright by designer/architect.

Plan #121092

Dimensions: 65'4" W x 52'8" D
Levels: 1
Square Footage: 3,225
Main Level Sq. Ft.: 1,887
Basement Level Sq. Ft.: 1,338
Bedrooms: 3
Bathrooms: 2½
Foundation: Basement
Materials List Available: Yes
Price Category: G

Images provided by designer/architect.

This is the design if you want a home that will be easy to expand as your family grows.

Features:

• Entry: Both the dining room and great room are immediately accessible from this lovely entry.

• Great Room: The transom-topped bowed windows highlight the spacious feeling here.

• Gathering Room: Also with an angled ceiling, this room has a fireplace as well as built-in

entertainment center and bookcases.

• Dining Room: This elegant room features a 13-ft. boxed ceiling and majestic window around which you'll love to decorate.

• Kitchen: Designed for convenience, this kitchen includes a lovely angled ceiling and gazebo-shaped breakfast area.

• Basement: Use the plans for finishing a family room and two bedrooms when the time is right.

Main Level Floor Plan

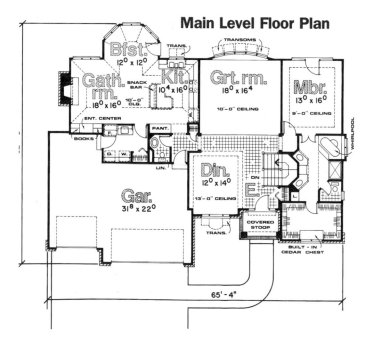

Basement Level Floor Plan

Copyright by designer/architect.

Let Us Help You Plan Your Dream Home

Whether you've always dreamed of building your own home or you can't find the right house from among the dozens you've toured, our collection of Downsized Luxury Home plans can help you achieve the home of your dreams. You could have an architect create a one-of-a-kind home for you, but the design services alone could end up costing up to 15 percent of the cost of construction—a hefty premium for any building project. Isn't it a better idea to select from among the hundreds of unique designs shown in our collection for a fraction of the cost?

What does Creative Homeowner Offer?

In this book, Creative Homeowner provides hundreds of home plans from the country's best architects and designers. Our designs are among the most popular available. Whether your taste runs from traditional to contemporary, Victorian to early American, you are sure to find the best house design for you and your family. Our plans packages include detailed drawings to help you or your builder construct your dream house. **(See page 230.)**

Can I Make Changes to the Plans?

Creative Homeowner offers three ways to help you achieve a truly unique home design. Our customizing service allows for extensive changes to our designs. **(See page 231.)** We also provide reverse images of our plans, or we can give you and your builder the tools for making minor changes on your own. **(See page 234.)**

Can You Help Me Manage My Costs?

To help you stay within your budget, Creative Homeowner has teamed up with the leading estimating company to provide one of the most accurate, complete, and reliable building material take-offs in the industry. **(See page 232.)** If that is too much detail for you, we can provide you with general construction costs based on your zip code. **(See page 234.)** Also, many of our plans come with the option of buying detailed materials lists to help you price out construction costs.

How Can I Begin the Building Process?

To get started building your dream home, fill out the order form on page 235, call our order department at 1-800-523-6789, or visit ultimateplans.com. If you plan on doing all or part of the work yourself, or want to keep tabs on your builder, we offer best-selling building and design books available at www.creativehomeowner.com.

Our Plans Packages Offer:

"Square footage" refers to the total "heated square feet" of this plan. This number does not include the garage, porches, or unfinished areas. All of our home plans are the result of many hours of work by leading architects and professional designers. Most of our home plans include each of the following:

Frontal Sheet

This artist's rendering of the front of the house gives you an idea of how the house will look once it is completed and the property landscaped.

Detailed Floor Plans

These plans show the size and layout of the rooms. They also provide the locations of doors, windows, fireplaces, closets, stairs, and electrical outlets and switches.

Foundation Plan

A foundation plan gives the dimensions of basements, walk-out basements, crawl spaces, pier foundations, and slab construction. Each house design lists the type of foundation included. If the plan you choose does not have the foundation type you require, our customer service department can help you customize the plan to meet your needs.

Roof Plan

In addition to providing the pitch of the roof, these plans also show the locations of dormers, skylights, and other elements.

Exterior Elevations

These drawings show the front, rear, and sides of the house as if you were looking at it head on. Elevations also provide information about architectural features and finish materials.

Interior Elevations and Details

Interior elevations show specific details of such elements as fireplaces, kitchen and bathroom cabinets, built-ins, and other unique features of the design.

Cross Sections

These show the structure as if it were sliced to reveal construction requirements, such as insulation, flooring, and roofing details.

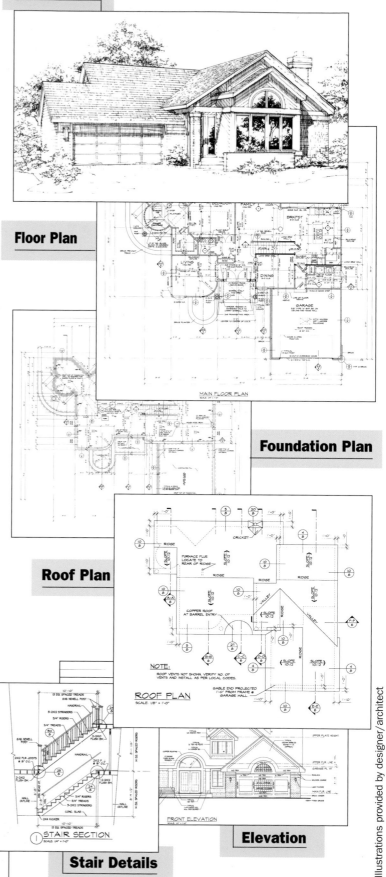

Frontal Sheet

Floor Plan

Foundation Plan

Roof Plan

Cross Sections

Stair Details

Elevation

Illustrations provided by designer/architect

Customize Your Plans in 4 Easy Steps

1 **Select the home plan** that most closely meets your needs. Purchase of a reproducible master is necessary in order to make changes to a plan.

2 **Call 1-800-523-6789 to place your order.** Tell our sales representative you are interested in customizing your plan. To receive your customization cost estimate, our modification company will contact you (via fax or email) requesting a list or sketch of the changes requested to one of our plans. There is a $50 nonrefundable consultation fee for this service. If you decide to continue with the custom changes, the $50 fee is credited to the total amount charged.

3 **Fax or email your request** to our modification company. Within three business days of receipt of your request, a detailed cost estimate will be provided to you.

4 **Once you approve the estimate,** a 75% retainer fee is collected and customization work begins. Preliminary drawings typically take 10 to 15 business days. After approval of the design, the balance of your customization fee is due before modified plans can be shipped. You will receive five sets of blueprints, a reproducible master, or CAD files, depending on which package was purchase.

Modification Pricing Guide

Categories	Average Cost For Modification
Add or remove living space	Quote required
Bathroom layout redesign	Starting at $150
Kitchen layout redesign	Starting at $120
Garage: add or remove	Starting at $600
Garage: front entry to side load or vice versa	Starting at $300
Foundation changes	Starting at $220
Exterior building materials change	Starting at $200
Exterior openings: add, move, or remove	$75 per opening
Roof line changes	Starting at $600
Ceiling height adjustments	Starting at $280
Fireplace: add or remove	Starting at $90
Screened porch: add	Starting at $300
Wall framing change from 2x4 to 2x6	Starting at $250
Bearing and/or exterior walls changes	Quote required
Non-bearing wall or room changes	$65 per room
Metric conversion of home plan	Starting at $495
Adjust plan for handicapped accessibility	Quote required
Adapt plans for local building code requirements	Quote required
Engineering stamping only	Quote required
Any other engineering services	Quote required
Interactive illustrations (choices of exterior materials)	Quote required

Note: Any home plan can be customized to accommodate your desired changes. The average prices above are provided only as examples of the most commonly requested changes, and are subject to change without notice. Prices for changes will vary according to the number of modifications requested, plan size, style, and method of design used by the original designer. To obtain a detailed cost estimate, please contact us.

Terms & Copyright

These home plans are protected under the terms of United States Copyright Law and may not be copied or reproduced in any way, by any means, unless you have purchased reproducible masters, which clearly indicate your right to copy or reproduce. We authorize the use of your chosen home plan as an aid in the construction of one single-family home only. You may not use this home plan to build a second or multiple dwellings without purchasing another blueprint or blueprints, or paying additional home plan fees.

Architectural Seals

Because of differences in building codes, some cities and states now require an architect or engineer licensed in that state to review and "seal" a blueprint, or officially approve it, prior to construction. Delaware, Nevada, New Jersey, New York, and some other states require that all plans for houses built in those states be redrawn by an architect licensed in the state in which the home will be built. We strongly advise you to consult with your local building official for information regarding architectural seals.

Before Customization

After

Turn your dream home into reality with

UltimateEstimate

When purchasing a home plan with Creative Homeowner, we recommend you order one of the most complete materials lists in the industry.

1 What comes with an Ultimate Estimate?

Quote

- Basis of the entire estimate.

- Detailed list of all the framing materials needed to build your project, listed from the bottom up, in the order that each one will actually be used.

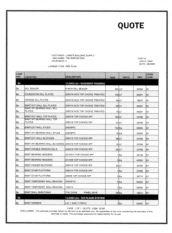

Comments

- Details pertinent information beyond the cost of materials.

- Includes any notes from our estimator.

Express List

- A version of the Quote with space for SKU numbers listed for purchasing the items at your local lumberyard.

- Your local lumberyard can then price out the materials list.

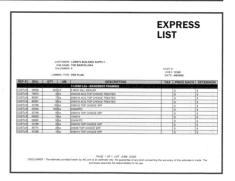

Construction-Ready Framing Diagrams

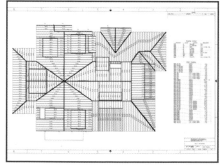

- Your "map" to exact roof and floor framing.

Millwork Report

- A complete count of the windows, doors, molding, and trim.

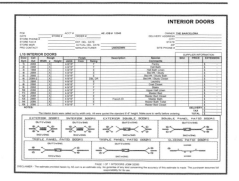

Man-Hour Report

- Calculates labor on a line-by-line basis for all items quoted and presented in man-hours.

Why an Ultimate Estimate?

Accurate. Professional estimators break down each individual item from the blueprints using advanced software, techniques, and equipment.

Timely. You will be able to start your home-building project quickly — knowing the exact framing materials you need to order from your local lumberyard.

Detailed. Work with your local lumberyard associate to complete your quote with the remaining products needed for your new home.

So how much does it cost?

Pricing is determined by the total square feet of the home plan — including living area, garages, decks, porches, finished basements, and finished attics.

Square Feet Range	UE Tier*	Price
Up to 5,000 total square feet	XB	$345.00
5,001 to 10,000 total square feet	XC	$545.00

*Please see the Plan Index to determine your plan's Ultimate Estimate Tier (UE Tier).
Note: All prices subject to change.

Call our toll-free number (800-523-6789), or visit ultimateplans.com to order your Ultimate Estimate.

What else do I need to know?

Call our toll-free number (800-523-6789), or visit **ultimateplans.com** to order your Ultimate Estimate.

Turn your dream home into reality.

Decide What Type of Plan Package You Need

How many Plans Should You Order?

Standard 8-Set Package. We've found that our 8-set package is the best value for someone who is ready to start building. The 8-set package provides plans for you, your builder, the subcontractors, mortgage lender, and the building department.

Minimum 5-Set Package. If you are in the bidding process, you may want to order only five sets for the bidding round and reorder additional sets as needed.

1-Set Study Package. The 1-set package allows you to review your home plan in detail. The plan will be marked as a study print, and it is illegal to build a house from a study print alone. It is a violation of copyright law to reproduce a blueprint without permission.

Buying Additional Sets

If you require additional copies of blueprints for your home construction, you can order additional sets within 60 days of the original order date at a reduced price. The cost is $45.00 for each additional set. For more information, contact customer service.

Reproducible Masters

If you plan to make minor changes to one of our home plans, you can purchase reproducible masters. These plans are printed on bond or vellum paper that is easy to alter. They clearly indicate your right to modify, copy, or reproduce the plans. Reproducible masters allow an architect, designer, or builder to alter our plans to give you a customized home design. This package also allows you to print as many copies of the modified plans as you need for the construction of one home.

CAD (Computer Aided Design) Files

CAD files are the complete set of home plans in an electronic file format. Choose this option if there are multiple changes you wish made to the home plans and you have a local design professional able to make the changes. Not available for all plans. Please contact our order department or visit our Web site to check the availability of CAD files for your plan.

Mirror-Reverse Sets/Right-Reading Reverse

Plans can be printed in mirror-reverse—we can "flip" plans to create a mirror image of the design. This is useful when the house would fit your site or personal preferences if all the rooms were on the opposite side than shown. As the image is reversed, the lettering and dimensions will also be reversed, meaning they will read backwards. Therefore, when ordering mirror-reverse drawings, you must order at least one set of the original plan unreversed. A $50.00 fee per plan order will be charged for mirror-reverse (regardless of the number of mirror-reverse sets ordered). Some plans are available in right-reading reverse, this feature will show the plan in reverse, but the writing on the plan will be readable. A $150.00 fee per plan order will be charged for right-reading reverse (regardless of the number of right-reading reverse sets ordered). Please contact our order department or visit our website to check the availibility of this feature for your chosen plan.

EZ Quote: Home Cost Estimator

EZ Quote is our response to one of the most frequently asked questions we hear from customers: "How much will the house cost me to build?" EZ Quote: Home Cost Estimator will enable you to obtain a calculated building cost to construct your home, based on labor rates and building material costs within your zip code area. This summary is useful for those who want to get an idea of the total construction costs before purchasing sets of home plans. It will also provide a level of comfort when you begin soliciting bids. The cost is $29.95 for the first EZ Quote and $19.95 for each additional one. Available only in the U.S. and Canada.

Materials List

Available for most of our plans, the Materials List provides you an invaluable resource in planning and estimating the cost of your home. Each Materials List outlines the quantity, dimensions, and type of materials needed to build your home (with the exception of mechanical systems). You will get faster, more-accurate bids from your contractors and building suppliers. A Materials List may only be ordered with the purchase of at least five sets of home plans.

CompleteCost Estimator

CompleteCost Estimator is a valuable tool for use in planning and constructing your new home. It provides more detail than a materials list and will act as a checklist for all items you will need to select or coordinate during your building process. CompleteCost Estimator is only available for certain plans (please see Plan Index) and may only be ordered with the purchase of at least five sets of home plans. The cost is $125.00 for CompleteCost Estimator.

Ultimate Estimate (See page 232.)

Order Toll Free by Phone
1-800-523-6789
By Fax: 201-760-2431

Orders received 3PM ET, will be processed and shipped within two business days.

Order Online
www.ultimateplans.com

Mail Your Order
Creative Homeowner
Attn: Home Plans
24 Park Way
Upper Saddle River, NJ 07458

Canadian Customers
Order Toll Free 1-800-393-1883

Mail Your Order (Canada)
Creative Homeowner Canada
Attn: Home Plans
113-437 Martin St., Ste. 215
Penticton, BC V2A 5L1

Before You Order

Our Exchange Policy

Blueprints are nonrefundable. However, should you find that the plan you have purchased does not fit your needs, you may exchange that plan for another plan in our collection within 60 days from the date of your original order. The entire content of your original order must be returned before an exchange will be processed. You will be charged a processing fee of 20% of the amount of the original order, the cost difference between the new plan set and the original plan set (if applicable), and all related shipping costs for the new plans. Contact our order department for more information. Please note: reproducible masters may only be exchanged if the package is unopened and CAD files cannot be exchanged and are nonrefundable.

Building Codes and Requirements

All plans offered for sale in this book and on our website (www.ultimateplans.com) are continually updated to meet the latest International Residential Code (IRC). Because building codes vary from area to area, some drawing modifications and/or the assistance of a professional designer or architect may be necessary to comply with your local codes or to accommodate specific building site conditions. We strongly advise you to consult with your local building official for information regarding codes governing your area.

Multiple Plan Discount

Purchase **3** different home plans in the **same order** and receive **5% off** the plan price.

Purchase **5** or more different home plans in the **same order** and receive **10% off** the plan price.

(Please Note: Study sets do not apply.)

Blueprint Price Schedule

Price Code	1 Set	5 Sets	8 Sets	Reproducible Masters	CAD	Materials List
A	$400	$440	$475	$575	$1,025	$85
B	$440	$525	$555	$685	$1,195	$85
C	$510	$575	$635	$740	$1,265	$85
D	$560	$605	$665	$800	$1,300	$95
E	$600	$675	$705	$845	$1,400	$95
F	$650	$725	$775	$890	$1,500	$95
G	$720	$790	$840	$950	$1,600	$95
H	$820	$860	$945	$1,095	$1,700	$95
I	$945	$975	$1,075	$1,195	$1,890	$105
J	$1,010	$1,080	$1,125	$1,250	$1,900	$105
K	$1,125	$1,210	$1,250	$1,380	$2,030	$105
L	$1,240	$1,335	$1,375	$1,535	$2,270	$105

Note: All prices subject to change

Ultimate Estimate Tier (UE Tier)

UE Tier*	Price
XB	$345
XC	$545

* Please see the Plan Index to determine your plan's Ultimate Estimate Tier (UE Tier).

Shipping & Handling

	1-4 Sets	5-7 Sets	8+ Sets or Reproducibles	CAD
US Regular (7–10 business days)	$18	$20	$25	$25
US Priority (3–5 business days)	$25	$30	$35	$35
US Express (1–2 business days)	$40	$45	$50	$50
Canada Express (3–4 business days)	$100	$100	$100	$100
Worldwide Express (3–5 business days)	** Call for price quote **			

Note: All delivery times are from date the blueprint package is shipped (typically within 1-2 days of placing order).

Order Form Please send me the following:

Plan Number: _____ **Price Code:** _____ (See Plan Index.)

Indicate Foundation Type: (Select ONE. See plan page for availability.)
- ❏ Slab ❏ Crawl space ❏ Basement ❏ Walk-out basement
- ❏ Optional Foundation for Fee _____ $_____

(Please enter foundation here)

Please call all our order department or visit our website for optional foundation fee

Basic Blueprint Package   Cost
- ❏ CAD Files $_____
- ❏ Reproducible Masters $_____
- ❏ 8-Set Plan Package $_____
- ❏ 5-Set Plan Package $_____
- ❏ 1-Set Study Package $_____
- ❏ Additional plan sets:
  __ sets at $45.00 per set $_____
- ❏ Print in mirror-reverse: $50.00 per order $_____
  Please call all our order department or visit our website for availibility
- ❏ Print in right-reading reverse: $150.00 per order $_____
  Please call all our order department or visit our website for availibility

Important Extras
- ❏ Ultimate Estimate (See Price Tier above.) $_____
- ❏ Materials List $_____
- ❏ CompleteCost Materials Report at $125.00 $_____
  Zip Code of Home/Building Site _____
- ❏ EZ Quote for Plan #_____ at $29.95 $_____
- ❏ Additional EZ Quotes for Plan #s_____
  at $19.95 each $_____
- **Shipping (see chart above)** $_____
- **SUBTOTAL** $_____
- **Sales Tax** (NJ residents only, add 7%) $_____
- **TOTAL** $_____

Order Toll Free: 1-800-523-6789   By Fax: 201-760-2431
Creative Homeowner (Home Plans Order Dept.)
24 Park Way
Upper Saddle River, NJ 07458

Name _____
(Please print or type)

Street _____
(Please do not use a P.O. Box)

City _____ State _____

Country _____ Zip _____

Daytime telephone (   ) _____

Fax (   ) _____
(Required for reproducible orders)

E-Mail _____

Payment ❏ Bank check/money order. No personal checks.
Make checks payable to Creative Homeowner

❏ VISA   ❏ MasterCard   ❏ American Express   ❏ Discover

Credit card number _____

Expiration date (mm/yy) _____

Signature _____

Please check the appropriate box:
❏ Building home for myself   ❏ Building home for someone else

SOURCE CODE | CB950

Copyright Notice

All home plans sold through this publication are protected by copyright. Reproduction of these home plans, either in whole or in part, including any form and/or preparation of derivative works thereof, for any reason without prior written permission is strictly prohibited. The purchase of a set of home plans in no way transfers any copyright or other ownership interest in it to the buyer except for a limited license to use that set of home plans for the construction of one, and only one, dwelling unit. The purchase of additional sets of the home plans at a reduced price from the original set or as a part of a multiple-set package does not convey to the buyer a license to construct more than one dwelling.

Similarly, the purchase of reproducible home plans (sepias, mylars) carries the same copyright protection as mentioned above. It is generally allowed to make up to a maximum of 10 copies for the construction of a single dwelling only. To use any plans more than once, and to avoid any copyright license infringement, it is necessary to contact the plan designer to receive a release and license for any extended use. Whereas a purchaser of reproducible plans is granted a license to make copies, it should be noted that because blueprints are copyrighted, making photocopies from them is illegal.

Copyright and licensing of home plans for construction exist to protect all parties. Copyright respects and supports the intellectual property of the original architect or designer. Copyright law has been reinforced over the past few years. Willful infringement could cause settlements for statutory damages to $150,000.00 plus attorney fees, damages, and loss of profits.

CREATIVE HOMEOWNER®

ultimateplans.com

Order online by visiting our Web site.

Open 24 hours a day, 7 days a week.

Still haven't found your perfect home?
With thousands of plans online at ultimateplans.com, there are plenty more to choose from. Using our automated search tools, we make the process even easier. Just enter your ideal home criteria, and let our search tools find the plans for you!

Other great benefits for many plans at ultimateplans.com include:

- **More photos of both the exterior and interior of many of our most popular homes**
- **More side and rear elevations**
- **More data and information about each particular plan**

In addition, you will find more information about the building process and even free step-by-step DIY projects you can do!

Index

For pricing, see page 235.

Plan #	Price Code	Page	Total Finished Area Square Feet	Materials List Available	Complete Cost	UE Tier
101004	C	183	4271	Y	N	XB
101005	D	181	4702	Y	N	XB
101006	D	177	4699	Y	N	XB
101009	D	175	5354	Y	N	XC
101011	D	10	5209	Y	N	XC
101011	D	11	5209	Y	N	XC
101012	E	35	5330	N	N	XC
101013	E	174	5966	Y	N	XC
101017	E	23	4948	N	N	XB
101019	F	138	5507	N	N	XC
101022	D	180	4917	Y	N	XB
101116	G	56	3012	N	N	XB
111004	G	19	3847	N	N	XB
111006	E	161	2241	N	N	XB
111007	H	225	4278	N	N	XB
111015	E	179	2208	N	N	XB
111031	F	215	5304	N	N	XC
111039	G	59	3335	N	N	XB
121001	D	28	3583	Y	N	XB
121003	E	216	5706	Y	N	XC
121007	E	204	5807	Y	N	XC
121008	C	202	3979	Y	N	XB
121018	H	159	3950	Y	N	XB
121019	H	208	6424	Y	N	XC
121022	H	219	3556	Y	N	XB
121023	H	211	7745	Y	N	XC
121024	G	16	3738	Y	N	XB
121025	E	142	5120	Y	N	XC
121026	H	141	3926	Y	N	XB
121029	E	143	4846	Y	N	XB
121034	E	67	5478	Y	N	XC
121046	F	220	3337	Y	N	XB
121047	G	91	5863	Y	N	XC
121048	F	64	2975	Y	N	XB
121049	G	134	4580	Y	N	XB
121050	D	31	6721	Y	N	XC
121061	G	140	8350	Y	N	XC
121062	G	39	10005	Y	N	XC
121063	G	176	10352	Y	N	XC
121065	G	213	9284	Y	N	XC
121067	F	156	7964	Y	N	XC
121069	F	226	6563	Y	N	XC
121071	F	30	3623	Y	N	XB
121072	G	65	6853	Y	N	XC
121073	E	222	7839	Y	N	XC
121074	E	218	5677	Y	N	XC
121078	E	37	2712	Y	N	XB
121079	F	43	3565	Y	N	XB
121081	H	157	7027	Y	N	XC
121082	F	205	6606	Y	N	XC
121083	F	94	3407	Y	N	XB
121085	D	15	4393	Y	N	XB
121090	F	54	5349	Y	N	XC
121091	F	52	4925	Y	N	XB
121092	G	228	6399	Y	N	XC
121093	F	34	7939	Y	N	XC
121095	E	33	5279	Y	N	XC
121100	H	207	8324	N	N	XC
131002	C	90	3838	Y	N	XB
131003	B	120	3332	Y	N	XB
131003	B	121	3332	Y	N	XB
131014	B	72	3532	Y	N	XB
131014	B	73	3532	Y	N	XB
131019	E	44	4926	Y	N	XB
131025	G	58	3204	Y	N	XB
131026	F	42	4646	Y	N	XB
131027	E	82	5284	Y	N	XC
131027	E	83	5284	Y	N	XC
131028	F	162	6367	Y	N	XC
131028	F	163	6367	Y	N	XC
131030	E	88	4193	Y	N	XB
131032	E	22	4364	Y	N	XB
131033	F	136	5803	Y	N	XC
131043	D	93	4132	Y	N	XB
131044	D	55	5158	Y	N	XC
131050	F	27	5920	Y	N	XC
131081	L	132	4958	Y	N	XB
131084	K	155	3309	Y	N	XB
141020	G	53	5235	N	N	XC
141032	E	63	2476	Y	N	XB
151001	G	137	7393	N	Y	XC
151002	F	209	5583	N	Y	XC
151004	E	223	5049	N	Y	XC
151011	F	224	4126	N	Y	XB
151014	F	182	3733	N	Y	XB
151015	F	41	5794	N	Y	XC
151018	F	95	2755	N	Y	XB
151019	F	38	3416	N	Y	XB
151030	F	130	2949	N	Y	XB
151031	F	172	9878	N	Y	XC
151032	C	203	3234	N	Y	XB

Index *For pricing, see page 235.*

Plan #	Price Code	Page	Total Finished Area Square Feet	Materials List Available	Complete Cost	UE Tier
151034	D	24	4839	N	Y	XB
151050	F	9	5648	N	Y	XC
151057	G	210	7053	N	Y	XC
151063	E	217	3285	N	Y	XB
151087	F	47	4228	N	Y	XB
151117	D	29	5330	N	Y	XC
151121	G	140	3108	N	Y	XB
151170	E	20	3056	N	Y	XB
151179	E	18	3918	N	Y	XB
151530	D	102	2934	N	Y	XB
151595	H	178	5854	N	Y	XC
151656	D	48	2635	N	Y	XB
151731	D	98	3242	N	Y	XB
161002	D	36	4231	N	N	XB
161011	C	57	4256	Y	N	XB
161012	C	70	4101	Y	N	XB
161013	C	60	3610	Y	N	XB
161014	C	16	4060	Y	N	XB
161015	C	46	1768	Y	N	XB
161016	D	214	4199	N	N	XB
161017	F	17	4548	N	N	XB
161018	F	40	6405	N	N	XC
161020	D	31	2349	Y	N	XB
161025	F	45	5135	N	N	XC
161028	H	227	6861	N	N	XC
161035	H	135	7702	N	N	XC
161036	H	149	3664	N	N	XB
161040	E	200	4580	Y	N	XB
161042	D	218	4564	Y	N	XB
161045	D	26	4455	N	N	XB
161051	E	14	4986	Y	N	XB
161052	C	66	4231	Y	N	XB
161061	H	108	6474	N	N	XC
161061	H	109	6474	N	N	XC
161072	D	85	5652	Y	N	XC
161073	D	56	4393	Y	N	XB
161080	F	113	5459	Y	N	XC
161153	F	107	5298	Y	N	XC
161184	F	51	4822	Y	N	XB
161224	F	106	6555	Y	N	XC
181061	D	130	4538	Y	N	XB
181078	E	97	4006	Y	N	XB
181079	J	160	5223	Y	N	XC
181080	E	62	3453	Y	N	XB
181081	F	117	4472	Y	N	XB
181085	E	89	4438	Y	N	XB
181137	E	112	4228	Y	N	XB
181151	F	86	4328	Y	N	XB
181253	H	154	5013	Y	N	XC
181640	G	155	4170	Y	N	XB
191001	D	96	2156	N	N	XB
191002	C	64	1716	N	N	XB
191003	C	92	2647	N	N	XB
191012	D	118	2123	N	N	XB
191017	F	114	2605	N	N	XB
191028	F	84	2669	N	N	XB
191029	F	84	2726	N	N	XB
191037	C	115	2562	N	N	XB
191068	D	48	3387	N	N	XB
211002	C	205	2696	Y	N	XB
211008	E	59	2902	Y	N	XB
211011	F	212	3910	Y	N	XB
211029	C	71	2569	Y	N	XB
211037	D	33	2809	Y	N	XB
211049	D	160	2843	Y	N	XB
211075	H	111	5117	Y	N	XC
211086	C	30	2628	Y	N	XB
211090	D	32	3174	Y	N	XB
211111	G	56	3948	Y	N	XB
221017	E	17	5010	N	N	XC
221018	D	186	4762	N	N	XB
221022	G	219	5246	N	N	XC
221023	H	144	6474	N	N	XC
221025	G	15	5829	N	N	XC
221079	F	49	3709	N	N	XB
221155	H	186	4746	N	N	XB
241008	E	21	2867	N	N	XB
261001	H	25	6565	N	N	XC
261004	F	69	5407	N	N	XC
271073	D	32	4134	N	N	XB
271076	D	131	4461	N	N	XB
271081	E	57	3691	N	N	XB
271094	G	107	5695	N	N	XC
271095	G	173	3220	N	N	XB
271096	G	178	3190	N	N	XB
271098	G	114	3382	N	N	XB
291013	H	47	6736	N	N	XC
311042	H	179	9094	Y	N	XC
321006	E	58	4076	Y	N	XB

Index

For pricing, see page 235.

Plan #	Price Code	Page	Total Finished Area Square Feet	Materials List Available	Complete Cost	UE Tier
321029	E	65	4517	Y	N	XB
321034	H	206	5451	Y	N	XC
321048	G	61	3878	Y	N	XB
321049	G	46	3806	Y	N	XB
321061	G	221	3766	Y	N	XB
331004	G	85	4438	N	N	XB
331005	H	139	4442	N	N	XB
351001	D	12	2946	Y	N	XB
351003	F	87	2416	Y	N	XB
351008	D	13	2851	Y	N	XB
351033	C	68	2319	Y	N	XB
371042	D	14	2825	N	N	XB
371092	H	145	8883	N	N	XC
441001	D	98	1850	Y	N	XB
441003	C	116	1580	N	N	XB
441004	C	110	1728	Y	N	XB
441005	D	103	1800	Y	N	XB
441007	D	131	2197	Y	N	XB
441008	D	112	2001	Y	N	XB
441010	F	119	3390	Y	N	XB
441012	H	100	5172	Y	N	XC
441013	G	115	3977	Y	N	XB
441024	H	158	3887	Y	N	XB
441025	G	101	3457	N	N	XB
441033	F	106	2986	Y	N	XB
441035	D	104	2692	Y	N	XB
561174	H	49	3753	N	N	XB
581028	H	50	5304	N	N	XC
581034	F	152	5591	N	N	XC
581035	G	150	6277	N	N	XC
581036	I	148	6367	N	N	XC
581090	F	153	5684	N	N	XC
581097	F	99	6111	N	N	XC
651132	E	105	3123	N	N	XB
651179	H	99	4900	N	N	XB
671063	F	161	5970	Y	N	XC
671066	G	154	3968	Y	N	XB
671102	E	150	3896	Y	N	XB
611016	C	194	2148	N	N	XB
611025	H	196	4929	N	N	XB
611036	G	199	3584	N	N	XB
611038	G	190	3964	N	N	XB
611041	H	191	4133	N	N	XB
611044	H	195	4369	N	N	XB
611045	H	195	4512	N	N	XB
611107	E	185	2955	N	N	XB
611112	F	198	3387	N	N	XB
611114	F	189	3339	N	N	XB
611115	G	187	3566	N	N	XB
611126	E	197	3186	N	N	XB
611133	G	199	4454	N	N	XB
611134	H	188	5052	N	N	XC
651047	F	151	2669	N	N	XB
651049	H	146	3769	N	N	XB
651050	G	147	3178	N	N	XB
651064	E	50	2504	N	N	XB
661001	C	190	2471	N	N	XB
661004	E	184	3346	N	N	XB
661006	E	184	3872	N	N	XB
661007	F	185	3652	N	N	XB
661010	F	192	3664	N	N	XB
661010	F	193	3664	N	N	XB
661013	G	187	4146	N	N	XB
661014	G	196	5399	N	N	XC
661046	C	194	2199	N	N	XB
661056	D	197	2486	N	N	XB
661073	D	206	2865	N	N	XB
661124	E	51	3487	N	N	XB
661125	E	203	3126	N	N	XB
661146	E	188	3446	N	N	XB
661165	F	198	4297	N	N	XB
661181	F	201	3312	N	N	XB
661182	G	189	4467	N	N	XB
661190	F	191	4279	N	N	XB
661191	E	133	2298	N	N	XB
661197	G	207	5176	N	N	XC
661205	G	204	3856	N	N	XB
661208	G	202	3876	N	N	XB
661210	G	113	5193	N	N	XC
661211	G	151	4515	N	N	XB
661218	E	141	3608	N	N	XB

Ultimate**Estimate**

The **fastest** way to get started **building** your **dream home**

One of the most complete materials lists in the industry

Work with our order department to get you started today

To learn more go to page 232
or visit

CRE▲TIVE
HOMEOWNER®

online at ultimateplans.com